UNVEILING THE NATION

UNVEILING THE NATION

The Politics of Secularism in France and Quebec

EMILY LAXER

McGill-Queen's University Press
Montreal & Kingston • London • Chicago

ISBN 978-0-7735-5628-7 (cloth)
ISBN 978-0-7735-5629-4 (paper)
ISBN 978-0-7735-5803-8 (ePDF)
ISBN 978-0-7735-5804-5 (ePUB)

Legal deposit second quarter 2019
Bibliothèque nationale du Québec

Printed in Canada on acid-free paper that is 100% ancient forest free (100% post-consumer recycled), processed chlorine free

This book has been published with the help of a grant from the Canadian Federation for the Humanities and Social Sciences, through the Awards to Scholarly Publications Program, using funds provided by the Social Sciences and Humanities Research Council of Canada.

Funded by the Government of Canada | Financé par le gouvernement du Canada

Canada Council for the Arts | Conseil des arts du Canada

We acknowledge the support of the Canada Council for the Arts, which last year invested $153 million to bring the arts to Canadians throughout the country.

Nous remercions le Conseil des arts du Canada de son soutien. L'an dernier, le Conseil a investi 153 millions de dollars pour mettre de l'art dans la vie des Canadiennes et des Canadiens de tout le pays.

Library and Archives Canada Cataloguing in Publication

Title: Unveiling the nation : the politics of secularism in France and Quebec / Emily Laxer.
Names: Laxer, Emily, 1983– author.

Description: Includes bibliographical references and index.
Identifiers: Canadiana (print) 20189066288 | Canadiana (ebook) 20189066296 | ISBN 9780773556287 (cloth) | ISBN 9780773556294 (paper) | ISBN 9780773558038 (ePDF) | ISBN 9780773558045 (ePUB)

Subjects: LCSH: Secularism – Political aspects – France. | LCSH: Secularism – Political aspects – Québec (Province) | LCSH: Religion and state – France. | LCSH: Religion and state – Québec (Province)

Classification: LCC BL2765.F8 L39 2019 | DDC 322/.10944—dc23

This book was typeset by True to Type in 10.5/13 Sabon

For my father

Contents

Acknowledgments

Research for this book was made possible by generous funding from the Social Sciences and Humanities Research Council of Canada. A postdoctoral fellowship at the University of Michigan from 2016 to 2018 allowed me the time to complete the first full draft of this work. I thank Kathleen Fraser and Jacqueline Mason at McGill-Queen's University Press for their guidance from submission to publication, Dara Greaves for her skilful edit of the final manuscript, and the anonymous reviewers for their helpful comments and suggestions.

I am indebted to several colleagues for lending me their ears, talking over ideas, and commenting on successive iterations of this project. The research from which this book sprang benefited immeasurably from the advice of mentors at the University of Toronto: Monica Boyd, Jeffrey Reitz, Erik Schneiderhan, and most especially Anna Korteweg. The book would also not have been possible without the support of my postdoctoral advisor at the University of Michigan, Geneviève Zubrzycki, who encouraged me to pursue publication, and Fatma Müge Gocek, who offered crucial guidance and support during my time in Ann Arbor. To my colleagues, Salina Abji, Jennifer Elrick, Paulina Garcia del Moral, and Marisa Young: thank you for being such constant sources of inspiration and for sustaining me throughout the process of research and writing. A special thanks also to Efe Peker, for carefully reading the entire manuscript and providing valuable feedback.

I am profoundly grateful for friends and family in and outside of Toronto for their companionship and encouragement in all of my research endeavours. To my mother, Sandy Price, and my siblings Jonathan, Kate, and Michael: thank you for always being there, and for showing me what it means to be thoughtful and engaged, ever with good humour.

This book is dedicated to my father, James Laxer, whose unquestioning love and support gave me the impetus, and gumption, to bring this work to fruition. His irreplaceable insights, humanity, and humour will continue to mark my path at every turn.

UNVEILING THE NATION

The Politics of Secularism in France and Quebec

An Introduction

In October 1985, France's weekly *Figaro Magazine* published an issue with the question "Will We Still Be French in Thirty Years?" splashed on its cover. The article to which this provocative title referred cited "never-before seen" evidence of declining birth rates, rising immigration, and the spread of Islamic religious institutions to proclaim that France was undergoing a crisis in its national identity.[1] A subsequent piece published by the same magazine in September 1991 drew similarly inflammatory conclusions. The article, whose eye-catching title "Immigration or Invasion?" drew readers' attention, called for measures to restrict the "invasive" effects of immigration on French society through quotas, deportation of the undocumented, and tightened requirements around family reunification.[2] The covers of both of these issues portrayed Marianne – France's iconic female republican figure who stands for liberty and reason – shrouded in an Islamic veil, thus demonstrating the connection often made between immigration-related concerns and the perception of an Islamic threat to French nationhood.

In the thirty years since the publication of *Figaro Magazine*'s 1985 article, French Muslims – who account for roughly 10 per cent of the national population – have been the objects of an unrelenting campaign to curtail religious signs in France's public spaces and institutions. Shepherded by highly publicized government-sponsored inquiries, this campaign has so far resulted in two key pieces of legislation. In 2004, the right-wing government led by President Jacques Chirac responded to public concern over Islamic headscarves in schools by banning "ostentatious" religious signs in public elementary and secondary educational institutions. Then, in July 2010, a subsequent right-wing government headed by Nicolas Sarkozy outlawed facial coverings in all public spaces. This measure was aimed primarily at banning the Islamic niqab and burqa – worn by fewer than 2,000 women across France. President Sarkozy defended the ban on the basis that France is "an old nation assembled around a certain ideal of human dignity, particularly women's dignity, and around a certain ideal of life in a community. The veil that entirely conceals the face threatens these values, which are for us so fundamental, so essential to the republican contract."[3]

Although subject to political contestations by the French left when they were enacted, both the 2004 and 2010 laws have since been framed by France's traditional political parties as the objects of widespread consensus. After the Socialist Party took office in 2012, the new government promised to uphold Sarkozy's law, invoking the same connection between it and France's republican roots. In July 2013, for example, then minister of the interior Manuel Valls described the 2010 ban as "an emancipatory law." He went on to suggest that the ban "fosters women's liberation" as well as "equality between women and men," and that "secularism is the law and the Republic is shared."[4]

Much like their counterparts in France, politicians in Quebec have extensively debated the effect of a growing Muslim minority on the province's distinct national identity, and considered the merits of legislation to restrict Islamic and other religious symbols in public spaces and institutions. However, these debates have produced different outcomes. While in France a political consensus has emerged that banning Islamic symbols (particularly the burqa and niqab in public space and the hijab in schools) is critical to the "Republican contract," no such political consensus exists in Quebec, where issues of Islamic dress and religious accommodation instead remain highly contested.

A former French and subsequently British colony with a pronounced history of Catholic Church dominance, Quebec has forged a distinct nation on the North American continent. Following two failed referenda to achieve sovereignty (in 1980 and 1995), its nationalist project has increasingly centred on the question of how to incorporate a large and ethnically and linguistically diverse immigrant population. This has led to the elaboration of "interculturalism," a discourse of nationhood and integration that diverges from the federal multiculturalism policy by emphasizing the need for a "common public culture" centred on the French language.[5] As the question of religion moves to the forefront of debates over immigration in Quebec, French republican themes – especially *laïcité*, the term for separation of church and state – have become increasingly relevant to public discourse.[6] Since the 1990s, these themes have regularly been invoked among intellectual and political groups considering whether and how to accommodate minority religious signs and practices in the province.[7]

This debate gained national and international attention in August 2013, when the minority government led by the pro-sovereignty Parti Québécois (Quebec Party, PQ) revealed the contents of its Charter of Values. Foremost among the document's proposals was a plan to prohibit public sector employees from wearing religious signs on the job (see figure 0.1).[8] Far from representing a consensus regarding the secular boundaries of the nation, Quebec's Charter of Values sparked a heated debate among politicians and civil society actors over appropriate ways to define national identity. As they explored the meanings of key principles – namely religious freedom and gender (in)equality – participants in that debate offered competing accounts of what it means to be Québécois.[9] Whereas advocates of the bill framed it as fulfilling a need to render more explicit the parameters of state religious neutrality and the terms of immigrants' belonging to the nation, those in opposition – particularly within the federalist Parti libéral du Québec (Liberal Party of Quebec, PLQ) – viewed it as part of a dangerous effort to project a closed and ethnic brand of Québécois nationalism. The struggle over these competing articulations came to a head in the provincial election of April 2014, during which the PQ lost the confidence of the electorate by raising the spectre of a third referendum on Quebec's independence. This led to a victory for the anti-Charter PLQ, which temporarily put the question of restrictions on religious signs on the back burner.

Subsequent attempts to legislatively curtail the wearing of Islamic symbols in Quebec's public sphere have invited similar conflict. In 2015, the new PLQ government tabled Bill 62, which prohibits the wearing of facial coverings among users and providers of public services.[10] Although the party's parliamentary majority enabled the bill to pass in October 2017, all opposition party members voted against it, on the basis that its proposals were insufficient to uphold state secularism. The debate continued when challenges to the legality of Bill 62 ultimately led a Quebec Superior Court judge to suspend its implementation, until clear accommodations guidelines could be established. When the PLQ government complied in May 2018, outlining a set of criteria for allowing exemptions to the law, it was once again

Figure 0.1 PQ poster outlining the religious garments that *would not* be permitted for public sector employees under the Charter of Values, 2013.
Source: Parti Québécois: http://nosvaleurs.gouv.qc.ca.

excoriated by the opposition for being insufficiently committed to protecting the religious neutrality of the Quebec state.

Unveiling the Nation aims to understand how the restriction of Islamic signs became the object of an alleged political "consensus" in France, while remaining a consistent source of political conflict in Quebec. Contrary to most studies, which prioritize the role of ideas and institutions in determining state actors' responses to immigration-related diversity, I examine how electoral politics – and particularly the contexts and processes of partisan conflict – shapes these outcomes. Through a historical and contemporary comparison of the French and Québécois secularism debates, I put forward a *politics-centred* approach to the production of nationhood, which underscores the contingent nature of attempts to circumscribe the boundaries of belonging in religiously diverse societies.

THE RELIGIOUS SIGNS DEBATE AS A SITE FOR DEFINING THE RACIALIZED AND GENDERED BOUNDARIES OF NATIONHOOD

An underlying premise of this book is that, apart from setting the legal parameters of religious expression and accommodation, the process of introducing, debating, and adopting laws that restrict religious signs in the public sphere shapes the racialized and gendered boundaries of nationhood in immigrant-receiving countries.[11] This emphasis on boundary drawing is in harmony with the contemporary scholarship on nations and nationalism, which has undergone a shift in recent decades away from static, realist perspectives – which view nations as stable collectivities held together by states,[12] ethnic ties,[13] or culture[14] – toward an understanding of the nation as a contingent cultural, discursive, and political formation,[15] whose boundaries crystallize as a result of transformative events.[16]

Like their equivalents at the ethnic group level, the boundaries of nationhood are heavily contested. They effectively separate the world – both physically and symbolically – into "us" and "them," thus capturing the affective sense of place that anchors distinctive "political communities of belonging."[17] Korteweg and Yurdakul define belonging as:

> the subjective feeling of being at home in one's country, of easily moving through its particular places and spaces, and the sense of

> comfort and joy in inhabiting a particular locale. Belonging, in this sense, also means being able to articulate complaint without renouncing the claim to belonging, or the freedom to complain about aspects of living somewhere without being told that you should leave, of not being trapped in a distinction between those whose home is unambiguously "here" and those who are seen as having either a primary or secondary home elsewhere.

As these authors suggest, belonging is thus "simultaneously highly personal and utterly political."[18]

The national boundaries produced via campaigns to restrict religious signs in the public sphere have important racialized and gendered implications. Regarding the former, they inscribe racialized images of particular religious groups.[19] Such is the process captured by the concept of "Islamophobia," which Hajjat and Mohammed define as "the complex social process of racialization/othering based on evidence (whether real or imagined) of belonging to the Islamic faith."[20] Scholars have deployed this concept to understand the role of racial prejudice and discrimination in constructing a "Muslim problem" in France and elsewhere.[21] Their findings point to the ways that elites manipulate popular images of Muslims in order to serve their larger political interests.[22]

As the images of a veiled Marianne referred to above suggest, the racialized boundaries that religiously restrictive laws inscribe are also highly gendered. In order to justify curtailing garments like the Islamic headscarf, niqab, and burqa, states have mobilized select understandings of women's equality, agency, freedom, and dignity.[23] Yet, as I will emphasize in later chapters, these terms and their meanings remain subject to intense debate among feminists.[24] Those on the pro-ban side have tended to frame Islamic coverings as obstacles to women's emancipation. In the process, many have gained access to state power, contributing to the rise of what Farris calls "femonationalism": an ideological formation that combines a neo-liberal outlook with feminist ideals in order to stigmatize and exclude Muslim minorities from the body politic.[25] Anti-ban feminists have responded by maintaining that restrictive laws violate veiled women's religious freedom as well as their right to choose. In some cases – with France being a prime example – these claims have been met with strong opposition from state actors intent on reducing the public visibility of Islam.

Postcolonial scholars have compellingly shown that colonial systems of meaning and relations of power inform the racialized and gendered dimensions of these debates. Indeed, several have underlined the ways in which "Western" feminist actors subjugate "Third World Women" in order to delegitimize practices – like the face veil – which they deem contrary to women's emancipation. This process of subjugation, many argue, has allowed for a falsely universalizing narrative to take hold, in which "Western" women are conceived of as superior, liberated, and better able to exert agency and control in their lives.[26] "Unveiling" the female colonial subject is essential to this universalizing project and to the national boundary-drawing projects that it upholds.

The colonial dimension of nation building is critical to understanding both the French and Québécois religious signs debates. A majority of French Muslim residents draw their origins from Tunisia, Morocco, and Algeria, all former French colonies. The 1962 Algerian war for independence played a key role in rendering the veil a symbol of the "stranger" in France.[27] The religious signs debate in Quebec is also infused with colonial meanings and relationships, but in different ways. Memories of French and British colonial rule are very much central to the Québécois collective imaginary. Yet, as a settler nation, Quebec is also complicit in global processes of colonial domination. This dual colonial legacy has informed the construction of two majority nations in the province: a francophone nation that constitutes a majority at the provincial level, and an anglophone nation that exercises majority control over the federal institutions of nationhood, while still having significant influence over provincial linguistic and national affairs. The political influence of these two majority nations further maps onto a multi-level structure of governance in Canada, in which questions of religion, secularism, and women's rights are decided by both the provincial and federal governments.

WHY POLITICS MATTERS: THE ARGUMENT IN BRIEF

Campaigns to curtail Islamic religious signs in the public sphere are thus important sites in which state and civil society actors delineate the boundaries of national belonging, particularly in postcolonial settings like France and Quebec. In trying to understand why such campaigns succeed in generating political consensus – and even legislation – in some societies but not in others, social scientists have underscored the importance of entrenched "models" of nationhood. In other words, the prevailing analytic story has been one in which discourses of national membership and the institutional frameworks that uphold them dictate the way political actors address issues of religious diversity.

Unveiling the Nation problematizes this prevailing story. Using France and Quebec as case examples, I argue that the competition among political parties for power and legitimacy impacts national debates over religious signs in ways that scholars have yet to fully appreciate. I make this case by bringing into conversation two literatures that rarely engage with one another. The first, which I have labelled the "prevailing story," attends to the role of ideas and institutions in determining how state actors approach questions of diversity and integration. The second body of scholarship that I deploy pertains to party politics, more specifically to the ways that, through the battles they undertake for electoral success, parties strategically fashion and refashion the boundaries of political space. Building on the burgeoning "political articulation" thesis within political sociology,[28] I propose that, rather than straightforwardly reflect extant ideational and institutional structures, parties mobilize those structures selectively and strategically in order to achieve their respective goals.

To better understand the mechanisms attending these mobilization processes, I pay attention to the *contexts* and *processes* of political articulation in the French and Québécois religious signs debates. By *contexts*, I refer to the established ideological dimensions that have historically prescribed parties' strategic calculations in different electoral settings – what political scientists often call the "axis of competition." In most western countries, that axis has largely been shaped by views regarding the distribution of material, economic resources, with left-wing parties advocating a degree of redistribution by the state, while their right-wing counterparts place greater faith in the distributive powers of markets. Yet, in many societies, contests over economic issues are undergirded by struggles around identity, diversity, and nationhood.

I propose that the presence of distinct axes of competition has led mainstream parties in France and Quebec to position themselves differently with respect to the Islamic veiling debate. In France, where class-based concerns have until recently constituted the main axis of electoral competition, traditional left and right parties have embraced a restrictive secularism in order to deflect an ultra-right political threat. In Quebec, where competing national projects have long dictated parties' electoral platforms, politicians have proffered competing approaches to secularism, ones that that reinforce their distinctive positions along a nation-centred axis of competition.

To theorize the *processes* behind parties' articulation of the religious signs issue in France and Quebec, I draw upon the additional concept of "issue ownership." This concept has primarily been used by political scientists to illustrate how emerging ultra-right political parties upset the established dynamics of competition in electoral systems. They do so, the argument goes, by enticing their mainstream right-wing rivals into seeking ownership of the issues that they – the ultra-right – introduce into political discourse, for example regarding the threat of Islam to national identity. What's been neglected in the study of issue ownership, however, is the extent to which, in the process of trying to win elections, parties also constitute and reconstitute long-term discursive formations around nationhood and identity.

I propose that, in competing to "own" the religious signs issue, political parties in France and Quebec have carved distinct boundaries around what comprises full membership in the nation. Although they may be hesitant to co-opt the economic programs of their ultra-right challengers, the traditional right and left in France have been amenable to holding onto support by attempting to "own" aspects of the ultra-right's anti-Muslim nationalist script. In Quebec, by contrast, the two parties that have traditionally dominated the electoral landscape have been disinclined to seek shared ownership of the religious signs issue. As the main pro-sovereignty force in provincial politics, the Parti Québécois has advanced a restrictive platform, based on shared national "values." Conversely, as the traditional federalist party, the Parti libéral du Québec has committed – although waveringly – to a secular program that leaves more room for expressions of religious difference.[29]

Recent sweeping shifts in the composition of both the French and Québécois electoral systems have brought new non-traditional contenders to the forefront of these debates. In 2017, France's primary right and left parties all but disappeared from the political landscape, as Emmanuel Macron's En Marche! (Onward!) movement captured voters' imaginations, defeating the ultra-right Front National (National Front, FN) led by Marine Le Pen. Likewise, Quebec's electoral system experienced a shock in 2018, when the Coalition avenir Québec

(Coalition for Quebec's Future, CAQ) – a relatively new centre-right party that advocates autonomy, but not sovereignty, in Quebec – obtained a majority government. While not the focus of this book, both events speak to the capacity of political parties to reinvent politics-as-usual, with significant implications for contemporary debates around nationhood and diversity.

By tracing the contexts and processes attending partisan conflicts over secularism in France and Quebec, *Unveiling the Nation* aims to introduce a more robust theoretical framework for analyzing the religious signs debate in cross-national perspective. While it prioritizes the role of political parties, the *politics-centred* approach I put forward does not reject prior ideational and institutional analyses. Rather, it sheds light on the selective and strategic ways that parties interpret extant ideas and institutions as they attempt to "own" the religious signs issue in distinct political settings. The resulting framework attends more explicitly to the contingencies, conflicts, and alliances that surround campaigns to curtail Islamic signs, and to the implications of such campaigns for constructing the boundaries of nationhood.

METHOD AND SITES OF ANALYSIS

The method of this study weaves together two traditions in the social scientific research on the construction of social identities. The first tradition highlights the importance of narrative or narrativity in the building of national sentiment.[30] This tradition arose out of scholars' desire to challenge research that, by relying on a "de-narrativized" and "naturalistic" reading of history,[31] generates abstract theories that escape "historicity, time and space"[32] and result in "invariant thinking."[33] Such theories, according to Tilly, frequently appear in "studies of nationalism, democratization, the disintegration of empires, social movements, transformations of states, wars, revolution, and other large-scale political phenomena."[34] To counteract this tendency toward abstraction, scholars using a narrative approach have insisted on the importance of the "storied dimensions" of social phenomena.[35]

The second methodological tradition utilized in this study situates contemporary phenomena in contingency, that is, in the "events" that redefine established modes of social interaction in transformative ways.[36] This tradition derives from scholars' desire to break free of path-dependent conceptions of temporality and change. Sewell –

the leading exponent of the sociological theory of eventfulness – describes events as able to "transform social relations in ways that could not be fully predicted from the gradual changes that may have made them possible." Such events, he further maintains, "reshape history, imparting an unforeseen direction to social development and altering the nature of the causal nexus in which social interactions take place."[37]

Whether and how an event will impact existing structures and practices cannot be known *a priori*. Rather, as Berezin suggests in relation to the causes underlying the spread of ultra-right parties in Europe, events are "*templates of possibility*," which "make manifest what *might* happen, rather than predict what *will* happen." The range of possible outcomes that an event can generate, however, depends in significant part on the collective evaluations that give it meaning. Those evaluations are, in turn, influenced by existing structures and practices. Thus, "events, evaluation and narrative are intimately connected."[38]

In order to understand how party competition informs the production of nationhood in the French and Québécois religious signs debates, I focus on two key contemporary "events": the 2010 ban of facial coverings in French public space and Quebec's 2013 Charter of Values. More than their historical antecedents, these two "events" constituted key moments in which the debate over Islamic signs became the focus of party political contention. Prior nationwide debates over this issue – most notably the 2003 Stasi commission, which preceded the 2004 law on religious signs in French schools, and the 2007–08 Bouchard-Taylor commission in Quebec – primarily involved intellectuals and "experts." By contrast, politicians were the key interlocutors in the debates surrounding the face veil ban and Charter of Values. Thus, while I pay attention to the historical and narrative significance of prior "events" in defining the discursive, institutional, and political terrain around the religious signs debate in each setting, I focus on these particular moments of conflict to capture the role of party political contention in defining state responses to this issue.

To analyze the French 2010 ban, I use the Gerin commission – the six-month parliamentary inquiry that preceded the 2010 face veil ban – as a point of entry. After a short reprieve following the 2004 law, Muslim religious symbols resurfaced as the subject of a national political controversy in 2008, when President Sarkozy denied citizenship to Faiza Silmi, a thirty-two-year-old resident of Moroccan origin, on the basis that her wearing of the face veil signalled a "radical" practice of Islam. When media coverage of the incident sparked a nationwide debate over whether to legally ban this practice on the French territory, Communist Party MP[39] and mayor of Venissieux (a suburb of Lyon) André Gerin wrote an open letter to the prime minister, François Fillon, demanding government action. On 19 June 2009, fifty-eight members of the National Assembly ratified Gerin's proposal to launch a government inquiry into the face veil, among them forty-three representatives of the Union pour un mouvement national (Union for a National Movement, UMP), seven Socialists, three Communists, and two representatives of the Nouveau Centre (New Centre) party.

Between June and December 2009, Gerin and thirty-one other members of parliament heard testimony from individuals representing various organizations and social groups; questioned ambassadors in all EU countries, the United States, Canada, Turkey and some Arab nations; and heard from all political parties represented in the National Assembly and Senate.[40] The resulting report, which the commission submitted to the French National Assembly on 26 January 2010, condemned the face veil on the basis that it contravenes the "universal" republican values of *liberté* (freedom), *égalité* (equality), *fraternité* (solidarity), and *laïcité* (the separation of church and state). Although tensions between the Socialists and UMP prevented the commission from claiming unanimous support for a legal ban, Sarkozy pushed ahead with the law, bringing a bill to the National Assembly in July 2010 that prohibits the "dissimulation of the face in public space."[41]

In order to study the effect of political competition on the production of nationhood in this debate, I examined not only the Gerin commission report itself, but also all of the transcripts of its deliberations, including presentations by its seventy-eight invited participants. I also spent the months of October 2012 and March, April, and October 2013 conducting interviews in Paris and Lyon, France. Of a total of twenty-nine interviews, nine were conducted with politicians involved in the commission (see appendix, table A.1), thirteen with organization representatives (see appendix, table A.2), and seven with other individual actors who either participated in the Gerin commission or played a key role in the surrounding public debate (see appendix, table A.3).

My analysis of contemporary democratic struggles around the governance of religious signs in Quebec focuses on debates pertaining to the Parti Québécois' Charter of Values in 2013–14. In addition to prohibiting "ostentatious" religious signs in public sector employment, the proposed legislation – Bill 60 – further promised to establish a duty of neutrality for all state employees; to make it mandatory to uncover one's face when providing or receiving public services; to entrench state religious neutrality and the secularity of state institutions in Quebec's Charter of Human Rights and Freedoms; and to implement a government policy to regulate demands for accommodation in state organizations. Controversially, the PQ government proposed to keep the crucifix in Quebec's National Assembly and the 100-foot electrified cross atop Montreal's Mount Royal, on the basis that these commemorate Quebec's Catholic heritage and do not constitute an unacceptable infringement of secularist principles.[42]

Responding to concerns by all three opposition parties about the Charter's proposals, the PQ government established a commission of inquiry in December 2013, inviting citizens and experts to share their positions on the proposed Charter. Although it received upwards of 200 briefs, the commission's proceedings were cut short when the PQ called a provincial election to take place in early April 2014. Not surprisingly, the Charter of Values became the central item in the party's campaign for re-election. Halfway through the election campaign, though, fears that the PQ would call a referendum on sovereignty if re-elected shifted the debate, allowing the PLQ to win a majority government and effectively putting an end to the Charter of Values debate.

To capture the political processes surrounding the Charter of Values debate, I analyzed parliamentary debates, press releases by the major political parties, and submissions by citizens and organizations to the public hearings on the Charter's legislative proposals, and I conducted interviews with key actors, including prominent politicians (see appendix, table A.4) and organization members (see appendix, table A.5). To elucidate the significance of earlier discussions of religious accommodation, I also interviewed four prominent figures in the 2008 Bouchard-Taylor commission, including both co-chairs (see appendix, table A.6).

My analysis of the French and Québécois religious signs debates also draws significantly from media reports in each setting. Newspapers and other media are important venues for observing the role of politicians in national boundary-formation processes. Indeed, studies show that media representations of salient political issues contribute to creating "a sense that the nation or national society has an ongoing existence" and that "nationhood is constituted over time."[43] Unlike party manifestos, which convey a unified image of parties' objectives, the media provide critical information on intra-party dissent around issues like diversity and inclusion, making it possible to gauge the influence of "deviant groups or factions" and to identify the "divergent positions of individual party members."[44] Media representations of party positioning also allow "analysis of how parties are presented to a larger audience in mass-mediated public debates."[45] Thus, where relevant, I supplement interviews and other textual data with analysis of media representations of party political battles around religious signs in France and Quebec.

PLAN OF THE BOOK

In a first, theoretical chapter, I situate the study within the larger social scientific conversation about what informs state actors' responses to religious diversity in different national settings. Beginning with a survey of prevailing ideational and institutional theories, I proceed to argue that scholars of religion, secularism, and nationalism should give greater priority to the political determinants of contemporary debates in these areas, particularly given the proliferation of ultra-right political contenders in Europe and North America.

After outlining the study's theoretical framework, I then turn to the substantive analysis, which unfolds in two parts. In part 1, I draw on secondary texts, media reports, political party documents, and interviews to trace the historical dynamics of party political contention and the emergence of the religious signs debates in France (chapter 2) and Quebec (chapter 3).

In part 2 of *Unveiling the Nation*, I tackle the more recent past and examine how political actors – both in and outside of the formal electoral sphere – have articulated the boundaries of the nation in the context of the two highly controversial and transformative "events" discussed above: the 2010 face veil ban in France (chapter 4) and the 2013 Charter of Values in Quebec (chapter 5). Although their precise consequences could not be predicted *a priori*, I argue, the articulations that political actors brought to these "events" in the public debate were critically informed by established "axes of competition" and by politicians' struggle for "ownership" of the religious signs issue in each setting.

A concluding chapter summarizes the theoretical contributions of the study. Drawing examples from the substantive chapters, it elucidates the analytic advantages of linking boundary drawing in the sphere of politics to the process of demarcating the boundaries of the nation.

In a final epilogue chapter, I discuss recent developments in the religious signs debates in France and Quebec. Further, I examine the implications of both the face veil ban and Charter of Values for contemporary politics, paying attention to the impacts of these "events" in reconfiguring the French and Québécois electoral systems since 2017.

1

Toward a Politics-Centred Approach to the Production of Nationhood

Debates over whether and how to incorporate religious minorities are a central focus of nation-building projects in numerous immigrant-receiving countries. The United States is a recent example of this trend. With the inauguration of Donald Trump as president and the subsequent executive order restricting entry from seven (later reduced to six) predominantly Islamic countries, the position of Muslims in that country has become highly tenuous. In Europe, portrayals of a Muslim "other" have pervaded movements aimed at preserving distinct national identities. Concern over immigration from Muslim countries was central, for example, to the 2016 Brexit campaign for the United Kingdom's withdrawal from the EU. Likewise, hostility to the Muslim presence played a key part in the 2017 Dutch election, in which the ultra-right populist Partij voor de Vrijheid (Party for Freedom) took second place, with 13 per cent of the vote.[1]

These broad-based debates over Muslims' national belonging are often accompanied by campaigns to legally restrict the wearing of Islamic signs in public spaces and institutions. In 2018, Denmark joined France, Belgium, and Austria in prohibiting full facial coverings in public areas. The Netherlands also entered the fray when it introduced a partial ban in 2015, and in 2016, German chancellor Angela Merkel endorsed her party's call to ban the full-face veil "wherever it is legally possible."[2]

Scholars seeking to understand the proliferation of these restrictive campaigns have placed significant stock in the role of institutionally embedded discourses or "models" of nationhood, leaving the role of party political conflict relatively unexplored. The principal task of this chapter is to sketch the parameters of an alternative, *politics-centred* approach to understanding why states respond the way they do to minority religious signs and practices within their territories.

In the first part, I outline prevailing social scientific approaches to this question, highlighting their strengths and limitations. The first, which I call the national "models" approach, underscores the ideological determinants of state responses to immigrant selection and incorporation. The second approach focuses on the ways that institutions, via existing laws and policy frameworks, enable and/or constrain the actions of states in the realm of religious incorporation. While they each shed some light on the ideational and institutional contours of contemporary debates, I argue that neither of these perspectives accounts for France's and Quebec's precise and distinctive trajectories regarding the political response to Islamic veiling.

In the second part of the chapter, I present an alternative, *politics-centred* framework, which addresses the role of electoral competition, interests, and strategy in shaping how party political actors interpret and frame established ideas and institutional frameworks in the process of debating the religious signs issue. Using this approach, I propose that entrenched "models" of nationhood and the laws and institutions governing the place of religion in the public sphere matter in shaping the politics of secularism in France and Quebec, but primarily insofar as they serve parties' struggles for "issue ownership."

THE NATIONAL "MODELS" APPROACH: REPUBLICANISM IN FRANCE; INTERCULTURALISM IN QUEBEC

The central tenet of the national "models" approach is that state decisions regarding immigrant selection and incorporation reflect systems of meaning that are bound up in countries' unique historical nation-building processes. Focusing on the discursive meaning(s) applied to nationhood,[3] this research suggests that national ideological structures define the "grand narratives,"[4] "philosophies,"[5] "scripts,"[6] and "cultural idioms"[7] that prescribe the social and political boundaries of the nation. Over time, they also shape the way nation-states incorporate differences related to class, gender, race, and religion. For example, adherents of this approach have examined how class and gender considerations inform, and are shaped by, the emergence of distinct welfare state regimes.[8] "Models" of nationhood also draw from and reinforce particular gendered and racial hierarchies.[9] Recently, religion has re-emerged as a key problematic around which ideologies of nationhood are defined. Indeed, given its role in framing state strategies for regulating difference and demands for recognition, the question of secularism is now seen as inextricably linked to constructions of nationhood and citizenship,[10] and as also playing a role in shaping the politics of gender across states.[11]

The national "models" approach has been an especially powerful tool in scholarly discussions of French immigration policy and, more recently, of the French state's response to religious signs. These discussions foreground the role of republicanism, suggesting that it advocates a restrictive approach to addressing diversity in France.

Rooted in the 1789 Revolution, French republicanism encompasses a Janus-faced set of ideals. On the one hand, it shares with Anglo-American liberalism a commitment to principles of justice and equality; the protection of individual rights through the separation of public and private spheres; and the notion that dignity lies in individuals' capacities to create their own conceptions of the good. Where republicanism parts ways with liberal citizenship, however, is in the relative "thickness" of the civic bond and the expansiveness of the public sphere that it condones.[12] The latter is rooted in the Rousseauist attempt to reconcile the active participation of free and equal citizens with a commitment to the common good in democratic polities. Fearing that unbridled liberalism threatens the polity by fostering a disproportionate emphasis on individual rights and interests, Rousseau sought to ensure citizens' political commitment under the Ancien Régime – which preceded the Revolution – by relaxing the liberal value of state neutrality and by defining civic virtue as a key aspect of citizenship. This advocacy of a strong public identity that transcends private preferences supplies the communitarian element of the republican discourse.[13]

The balance sought by Rousseau between the values of autonomy and civic virtue, or moral freedom and political obligation, is achieved via the intersection of *liberté*, *égalité*, *fraternité*, and *laïcité* in the French republican contract. France's Declaration of the Rights of Man and of the Citizen (1789) defines liberté as: "being able to do anything that does not harm others: thus, the exercise of the natural rights of every man or woman has no bounds other than those that guarantee other members of society the enjoyment of these same rights." Égalité refers to the notion that the law "must be the same for all, whether it protects or punishes. All citizens, being equal in its eyes, shall be equally eligible to all high offices, public positions and employments, according to their ability, and without other distinction than that of their virtues and talents." Finally, fraternité is described in the republican discourse as the sense of community or brotherhood fostered by a collective commitment to the principles of liberté and égalité. In other words, it is by embracing common notions of liberté and égalité that individual citizens come to form a community of "public similars."[14] The boundaries of that community are further encompassed by the notion of laïcité, the French republican term for the separation of church and state.

While they recognize that France's immigration laws have fluctuated over time, scholars have been keen to suggest that republicanism dictates the range of policy solutions that legislators adopt in this area. In his foundational study of French immigration policy, for instance, Brubaker identified republicanism as the key "cultural idiom," which prescribes an open and civic conception of nationhood. That "idiom," he suggested, has encouraged successive French governments to adopt a relatively permissive approach to naturalization and citizenship. Periodic rearticulations of republicanism, moreover, explain why France has fairly consistently naturalized the native-born children of immigrants according to a system of *jus soli*, which grants citizenship based on one's birthplace rather than ancestry.[15]

Subsequent research has corroborated the view that France's immigration and integration policies develop in consonance with the civic logic of republicanism. For example, Hollifield's historical study points to the impact of a "republican synthesis" – which is both universalist and nationalist – in granting legitimacy to legal immigration in France and in explaining the continuity of French immigration policy through periods of crisis.[16] The values embedded in republicanism have also been shown to permeate the juridical framings of immigration in France, leading to the entrenchment of social rights, including family reunification, in immigration policy,[17] and to the adoption of an assimilationist "philosophy of integration."[18] Each of these approaches to defining republicanism – as "cultural idiom," as "synthesis," and as "philosophy of integration" – reinforces the belief that this set of ideals encourages a comparatively open, inclusive definition of membership in France.

The recent scholarship on laws that restrict religious symbols in the name of laïcité has generated a more critical view of republicanism's role in shaping the terms of immigrants' belonging in France. Since the 2004 ban of religious signs in schools, a plethora of studies has been published, many of which attribute this law to a more restrictive aspect of the republican ethos. Using terms like "pretext,"[19] "technology of governance,"[20] or "tradition,"[21] these studies suggest that republicanism increases the "sensitivity" of the Islamic veil question,[22] bolsters the image of Muslim religious symbols as political weapons,[23] and determines which interpretations of gender and sexual equality civil society actors can legitimately deploy to confront Islam.[24] Some scholars propose that it is through its permeation into law and policy frames that republicanism dictates responses to the religious signs issue in France.[25] Others interpret the impact of republicanism in terms of its effect on the country's historical relations between church and state.[26]

Although they provide important insight into the discursive themes that French political actors bring to bear when debating issues like veiling, studies focusing on the causal effects of republicanism have not sufficiently problematized the multiple – even contradictory – conceptions of laïcité, the central republican value to appear in the French religious signs debate.[27] Laborde has helpfully grouped these conceptions of laïcité into three major strands. A first strand – laïcité as neutrality – calls for an end to state subsidization of religion. A second strand – laïcité as autonomy – sees laïcité as a doctrine of human emancipation, which takes shape through the liberalization of French society, in part through education. Lastly, laïcité as community is the least liberal of the concept's three interpretations. Guided by an obsession with social cohesion in the face of foreign "threats," proponents of this view apply the concept of laïcité not just to the state, but also to the behaviours of individual citizens.[28]

In focusing on republicanism – and particularly laïcité – as the driving force for France's restrictive response to religious signs like the face veil, many studies have glossed over the struggles, conflicts, and negotiations that underlie the diverse interpretations that political actors bring to these terms. Understanding how and why republicanism and laïcité became the hallmarks of a campaign to restrict certain Muslim religious practices requires a much more thorough investigation into the political contestations that surround issues of nationhood and belonging in France.

Like French republicanism, Quebec's developing – but still unofficial – intercultural "model" of nationhood is subject to multiple and contradictory interpretations. Emerging in the policy debates of the

1980s, interculturalism characterizes membership in the Québécois nation as a "moral contract" between immigrants and the host community. The aim of this contract is to establish a "common public culture" in which French is the language of public life; the participation and the contribution of everyone is expected and encouraged; and the contributions of diverse groups are welcome but only within the limits imposed by the respect for fundamental democratic values, and the necessity of inter-community exchange.[29] These three tenets amount to a "model" of nationhood, which relies for its content on both liberal and communitarian logics of membership. The emphasis on equal participation and insistence on adherence to democratic values (such as equality between the sexes) appeals to a universal and liberal notion of national belonging. Yet, at the same time, social cohesion, and indeed the practice of liberal citizenship itself, is viewed as predicated on a common commitment to unifying cultural characteristics, primarily language.

The intercultural "model" of nationhood differs from Canada's federal multiculturalism policy – and overlaps with French republicanism – in several key respects. Most significantly, its roots lie in a majority/minorities paradigm, which prioritizes the cultural survival of Quebec's francophone population. Thus, whereas Canada's federal multicultural approach does not in principle adhere to the idea of a majority culture, interculturalism is underpinned by concerns about social fragmentation and ghettoization that define the larger effort to ensure the primacy of the French language in Quebec. Interculturalism's emphasis on a "common public" culture also overlaps to some degree with the value attributed to "civic virtue" and public engagement by French republicanism. However, this approach distinguishes itself from the republican "model" in that it does not, according to its proponents, bestow a necessary precedence to the foundational cultural group.[30]

While it has not been officially adopted as policy in Quebec, interculturalism has been invoked in reports by government commissions,[31] by political parties,[32] and by prominent intellectuals in the province's religious signs debate.[33] As a result, it has also emerged as a key category of analysis in scholarly reflections on the production of Québécois citizenship and nationhood in the context of growing religious diversity.[34]

However, interculturalism is by no means the sole discourse informing political responses to the religious signs issue in Quebec.

For one, the past domination of the Catholic Church in Quebec remains visibly imprinted on the province's cultural, political, and architectural landscape, suggesting that religion – and not only language – remains a key source of collective identification.[35] Members of the National Assembly in Quebec City still enact laws under a cross that dominates the main wall of the chamber. In Montreal, a 100-foot cross lit by LED lights punctures the night sky atop the mountain at the centre of the city. The preservation of these prominent symbols has been defended in the name of protecting the province's cultural "heritage." Moreover, numerous politicians, academics, and political commentators in Quebec dislike the notion of interculturalism. When the Bouchard-Taylor report invoked the concept in 2008, many publicly rejected its ideals, on the basis that they too closely mirrored Canada's federal multiculturalism policy.[36]

In trying to understand the diverging outcomes of the religious signs debate in France and Quebec, therefore, it is tempting to turn to these nations' somewhat distinct "models" of nationhood. While French republicanism advocates a relatively strict separation between the public and private spheres, which politicians can cite to advocate restrictive laws, Quebec's intercultural discourse postulates a more interactive process for setting the parameters of integration, though one rooted in commitment to a "common public culture."

However, by themselves, these two "models" for incorporating newcomers cannot explain how France and Quebec embarked on distinct trajectories with respect to the religious signs issue. First and foremost, there is, as I have shown, no clear consensus as to the meaning of, or appropriate way of implementing, either French republican or Québécois intercultural nationhood. Both discourses remain subject to intense debate in the political sphere. Second, neither "model" provides a comprehensive explanation for the decisions surrounding religious signs. This is the case, in part, because both republicanism and interculturalism incorporate a diverse set of ideals. Some of those ideals align with a liberal conception of nationhood that prioritizes individual rights and freedoms. Others coincide with a communitarian logic that sees protection of the nation as a collective good. Because of the juxtaposition of these logics, it is difficult to draw causal inferences from the republican or intercultural "models" of nationhood. Finally, it is not sufficiently clear, from the events and processes that have occurred, how any differences that might exist between republicanism and interculturalism – such as the emphasis placed by the latter on the interactive character of integration – explain the divergent outcomes of campaigns to curtail religious signs in France and Quebec.

THE INSTITUTIONS APPROACH: THE 1905 LAW SEPARATING RELIGION AND THE STATE IN FRANCE; THE 1975 QUEBEC CHARTER OF HUMAN RIGHTS; AND THE 1982 CANADIAN CHARTER OF RIGHTS AND FREEDOMS

Institutional approaches to explaining state responses to religious diversity stem from an established research that sees decision-making by states as constrained by prevailing institutions such as constitutions, as well as by existing laws and policies. In specifying the mechanisms whereby "policies produce politics," studies in this vein highlight the impact of "feedback effects," arguing that entrenched policy frameworks determine which new policies "fit" – first, by creating resources and incentives that constitute a "sunk cost," and, second, by informing the ways that actors navigate choices in contexts of information asymmetry.[37]

Expanding upon the latter argument, much work in institutional theory has focused explicitly on the ideational effects of institutions. This research shows that existing policy programs regulate future outcomes by informing the cognitive and normative schemes that motivate political action.[38] Peter A. Hall describes this effect by arguing that "politicians, officials, the spokesmen for social interests, and policy experts all operate within the terms of political discourse that are current in the nation at a given time, and the terms of political discourse generally have a specific configuration that lends representative legitimacy to some social interests more than others, delineates the accepted boundaries of state action, associates contemporary political developments with particular interpretations of national history, and defines the context in which many issues will be understood."[39] This emphasis on the cognitive dimensions of policy feedback mechanisms also dovetails with research on the role of political and discursive opportunities in social movement research.[40]

The concept of institutional "feedback effects" – whether these take the shape of material "sunk costs" or entrenched ideational systems – informs analysis of policy in multiple fields, from social welfare to immigration. Pierson convincingly argued that feedback effects account for the relative success of pension reform efforts in Britain compared to the United States in the 1980s. In contrast to Britain, where the fragmented and underdeveloped structure of old-age pension programs precluded the mobilization of a powerful opposition to reform, the larger scope of coverage in the United States made possible the emergence of an influential elderly lobby capable of successful resistance to attempts to dismantle the program.[41] Addressing the role of institutions in shaping state responses to immigration, Bleich has shown that feedback mechanisms crucially inform contemporary discrimination policies in France and Britain. In particular, the desire for conformity with preexisting institutional templates explains in part why, in France, the fight against racism is the shared responsibility of the state and civil society, while in Britain, a quasi-governmental organization is responsible for dealing with concerns about race relations.[42]

Although a useful tool in comparative research, institutionalism provides only a partial explanation for the diverging responses to religious signs in France and Quebec. In France, for example, legal interpretations of laïcité have fluctuated over time. The Jules Ferry laws of the 1880s removed the Catholic Church from French schools, thus establishing a system of free, mandatory, and secular education. By requiring public school teachers to be lay people (not priests) and instituting a secular curriculum in the classroom, these laws laid the foundation for French schools to become sites for educating citizens and integrating them into a sense of national belonging that is free from religion. Then, in 1905, the French government under the leadership of prominent Socialists further entrenched the secular meaning of national belonging by introducing the Law of Separation between Church and State. The first article – which guaranteed the individual right to the free exercise of religion – inscribed laïcité as a principle that protects private beliefs and behaviours. The second article – the one that established the non-subsidization of religion by the state – expanded the reach of laïcité over public expressions of belonging by applying the institutional separation of church and state to the whole of the public sphere.

In practice, however, this institutional separation has been somewhat limited. Because the principle of equality enshrined in France's 1905 law was not retroactive, it has allowed the Catholic Church certain advantages not possessed by other religions that are newer to French society. For example, since Church property belonged to the state in the first place, the French state today continues to be responsible for its upkeep. The current regime of church-state relations also includes a great deal of government activity on behalf of certain religions, including: government funds to finance the upkeep of religious buildings that existed in 1905; government management and financing of chaplains' offices for major religions; explicit provisions for religious representation in a number of domains; and government funds to pay teachers' salaries in private confessional schools that have entered into contract with the state.[43]

Contemporary debates over minority religious signs have added further nuance to the definition of laïcité. In 2003, politicians intent on removing headscarves from schools began calling forth an alternative secular discourse, one that aims to integrate newcomers by limiting their practice of religion to the private sphere. The contours of this approach were drawn during the proceedings of the 2003 Stasi commission, the state-appointed inquiry into the status of secularism in schools, which heard testimony from teachers, intellectuals, politicians, and activists. The commission's final report, which recommended a complete ban of "ostentatious" religious signs in the public school system, departed from prior definitions of laïcité by suggesting that headscarves not only violate the secularity of the school as *public* institution; they also threaten students' *private* religious rights by subjecting them to proselytization. In this way, the Stasi commission severed the divide that previously existed between *providers* of public services – who are required to physically embody the neutrality of the state – and *users* – whose conduct had until this period been defined according to the principle of freedom of conscience.

As I will demonstrate in subsequent chapters, the meaning(s) attached to laïcité shifted once again in the context of France's recent face veil debate. Aware of the legal obstacles to using laïcité as a basis for regulating individual behavior outside of public institutions, proponents of the 2010 ban opted to construct the law around the more neutral principle of "public order," which was deemed to override the right to religious freedom. Yet, this did not prevent a significant backlash from the courts. In its March 2010 consultative ruling, for example, the Conseil d'État (Council of State, France's highest administrative court) declared that a general ban would violate non-discrimination and other fundamental rights, including the right to religious expression.[44] Adopting the 2010 face veil ban thus required significant effort on the part of politicians to override the institutional framework of the French legal system.[45]

Just as they cannot explain the expression of a "consensus" in France, principles institutionalized in legal texts cannot explain the conflict-ridden debate over religious signs in Quebec. The main legal principle to shape the debate over legal restrictions in that setting is that of "reasonable accommodation." This term first appeared in Canadian jurisprudence in the Supreme Court judgment in *O'Malley and Ontario Human Rights Commission v. Simpsons-Sears Limited* (1985). In this case, the appellant, O'Malley, alleged discrimination by her employer because she was periodically asked to work Friday evenings and Saturdays, preventing her from observing her religion. The Court ruled in favor of the appellant, finding that "An employment rule, honestly made for sound economic and business reasons and equally applicable to all to whom it is intended to apply, may nevertheless be discriminatory if it affects a person or persons differently from others to whom it is intended to apply. The intent to discriminate is not a governing factor in construing human rights legislation aimed at eliminating discrimination. Rather, it is the result or effect of the alleged discriminatory action that is significant."[46] Subsequent Supreme Court decisions have more fully clarified "reasonable accommodation" as a basis for adjudicating requests for religious exemptions in Canada.[47] In *Alberta v. Hutterian Brethren Church of Wilson* (2009), for example, the Court denied a request by Alberta's Hutterite community to be exempt from driving licence photographs, on the basis that granting such an exemption might elevate the risk of identity theft.[48]

Because it challenged the principle of "reasonable accommodation," by proposing to outlaw religious coverings from public sector employment, Quebec's 2013 Charter of Values drew opposition from several high profile legal associations. These include the Quebec Bar Association and the Commission des droits de la personne et des droits de la jeunesse (Human Rights and Youth Rights Commission, CDPDJ), which argued that the proposed legislation would contravene both the Quebec Charter of Human Rights and Freedoms and the Canadian Charter of Rights and Freedoms.[49]

The Quebec Charter of Human Rights and Freedoms is a statutory human rights code enacted in 1975. It is older than the constitutionally enshrined Canadian Charter of Rights and Freedoms, adopted in 1982. While it is technically only a statute, it is interpreted by the courts as having quasi-constitutional status. It is also symbolically important because Quebec never agreed to the 1982 amendment to the federal constitution, which brought about the federal Charter of Rights and Freedoms, though the federal constitution nonetheless applies in the province.[50] When litigants challenge Quebec legislation under both the Quebec Charter of Human Rights and Freedoms and the federal constitution, Canadian courts consider the Quebec Charter first.[51]

Confronted with the challenge that the Charter of Values was contrary to the Quebec Charter of Human Rights and Freedoms *and* the federal Charter of Rights and Freedoms, its advocates proposed to circumvent both. Since the Quebec Charter of Human Rights and Freedoms is a statutory enactment, the National Assembly could amend the statute to avoid a conflict. As to the federal constitution, advocates of the bill urged the Parti Québécois government to invoke the notwithstanding clause.[52] This clause allows the federal parliament and provincial legislatures to override certain sections of the Canadian Charter of Rights and Freedoms – including those regarding freedom of expression, freedom of religion, and equality – for a period of up to five years.[53]

These solutions (amending the Quebec Charter and invoking the notwithstanding clause) carry significant risks. For a government to invoke these options to override fundamental rights and freedoms, it must be certain there is widespread support for its position. Thus, both the Quebec Charter of Human Rights and Freedoms and the Canadian Charter of Rights and Freedoms posed a significant obstacle to the Charter of Values.

However, it was not the *legal* but rather the *political* process that doomed the Charter of Values – specifically, the failure of the Parti Québécois to secure a sufficient number of seats in the 2014 provincial election. In the lead-up to the election, Premier Marois and her colleagues mobilized a discourse of values and cultural threat to generate public support for the Charter of Values. In contrast, the PLQ leader, Philippe Couillard, drew upon a rights-based and pluralist understanding of national belonging to raise doubts about the PQ's capacity to serve the interests of all Québécois, especially minorities. As the electoral campaign wore on, these conflicting images of nationhood became entangled in debates over whether to pursue a third referendum on Quebec's independence from Canada. Although the PQ's official platform did not promise a referendum, a star candidate and future leader of the party, Pierre Karl Péladeau, injected this issue into the public debate when he raised a clenched fist at a campaign rally, declaring his desire to "make Quebec a country."[54] Although Marois skirted around the issue, promising not to hold a referendum until the Québécois "are ready," the uncertainty that Péladeau's gesture aroused was enough to propel the Parti libéral du Quebec into government.

Institutional analyses reveal a great deal about the real pragmatic constraints that state actors face in advocating policies regarding religious signs. However, they cannot fully account for the precise trajectories of political debates in this area. In France, for example, laws relating to the separation of religion from the state have traditionally provided that individuals are free to express their religious beliefs so long as they do not infringe the neutrality of the state. Yet, politicians determined to restrict Muslim dress were able to override these principles and use other values, like public order, to invoke a different conception of laïcité. Existing policy frameworks are of similarly limited use in understanding the trajectory of Quebec's religious signs debate. Although the Charter of Values would have faced significant legal obstacles had it been adopted by the National Assembly, it was on-the-ground political contestations over sovereignty that ultimately defeated its proposals.

BRINGING POLITICS IN: CLASS-BASED POLITICS IN FRANCE; NATION-CENTRED POLITICS IN QUEBEC

Having concluded that neither the national "models" nor the institutional approach fully illuminates the bases of state decision-making in the French and Québécois religious signs debates, I turn to an alternative area of research: the dynamics of party political competition. I utilize this literature to propose that entrenched "models" of nationhood and the laws and institutions governing the place of religion in the public sphere matter primarily insofar as they map onto the strategic interests of political parties. The framework I develop extends the political "articulation" thesis in the sociological study of electoral politics to emphasize parties' capacity to generate the meanings of secularism and national identity.

Social scientific researchers broadly agree that politics and "political elites" play a role in immigration debates and policy-making.[55] Yet, very few have directly explored the impact of political parties in shaping the terms of migrants' cultural, political, or economic incorporation across different national settings.[56] Critics attribute this omission to the fact that "the political science communities working on asylum and immigration, on the one hand, and [those studying political] parties, on the other, have traditionally sat at separate tables."[57] Whatever its origins, the dearth of research on parties' roles in debates around immigrant incorporation has led studies to downplay the contestations that arise around questions of belonging and citizenship.[58] It also results in a neglect of the fact that "it is through the agency of political parties that the issues of immigration are often politicized."[59] Before presenting my approach to studying the role of political parties in the French and Québécois secularism debates, a review of some broad developments in the social scientific theorizing of party politics is necessary.

Over the last several decades, there has been considerable debate among social scientists about whether and how parties impact social change. In the post-war period, the dominant approach – which originated in the work of Lipset and Rokkan (1967) – conceived parties as generated by, and ultimately reflecting, extant social identities and cleavages.[60] Although studies based on this "reflection thesis" paid some attention to social cleavages not directly related to class, scholars saw income and occupational hierarchies as the primary sources of voter-party alignment.

The sociological focus on political parties experienced a marked decline in the 1970s and 1980s, when non-party political phenomena – mainly states, state-building, and social movements – began to take precedence.[61] This shift in emphasis was partly motivated by evidence of parties' diminishing significance to policy-making, and by a perception that "post-material" concerns – such as environmentalism, gender equality, self-expression, and freedom of speech – were supplanting traditional class-based electoral coalitions. According to scholars, the impact of these concerns on voting patterns, social movement platforms, and civic participation indicated the advance of a "new politics," in which individual characteristics superseded structural location as correlates of political behaviour. Thanks to these shifts, social classes, and the "material" values associated with them, were no longer seen as the key referents for ideology, social division, and political activism.[62]

While much of the literature on "post-materialism" focused on social movement activity, its impacts were also observed in the changing structure of party political alignments. Left-right party distinctions have remained essential to many democratic systems.[63] Yet, studies also show that cleavages linked to class are no longer the main driving forces behind parties' electoral platforms.[64] In their effort to draw support from growing middle class strata, for instance, left-wing parties have largely abandoned explicitly socialist agendas in favour of programs targeting social issues,[65] deploying discourses of equal recognition over redistribution.[66]

The 1990s marked another sea change in the social scientific study of political parties, one that informs my analysis of party political debates over secularism in France and Quebec. In that decade, scholars began recasting political parties as playing a constitutive – rather than just derivative – role in the elaboration of social identities and divisions. More than mere conduits of public opinion, they argued, parties "help to structure as well as to reflect voter opinion – not only in terms of what citizens think but also what they think *about*."[67] Despite becoming increasingly disconnected from citizens and the class struggle, political parties were deemed crucial in defining and enacting political cultural norms.[68] Through their interactions with the media, for instance, parties were shown to provide "powerful journalistic heuristics" that influence reporters' stories on political conflict[69] and contribute to the proliferation of media-produced "imagined communities."[70] Taken together, these discoveries amounted to a revelation that parties define, as well as reflect, political cleavages and identities.

Evidence that political parties play a critical role in constituting the boundaries of political space ultimately spawned a new analytic perspective, which rejects the "reflection" thesis of the postwar period in favour of a conception of parties as vehicles for "articulating" social meanings. De Leon and colleagues – the main architects of this approach – posit that, by assembling, disassembling, and reassembling disparate constituencies into politically salient voting "blocs," parties fashion various social formations, creating "unity out of disparity."[71] In arriving at this conclusion, the authors take seriously the Gramscian and Laclauian notion that class cleavages take shape and become "naturalized" through political struggle. They further draw on Althusser's concept of "interpellation" to suggest that "political parties reconstruct certain issues as grievances through the differential interpellation of subjects, defined as the process of recognition of an individual as a concrete subject by ideological-political practice ... Outside this process of recognition, individuals or groups do not possess clearly specified political issues or grievances. Politics (re)defines what the grievance is and who the sufferers (and thus the people who should be mobilizing) are."[72] The articulation model thus marks a clear departure from the reflection thesis: rather than serve as vehicles for the expression of extant social divisions, political parties exercise significant control over the production, articulation, and ultimate meanings of those divisions.

Central to the articulation thesis is the notion that contemporary processes of political articulation are marked by the contestations among "traditional" parties – that is, those that "orient toward minor questions, the resolution of which tends to maintain the existing social order" – and "integral" parties – that is, those that "orient to transformational questions" and, in doing so, "politicize hitherto apolitical social identities."[73] In the current political climate, ultra-right parties are among the "integral" parties receiving the most scholarly attention. These parties share several distinguishing characteristics.

First, ultra-right parties favour an explicit or implicit anti-immigrant stance, which they use to mobilize "a deeper protest about the nature of postwar politics in general."[74] Resentment toward immigrants – for "stealing" jobs from the native-born and threatening to dilute the nation's ethnic and cultural character – are often conflated with other salient issues in these parties' platforms. In the case of France's Front National, for example, hostility to immigrants is intertwined with the party's critical stance on European integration and its alleged threat to national sovereignty.[75]

A second distinguishing feature of ultra-right parties is their tendency to combine anti-systemic positions with centralized organizational structures aimed at ensuring their electoral survival. In other words, these parties' anti-elitist – even anti-political – platforms do not deter them from centralizing leadership in highly personalized and charismatic individuals capable of garnering much-needed media attention.[76]

Third, because they emphasize the need to foster a "different kind of politics," ultra-right parties are able to attract a wide range of constituencies, from the working class to disenchanted skilled workers, the unemployed, and pensioners. They achieve this "assembling" of voters in part by borrowing from, and rearticulating, the narratives of their mainstream competitors.[77]

Due to a cross-national diffusion of their frames, ultra-right parties now constitute a new "party family" in Western Europe,[78] one that scholars hold (at least partially) responsible for the rise in anti-foreigner and anti-Muslim sentiment[79] and of exclusionary citizenship and integration policies.[80] But the sources of ultra-right parties' electoral success in Europe and elsewhere go beyond these issues. For one, these parties appeal to voters' growing apathy around mainstream political organizations. Disillusionment with such organizations is at the root, for instance, of the Front National's political ascent in France. With attachment to mainstream parties on the decline, and an overall rise in support for a less important role for parties in government, this party has managed to profile itself as a protest party, gaining legitimacy in the process.[81]

The rising success of ultra-right parties is also tied to the value shifts associated with "post-materialism." According to scholars, ultra-right political rhetoric is the result of a "silent counter-revolution," which opposes the egalitarianism and cultural libertarianism of the "new left."[82] Capitalizing on their populations' distrust of social and political institutions and a growing fear that ethnic and racial minorities pose a threat to national identity, parties such as the Front National, the Partij voor de Vrijheid (Party for Freedom, Netherlands), and the United Kingdom Independence Party have resonated with many voters.

The messaging of ultra-right parties is also rendered more salient by larger macro-structural changes. Welfare-state retrenchment combined with the emergence of a global economic infrastructure has produced "winners" and "losers." "Winners" include "entrepreneurs and qualified employees in sectors open to international competition," as well as "cosmopolitan citizens." The "losers," by contrast, include those "in protected sectors," as well as "citizens who strongly identify themselves with their national community."[83] Attempts by these "losing" groups to regain their social and economic foothold explain in large part why ultra-right parties in Europe have gained popularity since the 1980s and 1990s.[84] In 1984, France's Front National saw an important breakthrough when it attracted 11 per cent of the vote in the European elections.[85] In 1991, Sweden saw the rise of Ny Demokrati (New Democracy), a sibling to the long established and anti-taxation Fremskridtspartiet (Progress Party) in Denmark and Fremskrittspartiet (Progress Party) in Norway. That same year, the radical nationalist Vlaams Blok (Flemish Bloc) saw its best-ever performance in the Belgian elections. By 1994, Austria's

Freiheitliche Partei Österreichs (Freedom Party) went from near dissolution to gaining 23 per cent of the vote, its highest share of the national vote until that point.[86] Italy's Alleanza Nazionale (National Alliance) reached equal if not superior heights, when it won 14 per cent of the vote in the 1994 legislative election, and thus acquired five cabinet posts in Berlusconi's government.[87] And in 2002, the French Front National shocked many when its leader, Jean-Marie Le Pen, beat out the Socialist candidate Lionel Jospin to make it into the second round of the presidential election, though he ultimately received a paltry 18 per cent of the vote.

Concern over Europe's ability to handle the 2008 economic crisis has led ultra-right parties to take on even greater significance on the world political stage. According to Müller, governments' reliance on technocratic solutions to the Eurocrisis has contributed to these parties' rise, by legitimizing an apolitical, and ultimately undemocratic, approach to policy-making.[88] Since the 2008 crisis, there has been an upsurge in ultra-right party representation at the continental level. For instance, in March of 2014, European politics were jolted when a record fifty-two candidates representing ultra-right populist parties were elected to the European Parliament. What's more, two ultra-right parties – France's Front National and the Dansk Folkeparti (Danish People's Party) – gained the highest percentage of votes in their respective nationwide elections. In the French case, this entailed a quadrupling of the Front National's share of the vote from 6 per cent in 2009 to 25 per cent in 2014.[89]

By tapping into voters' disenchantment with their mainstream representatives, and by mobilizing public discontent over the economic and cultural impacts of globalization, ultra-right parties have thus made significant electoral gains, especially in Europe. In the process, they have contributed to the production of hostile discursive environments surrounding issues of diversity, religion, and belonging. Yet, the mechanisms by which ultra-right contenders inform "traditional" parties' articulation of these issues remain poorly understood. Moreover, scholars' focus on ultra-right political discourses and platforms has come at the expense of understanding how debates over religious signs shape up in democratic systems – like Quebec's – that lack a strong ultra-right contender. I address these unanswered questions by drawing an analytic distinction between the *contexts* and *processes* that shape parties' articulation of cleavages around religious diversity.

Contexts of Partisan Conflict: The "Axis of Competition"

In their initial formulation of the articulation thesis, de Leon and colleagues contended that class, ethnic, and racial formations "do not naturally carry a political valence," but are rather "deployed by parties to aggregate minorities through processes of 'interpellation.'"[90] Recent adaptations have tempered the voluntarism attributed to parties in this approach, by taking seriously the constraining effect that extant political cleavages, cultures, and institutions – what I call *contexts* of partisan conflict – have on party behaviour and decision-making. According to Eidlin: "While emphasizing parties' centrality, articulation models must also recognize that parties' actions are constrained by prior political identities, cultures, and institutional arrangements. These establish a range of possible identities or coalitions that exist prior to parties. But there is a gap between this range and the coalitions/identities that actually develop. Parties' actions bridge the gap between possible and actual outcomes."[91] Eidlin's analysis of party conflict differs from that of de Leon and colleagues in that it hinges on already-bound constituencies, which parties can either incorporate or ignore in their representation of political issues. In other words, pre-existing political coalitions "set limits on parties' scope of action,"[92] shaping – though not determining – their strategic choices.

In thinking about how established coalitions inform the strategic choices of parties in the religious signs debate, we can draw insight from the research on "axes of competition." In every political system, parties derive their strategic calculations from the positions they occupy along theoretically and empirically separable ideological dimensions or "axes." Set in place by prior conflicts, these dimensions "provide a common, simplified language for expressing political values," and infuse "the political system with stability, by constraining political actors, as well as with legitimacy of rule, by granting them a political mandate."[93] In most western electoral systems, the prevailing "axis of competition" largely centres on issues of class and the distribution of economic resources. However, as I mentioned above, an alternative axis of competition has emerged in many societies, along which parties take position vis-à-vis issues – such as the environment and identity – that diverge from class-based concerns.

Like Britain, France's electoral system has, until very recently, centred around a class-based axis of competition, with factors like religion, ethnicity, and language having only minor cross-cutting effects.[94] As the hegemonic party of the left from the late 1970s to 2017, the Parti socialiste (Socialist Party, PS) has traditionally vied for electoral success on the basis of an economic vision that prioritizes diminishing class inequality. Thanks to its focus on this issue, the party has also historically fared much better than its right-wing opponents in constituencies with a large number of immigrant residents, particularly those of North African origin. Meanwhile, as the predominant voice of the right in France, the Union pour un movement populaire (renamed Les Républicains, or "The Republicans," in 2015) has tied its economic vision to free market principles. As a result, it has attracted voters who are economically more conservative, especially shopkeepers, craftsmen, and farmers.

The growing political salience of post-material values has affected public opinion in France, with some effect on these parties' positioning. Like left parties elsewhere, the Socialists have taken up post-materialist issues, from feminism to anti-nuclear energy. This shift has complicated the party's relationship to the working class and to class ideology more generally. Although it still competes with the Parti communiste français (Communist Party of France, PCF) for working class support, the Socialist Party has increasingly become one of white-collar, middle-class membership and votes.[95] The UMP has, for its part, taken up the issue of national identity with increasing fervor, thus attracting more votes from practising Catholics.[96] However, with the exception of the emergence of the ultra-right Front National, the French political system has, from the postwar period until the recent 2017 presidential election, remained relatively stable. This is because, in their effort to distance themselves from their new competitors, moderate right parties have enforced a somewhat artificial institutional distinction, which masks the similarities in their own and the far right's ideological programs.[97]

By comparison, party political divides in Quebec have traditionally been much less influenced by class-based affiliations or interests. For one, class voting is less prominent in countries (like Canada) with multi-level governance structures, where responsibility for economic outcomes is shared across levels of government.[98] More importantly, party tensions in Quebec are instead dominated by attitudes to the "national question."[99] The Parti libéral du Québec has for decades been the predominant federalist voice in Quebec provincial politics. A centre-right party, it mainly draws votes from urban ridings, particularly in Montreal, and from those with a large number of non-francophone inhabitants. The party also has strong ties to its federal-level counterpart, the Liberal Party of Canada.

Until the provincial election of 2018, which saw it lose its official party status with less than 20 per cent of the vote,[100] the Parti Québécois was the predominant nationalist voice in electoral politics in Quebec. Since its creation in 1968, the party has governed the province through two failed referenda on sovereignty, one in 1980 and the other in 1995. In the case of the 1995 referendum, the pro-sovereignty option lost by a margin of less than 1 per cent. Although the Parti Québécois' sovereigntist agenda historically coincided with a left, welfare-statist view of governance and an inclusive national identity, the current leadership has broken somewhat with that tradition by shifting its economic program to the right and, most importantly for our purposes, by advocating a more closed national identity, which the proposed Charter of Values embodied.

Two relatively new parties – the Coalition avenir Québec (Coalition for Quebec's Future, CAQ) and Québec solidaire (Quebec in Solidarity, QS) – have begun to occupy a much more prominent role in Quebec's electoral politics. Both parties identify as nationalist, but only QS supports independence as the most appropriate solution to the "national question." Moreover, while QS advocates a welfare-statist approach to social, economic, and environmental issues, the CAQ campaigns on conservative economic policies and, increasingly, a restrictive immigration agenda. This latter vision succeeded in capturing voters' imaginations in the provincial election of 2018, when the CAQ swept unexpectedly to power, earning an unprecedented 37.41 per cent of the vote.[101]

Although they advocate different policies of redistribution, Quebec's traditional and newer political parties are largely known for their distinctive approaches to questions of recognition, whether geared to the nation as a whole or to its distinct minorities. Scholars argue that the significance of nationalism as a driver of party politics in Quebec draws the attention of subordinate social classes away from social democracy, a fact which until recently was reflected in relatively low support for the New Democratic Party in federal elections.[102] Combined with the importance of linguistic and religious cleavages, this contributes to the relatively limited effect of class on voting in Quebec.[103]

Processes of Partisan Conflict: Contests for "Issue ownership"

Contexts of partisan conflict significantly shape the long-term trends in voter-party alignment across different political settings. Yet, as the political articulation thesis emphasizes, parties play an active role in refashioning those structures. In the process, they redefine the boundaries of electoral debate and, I will argue, shift the parameters of nationhood and national belonging.

Particularly in electoral systems that feature emerging ultra-right competitors, party competition is constituted by struggles over the dimensional configuration of political space. In election periods especially, parties must decide whether to compete along the main axis of competition or whether to challenge that axis by highlighting other, unaligned issues. Because they tend to have long-standing societal roots and organizational apparatuses, "traditional" parties are apt to reproduce existing issue linkages. By contrast, "integral" parties have an interest in bundling political issues in such a way as to divide incumbent parties and produce additional planes of party competition by creating systemic instability.

When "integral" parties on the ultra-right threaten the dimensional status quo by injecting new themes into political debate, "traditional" parties have two options. One response they can bring to this challenge is to compete for ownership of the issues that their new competitors inject into the political discourse.[104] Since they typically already "own" the ethno-nationalist discourses that inform opposition to immigration, right-wing parties are most directly threatened by the ultra-right's anti-immigrant stance. However, left-wing parties are also susceptible to "contagion from the right" in this area. Studies show that, in response to pressure from their mainstream and ultra-right political foes, left parties have increasingly gotten "tough on immigration" and begun to advocate policies that narrow the boundaries of national membership and belonging.[105]

Parties' efforts to "own" the issues raised by new competitors can coexist with attempts to rebuild the boundaries of legitimacy among parties. Indeed, a second solution that "traditional" parties bring in combatting new challengers is to reassert the frontiers of "legitimate" politics in ways that exclude those challengers. As Hagelund explains, parties of the mainstream right and left often retaliate against their ultra-right opponents by identifying them as the "indecent other" whose very existence bolsters their own "decency." This process of erecting boundaries around what constitutes "decent" politics has been illustrated in the case of Norway's anti-immigrant Fremskrittspartiet (Progress Party). In addition to its actual proposals, this party has influenced the Norwegian party system through what it has been "made into" by the other parties. Ironically, the presence of this party has contributed to a sense of unity in electoral politics, by serving as the outsider "against which all other parties contrast themselves."[106]

This process of discursively separating the "insiders" and "outsiders" of electoral politics closely mirrors the interplay between "sameness" and "difference" in national boundary drawing. At the root of all boundary formation projects – whether these apply to ethnic, religious, or other groupings – is the attempt to distinguish "us" from "them."[107] Likewise, belonging to the nation is "always constituted vis-à-vis what or who we are not." In producing a bounded sense of national identity, therefore, national actors must construct a kind of "imagined homogeneity" that downplays "the realities of difference in the populations constituting the nation."[108]

The struggle to demarcate electoral boundaries can also *shape* national boundary drawing. According to research, political parties not only contribute to the proliferation of media-produced "imagined communities";[109] they also influence public opinion on various matters, including immigrants' belonging to the nation[110] and group identity.[111]

I utilize these insights to contend that differing *contexts* of partisan conflict – which are tied to the historic prevalence of distinct axes of electoral competition – have contributed to producing different *processes* of contention among the major parties involved in the French and Québécois secularism debates. In France, where class conflicts have until very recently dominated voter-party alignments, the traditional political parties have been willing to claim consensus – whether real or imagined – around questions of national identity and minority integration if it enables them to deflect the ultra-right political threat. In Quebec, however, where distinct nationalist visions dictate much of the battle among parties, consensus around matters of identity and integration has been far more elusive.[112]

In placing the *processes* of partisan conflict at the centre of the analysis, I do not deny the influence of established ideas or institutions over the politics of secularism and the production of nationhood in France and Quebec. I take seriously the notion that the political mention of ideas and institutions is a highly strategic and goal-oriented endeavour. However, I also appreciate the important role that these factors play in setting the "overall constitutive rules, the ideological terrain of taken-for-granted assumptions, within which strategic action occurs."[113] These "rules" and "assumptions" are not necessarily always coherent. In this regard, I suggest that, as they become bases for political action, overarching ideas like republicanism and interculturalism, and the institutional frameworks that sustain them, can and do take on shifting meanings.[114] I in turn propose that those meanings are profoundly influenced by interests,[115] in particular by parties' strategic efforts to "own" salient political issues in order to gain control over what constitutes "legitimate" politics.

CONCLUSION

Given the significant shortcomings of the national "models" and institutional approaches in explaining the trajectories of the religious signs debate in France and Quebec, I have proposed in this chapter a *politics-centred* framework for examining these processes. This framework foregrounds the linkages between attempts by political parties to "own" the religious signs issue – reshaping the boundaries of the political sphere in the process – and the demarcation of national boundaries. A central tenet of this approach, moreover, is that the extent to which class-based versus nation-centred social cleavages motivate electoral competition affects parties' articulations of – and positioning around – secularism and religious diversity. Over the next several chapters, I will employ this politics-centred framework to argue that the differing *contexts* and *processes* of partisan conflict in France and Quebec have led parties to articulate the religious signs issue in different ways, with implications for representing Muslims' belonging to the nation.

PART ONE

Demarcating the Boundaries of Politics

2

"Neither Right nor Left: French!"

Meeting the Ultra-Right Challenge in French Politics

This chapter analyzes the historical and contemporary contestations around religious signs in the French political system. Utilizing secondary historical data, government documents, and newspaper reports, and drawing further insight from the literature on political articulation, I argue that party political battles over who gets to "own" the religious signs issue in France have shaped the meaning(s) that politicians apply to republicanism in contemporary debates over the face veil.

My analysis focuses on critical historical junctures in which alliances and conflicts formed among three political parties: the right-wing UMP (since renamed Les Républicains, "The Republicans"), the left-wing Socialists, and the ultra-right Front National. Highly established and institutionalized, the former two parties have traditionally profiled themselves in terms of their contrasting economic agendas. Although periodically relevant, the issues of secularism and religious integration have not traditionally shaped the "axis of competition" between them. By contrast, the Front National is known for profiling itself in ways that intentionally defy established norms of party political contention in France. Founded in the early 1970s, but rising in electoral significance since the 1980s, this political party has largely branded itself according to "non-material" issues, like the threat of immigration to French national identity and culture.

I argue below that the dynamics of contestation that have arisen among these three parties shape the meaning(s) that politicians attach to republicanism - particularly laïcité – in France, with important consequences for articulating the gendered and racialized parameters of nationhood in the face veil debate. In particular, I maintain that by linking immigration to a proclaimed "crisis" in French national identity, the Front National put pressure on its competitors to take more explicit – and indeed more restrictive – positions on issues, like veiling, that have not traditionally been bases of contention. As they struggled to maintain their political territories in the face of this ultra-right challenge, both the UMP and the Socialists embraced the curtailment of religious signs in French public space as a way of promoting both laïcité and other values commonly associated with republicanism. These commitments in turn justified a closed conception of French nationhood, which, as I show in later chapters, rests on exclusionary notions of belonging and citizenship.

THE FRENCH REVOLUTION: BIRTHPLACE OF TWO COMPETING NOTIONS OF NATIONHOOD

Successive and highly conflict-ridden nation-building periods have been pivotal to laying the ideational and institutional foundations of parties' contemporary struggle to "own" the religious signs issue in France. To fully understand that struggle, we must look back at the event that gave birth to the republican discourse of French nationhood: the 1789 Revolution.[1] This event crystallized two competing visions of church-state relations, which have since underpinned the politics of secularism in France. Put forward by conservative counter-republicans, the first vision invoked the Gallican (the title assigned to the Catholic Church of France from 1682–1790) tradition, to promote an institutionalized state religion under the joint control of the Pope and the French monarch. This view contrasted sharply with that of a second group, the revolutionaries, whose nationalist vision centred on opposing the Catholic Church's control over public affairs.[2] In the centuries since, strategies for delimiting the relationship between religion and the public sphere in France have oscillated between these two opposing conceptions.

In the immediate aftermath of the 1789 Revolution, the French state maintained a degree of control over the Catholic Church, requiring priests to demonstrate their allegiance to the constitution and persecuting those who refused. However, after the 1795 fall of Robespierre – a leading figure in the French Revolution – the state withdrew its support of all religions, guaranteeing religious freedom to all, but forbidding public religious expression, including the wearing of religious clothing, funeral processions, and bell ringing. However, this regime, which instituted a strict, privatized notion of faith and religious belief, was short-lived. In 1801, Napoleon introduced a renewed form of Gallicanism through a Concordat (an agreement between the Catholic Church and the state) with the pope, which required that the French state officially recognize Catholicism. However, the Napoleonic Civil Code established in 1804 also restricted the powers of the Church by requiring that a civil authority perform marriages, by permitting divorce, and by introducing state regulation of inheritance. This regime also granted the state control over secondary schools and universities, but left primary schools in the hands of the Church.[3]

Although they specified the terms of church-state relations, arrangements established during the Napoleonic era left unresolved the underlying tension between the religious anti-republicanism of the French countryside and the growing anti-religious sentiment in urban centres.[4] This tension coincided with the antagonism emerging between "two Frances": the conservative and Catholic tradition of the provinces and atheistic and socialist Paris.[5] This antagonism was manifested in the growing gap between institutional, state-driven secular initiatives and the remaining cultural and moral salience of religion. With the Napoleonic Civil Code, the Catholic Church lost much of its institutional hold over the terms of public life in education, medicine, and law. Increasingly, governance over these spheres became inscribed in the logic of nation-statehood. Yet, religion remained highly significant as a moral and symbolic foundation for national belonging. Under Napoleon's reign, Catholicism gained recognition as "the religion of a large majority of Frenchmen," while minority religions – namely reformed and Lutheran Protestantism and Judaism – were, due in part to their militantism, credited with recognition by the state.[6]

The "double logic"[7] thus instilled during the Napoleonic era served as the basis for a continuing oscillation between republican and counter-republican discourses of nationhood in nineteenth-century France. That conflict came to a head in the violent uprisings of the Paris Commune that followed the country's defeat in the Franco-Prussian War. These events launched the Third Republic (1870–1940), an era of massive social and ideological transformation, during which rapid industrialization, advances in transportation and communications technology, and eroding local sources of belonging –

such as churches and local professional bodies – combined to produce a sense of nationhood that transcended geographic boundaries. Rural regions previously isolated from urban centres became the main targets of a state-led "civilizing" and modernizing project, which aimed to reorient France's diverse populace toward national, rather than local, concerns.[8] Along with the legacy of the Franco-Prussian War, the creation of the national anthem and the 1880 introduction of 14 July – "Bastille Day"[9] – as a national holiday solidified the perception of a shared national identity. A consolidated public education system helped to disseminate these national symbols to the masses, creating an unprecedented and publicly visible sense of "national community."[10]

Steps toward institutionalizing the religious neutrality of the French state served this broader quest to instill the conception of a national "we." With the Jules Ferry laws of the 1880s – which established free, mandatory, and secular education – the school replaced the church as the key source of knowledge about the world, becoming the inculcator of nationhood and patriotism on a national scale.[11] From this point forward, teachers in France's public schools would have to be lay people (not priests), and only secular teachings were allowed in the classroom.[12] Within a decade, an entire generation of previously "uncivilized" French school children would gain knowledge and competencies – including proficiency in the French language – that transcended the needs, and indeed the horizons, of their local communities.[13]

Yet, attempts to secure a state monopoly over education in the 1880s were only partly successful. Even though many no longer adhered to the moral dogmas of Catholicism, 97 per cent of French citizens remained notionally Catholic during this period. As a result, there was significant popular interest in maintaining the religious rites surrounding baptism, marriage, and burial.[14] Therefore, and despite the measures adopted through the Ferry laws, there remained for many decades "two school systems" – one religious and the other secular – whose curricula cultivated distinct visions of French society. In this way, the tension between a secular and a religious conception of nationhood remained notwithstanding state-led secular initiatives at the legal and institutional levels.[15]

The institutionally embedded tension between "two Frances" also took on important gendered dimensions with the sweeping secularizing reforms of the nineteenth century. While contemporary advocates of religious restriction have framed gender equality as the fruit of secularism, Scott has challenged that interpretation, demonstrating that secularization also brought about new and distinct forms of gender *in*equality, which were predicated on the division carved between the public and private spheres. Whereas the public sphere became the locus of male activity – in which reasonable debate was to take place, and where matters of state, rights, and citizenship were to be addressed – the private sphere became the home of passion and religious tradition, two traits that were read as feminine in the national cultural repertoire. In other words, the secularizing initiatives that marked nation-building in nineteenth-century France enabled a relegation of femininity to the private sphere, as women became "angels in the house," while men occupied the realm of the public and the political.[16]

The newly formed and increasingly secular French national identity of the nineteenth century was put under increased pressure by intensifying immigration levels in the 1870s and 1880s. Without the mass rural exodus that had urbanized Germany and Britain's populations, French capitalists sought to fill labour shortages by drawing on foreign workers, whom they largely recruited from other European countries such as Italy, Poland, and Spain. The resulting influx of migrants provoked a backlash from the native-born working classes, prompting professional bodies to organize around questions of nationality, seeking to keep out foreigners.[17] Aware of the electoral payoff to be gained from drawing on fear of incoming foreigners, politicians proposed legislation to limit the benefits of French citizenship for newcomers.[18] Although the native-born children of parents born outside France were allowed to naturalize as of 1889, these new citizens did not share all of the rights of French nationals; a line was drawn internally between citizens who were "nationals" and those who remained "outsiders."[19]

Tensions around immigration intersected with ongoing struggles over church-state relations in the Dreyfus Affair of 1898–99. This event, which involved accusations of treason against a Jewish military captain, brought to the fore the anti-Semitic sentiment that underlay much of the counter-republican movement.[20] Pro-Church forces took advantage of this scandal to cast a negative light on the institutional separation of church and state and to call for the re-establishment of Catholicism's governing powers. However, the vindication of Captain Dreyfus, combined with the advance of public secular education in the 1880s, forced Catholic conservatives to concede ground, eventually leading them to accept republicanism in some form. The resulting republican "synthesis" combined elements of the socialist left and the Catholic right and shaped the definition of French national identity until the Vichy regime dismantled it in the Second World War.[21]

However, partisan divisions continued to play an important role in articulations of French nationhood during this period. Seeking to offset the growing political influence of the industrial working class, right-wing conservatives crafted a narrative that emphasized the rural and Catholic dimensions of belonging, and romanticized a way of life increasingly threatened by modernization, immigration, and international conflict.[22] Actors deploying this script portrayed immigrants and Jews, two groups widely deemed incapable of true loyalty to France, as the "other."[23] An emerging leftist contingent opposed this vision, offering its own future-oriented national script, which saw public education as crucial to producing a literate, autonomous, and rational populace, capable of resisting religious dogmatism and opposing the determinism of the conservative ethos.[24]

These public figures on the left, many of them part of a coalition known as the Bloc des gauches (Leftist Bloc), became the main architects of the 1905 Law of Separation between Church and State, which abolished the power of the Concordat to regulate relationships between the French state and "recognized religions." The final version of the law defines secularism in terms of individuals' right to the free exercise of religion (article 1) and the non-subsidization of religion by the state (article 2).[25] By adopting these measures, the 1905 law marked the end of the Concordat, which gave semi-official status to Catholicism in France. Yet, two exceptions remained. First, the law contained a provision promising to maintain chaplaincy services in isolated spaces such as prisons, hospitals, the army, and boarding schools. The second exception to the 1905 law concerns the attribution of state funds to maintain religious buildings – churches, temples, and synagogues – that had previously been public property.[26]

Importantly, the institutional secularism established by the 1905 law also did not apply in French colonial territories, such as Algeria. In these jurisdictions, religion continued to be promulgated as a basis of attachment and loyalty to the French Empire. Even the anticlerical forces of the metropolis favoured the maintenance of

Catholic schools in colonized territories as spaces in which to educate future elites.[27]

Although the 1905 law embodied a pragmatic and liberal interpretation of secularism,[28] it was not the object of a complete consensus in the French parliament. Three other interpretations of laïcité also prevailed during this period. The first saw laïcité as a vehicle for destroying the Catholic Church and de-Christianizing French society. A second view, advocated by followers of Emile Combes, who was leader of the leftist cabinet at the time of the 1905 law, emphasized the need to end privileges for clergymen, but maintained that the state should have control of the church. A third and final interpretation sought to republicanize or democratize the church itself.[29]

The ideological tensions around the meaning(s) of laïcité and nationhood that were established during the nineteenth century – most notably that between a republican secular outlook based on freedom of religion and expression, and a counter-republican image of France emphasizing its Catholic roots – laid the ideational foundations of the current struggle over Islamic signs. Indeed, as I will show, these tensions continue to orient partisan debates around ways to apply laïcité in the context of rising immigration to France. At the same time, because of competition among parties to "own" the religious signs issue, those debates have been obscured by a proclaimed cross-party consensus around the need to protect laïcité by restricting (certain) religious signs in France's public sphere.

FRANCE: A NATION OF IMMIGRANTS?

Although France is now considered a country of immigration, permanent resettlement "has *never* achieved the legitimacy that it has enjoyed in the United States or Canada," for example.[30] This is partly due to the fact that, until relatively recently, immigration to France was conceived in largely temporary terms, as a mechanism through which to fill short-term labour shortages. In more recent decades, the proliferation of long-term settlement, combined with the shift in immigrant origins from primarily European countries to former North African colonies, has introduced new controversies around immigration in France, a partial outcome of which is the debate over Islamic religious signs.

Until the mid-twentieth century, French employers were the primary actors responsible for organizing immigration to France, with the state occasionally intervening to halt arrivals in large numbers. The country's first major wave of migration began in the latter decades of the nineteenth century, when declining fertility and a delayed rural exodus prompted French industrialists to seek foreign labour. By 1900, the largest proportion of foreigners hailed from Belgium and Germany, with increasing numbers arriving from Italy and Poland by the 1920s.[31] Changes in the characteristics of French immigration – including a shift in settlers' origins and their growing tendency toward long-term stay – prompted virulent nativist and anti-immigrant campaigns in the postwar period. Beginning in 1946, the French state began to fill labour shortages by accepting increasing numbers of temporary workers from its colonies in Tunisia, Morocco, and Algeria (a protectorate of France until 1962). Mostly men looking to send remittances and eventually return to their countries of origin, these temporary workers were treated as "visitors" to France. Keeping their practice of Islam minimal, they did not expect, nor receive, permanent rights or recognition from the French state.[32]

As immigration from France's North African colonies accelerated and took on a more settled character in the 1960s, the tenor of anti-immigrant campaigns became especially hostile. Despite initially being granted a privileged legal status due to their countries' colonial ties to France, newcomers from this region became the subjects of increasingly concerted attempts to thwart access to permanent citizenship.[33] These attempts coincided with a new phase in the struggle over French national identity, one that has defined the terms of struggle over the boundaries of French politics ever since. During this period, the resurgence of capitalism and the construction of a global diplomatic infrastructure fostered a forward-thinking republican narrative centred on universal rights. Although conservative politicians did not abandon their concern about foreigners and immigration, they refrained from orienting their political platforms around these issues, recognizing the destructive effects of xenophobic attitudes.[34] The postwar generation also bore witness to a period of wide-scale social upheaval, with previously isolated rural populations navigating their way to France's growing urban centres.

The resulting identity struggles culminated in the protests of May 1968, which solidified a left-wing vision that broke significantly with the prior leftist script. Rather than seeing national identity as simply the product of historical fact, participants in this movement saw it as demanding a critical rethinking of the republican social project, one that would embrace previously marginalized populations and identities. An emerging multicultural discourse thus became the vehicle for a postcolonial denunciation of the assimilationist practices of the French state, particularly those directed at France's Algerian, Tunisian, and Moroccan populations.[35]

This vision provoked a backlash among right-wing conservatives who, by the 1980s, were less able to contain anti-immigrant sentiment within their ranks. The increasing visibility of the Arab-Muslim population, mostly from Algeria, contributed to the conflict over French national identity. Two factors exacerbated tensions around this community. First, economic recession embittered French-born citizens who believed that Algerian workers, whom many continued to view as former colonial subjects rather than full-fledged French citizens, were taking precious jobs away from those born in mainland France. By the 1950s, male French citizens from Algeria, and migrants from Tunisia and Morocco, were increasingly being joined by their spouses and children, giving the French North African community a more settled character. The oil crises of the 1970s hit this community hard, creating high joblessness rates and intensifying the reliance on social services.[36] Second, the native-born children of Algerians – known as "Beurs" – were beginning to demand their rights as full-fledged French citizens, marching across France in 1983 in a national call for labour market equality and an end to racist violence. The "Beurs" were split into different camps. One contingent sought mainstream representation and campaigned for colour-blind equality in the Socialist Party and civic organizations like SOS Racisme, an anti-racist NGO founded in 1984. A second contingent sought more meaningful recognition of the community's Muslim identity, which it fought for through activism in pro-Islamic associations. Committed to demonstrating that one can be both Muslim and French, members of the latter group engaged in increasingly public forms of religious practice, by building mosques, participating in public rituals such as group prayer, and adopting religious dress.[37]

Public concern over the integration of French North Africans – who are concentrated mainly in city suburbs where rates of unemployment are high and housing is deteriorating – has continued to foster efforts to limit access to French citizenship. "Franco-Algerians" and their children were the central targets of the debate surrounding France's Nationality Code, which culminated in the highly restrictive Pasqua Laws of 1993.[38] Among other things, these laws revoked the automatic attribution of citizenship to children born in France to foreign-born parents. Although this and other restrictive aspects of the law were later modified, new restrictions have since been introduced. Following the right-wing return to power in 2002, the French government issued new limitations on foreigners' access to French visas and nationality, particularly for foreign spouses.[39]

Citizenship rates – particularly among North African migrants – remain remarkably low in France. According to the results of the 2008 *Trajectories and Origins* survey, the proportion of those with French nationality ranges from 45 per cent among Algerian migrants to 47 per cent among those arriving from Morocco and Tunisia.[40] These low rates are partly due to the substantial practical and administrative barriers that applicants face in gaining citizenship. In order to be approved, an applicant must pass several thresholds and meet requirements set by various governmental agencies. One of the main obstacles stems from the criterion of "acceptability," which requires applicants to justify their "assimilation into the French community, primarily by sufficient knowledge of the French language."[41] This criterion became especially important following the rise in immigration from Sub-Saharan Africa in the 1970s. During this period, the definition of assimilation was expanded to include "accepting French values, especially when candidates practiced polygamy or wore Islamic headscarves, despite the fact that administrative tribunals discourage such approaches."[42]

Just as the Franco-Prussian War served as a reference point for the definition of French national identity in the Third Republic, "Arabs" and "Muslims" became the "other" that shaped the terms of political debate regarding national belonging from the 1980s onward.[43] It is in this political climate that the populist and ultra-right Front National gained strength and, through its adoption of a nation "in crisis" script, launched a period of heightened contestation over the configuration of French politics and of French nationhood itself.

NAVIGATING A CLASS-BASED POLITICS: THE SOCIALIST AND UMP PARTIES

In order to understand how political parties' articulation of the boundaries of the electoral sphere has shaped the unfolding of France's secularism debate, it is necessary to first identify the particularities of the French electoral system. This system is highly unique in that it utilizes a two-round approach to electing both presidential and parliamentary candidates. As I will show below, the mechanical and psychological effects of this system[44] have helped to crystallize the contemporary right and left political camps in France, which until very recently have been overwhelmingly dominated by the UMP and Socialist parties.[45]

The French political system favours large parties and parties that can foster a broad consensus. In the case of presidential elections, the top two candidates advance to a run-off election in the second round – unless a candidate receives more than 50 per cent on the first ballot. In legislative elections, all candidates who receive the support of at least 12.5 per cent of registered electors are considered in the second round – unless, once again, the 50 per cent threshold is surpassed in the first round.[46]

Under this two-round system, large parties tend to be systematically overrepresented. In particular, parties that attract 20 per cent or more of the vote receive a higher number of seats than is warranted by their actual representation in the electorate. Parties involved in coalitions, which are common in the French political system, also benefit.[47] From a psychological standpoint, France's two-round system encourages majority outcomes by incentivizing strategic voting in two ways. First, voters who favour a party that has little chance of reaching the second ballot may choose to vote for a party that stands a better chance of passing this threshold. Second, voters whose preferred party is likely to enter the second round may choose to vote for a party against which they believe their candidate will have the strongest chance of winning.[48]

By advantaging large political parties, France's two-round electoral system has helped to solidify two "antagonistically related ideological camps."[49] The make-up of those camps has changed dramatically since the 1970s. Beginning in that decade, the left-wing camp saw a marked shift in power from the Parti communiste français (Communist Party of France, PCF) to the Socialists. Meanwhile, on the right side of the aisle, the key development has been the consolidation of (most) opposing parties under a single roof – the UMP – since 2002.

Until the late 1970s, the PCF enjoyed an advantage over the PS in legislative elections. This advantage came to an end with the rise of the Socialist Party in the 1978 legislative and 1981 presidential elections.[50] After becoming the leading voice of the left in electoral politics, the Socialist Party worked hard to consolidate diverse progressive viewpoints and incorporate radical and dissenting voices into its platform. Beginning in the 1970s, "new social movements" focusing on issues from feminism to the environment emerged as an alternative to the traditional axis of electoral contention in France. Despite the initial hostility of the major parties to competition from these alternative perspectives, Socialist Party elites largely succeeded in neutralizing or co-opting these issues for political gain.[51] Two main motivations underlay this attempt at co-optation. First, "new" political issues appealed to France's growing middle class, a key constituency of interest to the party. Second, there was "electoral capital" to be gained from these attempts at ownership. In particular, the necessity of attracting votes in the second round of elections encouraged the party to appear "open" to other currents within the left.[52] In this way, the Socialists' desire to diffuse opposition from left-wing competitors is partly accounted for by the two-round system and the constraints it imposes on the success of small parties.[53]

Attempts to gain ownership of "new" political issues, in part as a way to attract the growing middle class vote, have produced a complex relationship to the working class – and to class ideology more generally – within the French Socialist Party. In his attempts to make the PS the "hegemonic party" of the left, for instance, the Socialist leader in the 1970s, François Mitterrand, challenged the "materialist" orientation that had been the hallmark of the Communist Party brand and pursued an "ideological renovation" that has shaped the Socialists' role in French politics ever since. Although continuing to compete with the PCF (and with other further left parties) for blue-collar votes, the party effectively became one of "white-collar middle-class membership and votes."[54] Ironically, the more successful the party's leadership has been in rebalancing the left electorally, the more conservative it has become in promoting the "post-material" issues that served to differentiate it from its Communist competitor.[55] For example, as it increased its electoral support, the Socialist Party has become less open to the influence of dissenting feminist voices. The dominance of national electoral concerns has frustrated many members of this group who regret the party's militant "de-mobilization."[56]

The ongoing tendency toward "de-mobilization" – and the related strategy of downplaying traditional class concerns – has diluted the Socialist Party brand in the long run. In the 2002 election, the party became destabilized when its presidential candidate, Lionel Jospin, announced that he was "not a Socialist."[57] This comment, combined with Jospin's general reluctance to engage with the struggles of the industrial working class,[58] alienated left-wing voters and contributed to the Socialists' failure to reach the second ballot in that election. Nonetheless, while the Socialist Party became more centrist in its economic platform and less anti-capitalist, it remained focused on "bread-and-butter" issues, that is, on advancing the economic interests of its constituents, for example through policies regarding retirement and pensions, workers' pay, benefits, purchasing power, and hours of work. This was not surprising, given that unemployment rates began to rise in the early 1980s and have remained high ever since.

While the trajectory of France's left-wing political bloc has been driven by efforts at co-optation, on the right the key struggle has been over the consolidation of numerous and competing political parties. The central plot line in this regard has been the growing predominance of the Rassemblement pour la république (Rally for the Republic, RPR), particularly from the late 1980s onward, and the related electoral decline of other right-wing parties, including the more centrist Union pour la démocratie française (Union for French Democracy, UDF).[59] The RPR consolidated its power in 2002 when its leadership launched a new party – the UMP – whose membership combined representatives from numerous parties, though principally the RPR.[60] The impetus for the party's formation was twofold. The first motivation was to restore the authority of the RPR president, Jacques Chirac, following a poor performance in the first round of the 2002 presidential elections. The second, more institutional imperative underlying the creation of the UMP was to tighten the connection between the legislative and presidential aspects of the French political system. Although a normative system of cooperation dictated that parties on the right support each other in various ways – including by not threatening other parties' incumbency in particular ridings – adherence to these norms was not guaranteed.[61] As such, following his election to the presidency in 2002, Chirac felt he could no longer rely solely on the RPR for predominance in the legislative elections, and thus sought to consolidate his power through the creation of the UMP.

The positioning of the two traditional parties – the Socialists and the UMP – on key issues such as immigration is at least in part informed by the economic or class interests of their constituents. As the all-encompassing party of the left until 2017, the Socialists have traditionally fared much better in low-income constituencies, many of which comprise large numbers of residents of North African origin.[62] By contrast, the UMP has drawn much of its support from shopkeepers, craftsmen, and farmers, who tend to concentrate in more rural, less diverse areas.[63] In theory, therefore, appealing to a discourse of national identity "crisis" should raise more difficult dilemmas for the Socialists than for the UMP, by threatening to alienate the party's core constituencies, including Muslims. At the same time, however, Muslims' support for the Socialists is so overwhelming that the party has been able to rely on this constituency in elections. In 2012, for example, an extraordinary 93 per cent of French Muslims cast their votes in favour of the Socialist candidate for president, François Hollande.[64]

ENTER THE FRONT NATIONAL

Founded on the heels of the 1973 oil crisis, which hit France's industrial working class regions particularly hard, the Front National began as a party committed to protecting France from "foreign" political, economic, and cultural threats,[65] particularly those associated with communism and Marxist thought.[66] In its early stages, the party also drew significantly from themes associated with the Poujadiste movement, an anti-parliamentarian, xenophobic, and anti-Semitic group formed in the 1950s and backed by artisans and shopkeepers. The Front National's founding leader, Jean-Marie Le Pen, was himself a Poujadiste MP in the National Assembly during his youth. When he created the party, Le Pen invoked Poujadiste themes as a way of drawing together a heterogeneous collection of actors, including monarchists, former Nazi collaborators, traditionalist Catholics, and counter-revolutionaries.[67]

The Front National remained a sort of loose-fitting and relatively ineffective coalition of such groups until 1983, when its electoral breakthrough in the municipal elections of Dreux, a town in Northern France, marked its real take-off. Three years later, the party gained an unprecedented thirty-five seats in the National Assembly. This victory was partly enabled by President Mitterrand's introduction of proportional representation.[68] But it also stemmed from what Schain calls the FN's "reservoir of legitimacy."[69] From his party's inception, Jean-Marie Le Pen was able to capitalize on the anti-immigrant discourses that distinguished the Communist Party brand until its decline in the late 1970s. Indeed, prior to the creation of the FN, the Communist Party had been a principal vehicle "through which the immigration issue had been politically defined."[70] When the party lost electoral ground, the FN became the primary spokes-vehicle for anti-immigrant concerns, which by then had begun to resonate with voters.

The strength of attitudes to immigration in predicting the FN vote quickly distinguished the party as one whose fate would be determined by "issue voting." Yet, from its inception, the FN also managed to secure a relatively loyal following. In the 1980s, the party drew much of its support from artisans and shopkeepers, but also many in the liberal professions earning high incomes. In addition, more than two-thirds of its voters were non-practising Catholics, 60 per cent were male, and a majority were between the ages of thirty-five and sixty-five. Thus, in terms of age, sex, and income, early supporters of the Front National were "more likely than most voters to be stable and committed partisans."[71] By attracting these constituencies to his party, Le Pen built a base that expanded through the 1980s.

Although the revocation of proportional representation in 1986 put an end to the Front National's early success in the National Assembly, the party continued to increase its support in regional and presidential races, with Le Pen making a stunning breakthrough to the second round of the 2002 presidential elections, with 16.86 per cent of the vote in the first round, and his daughter and successor, Marine Le Pen, polling 17.9 per cent of votes in 2012[72] before advancing to the second round of the 2017 race for the presidency.[73]

In its more than forty years of existence, the Front National has varied its methods for articulating the concerns of French voters. In the 1990s, the party shifted its focus from the dangers of communism, Marxist thought, and Soviet Russia to the ways that Europeanization, and the global capitalist relations to which it contributed, threatened France's ability to govern its own cultural and economic affairs. Of growing concern to voters across the ideological spectrum, the question of France's future within a consolidated Europe became the key discursive vehicle by which Jean-Marie Le Pen and his associates presented themselves as capable of "overcoming the sectarian tendencies of the mainstream French left and right."[74] The significance of this tactic to the Front National's political brand became evident in its 1997 congress in Strasbourg, when the party adopted the slogan "Neither right nor left: French!"[75]

This rejection of left-right terminology – and consequently of the established class-based axis of competition – enabled Le Pen to claim, in the context of debate over Europe's expanding competencies in areas like immigration, security, and currency, that "a vote for him was a vote for France."[76] This strategy proved increasingly successful as the mainstream parties on the right and left converged around a program that was pro-Europe and, by extension, pro-globalization. That convergence was pivotal to the Front National's positioning within the French electoral system, as it enabled Le Pen to utilize elements of left-wing rhetoric – such as anti-capitalism – in forging a discourse that he could then market as broadly "French."[77]

With the start of the new millennium, a second of the Front National's most defining political claims – that immigrants are taking precious jobs away from native French citizens and thus threatening the social fabric of the nation – gained prominence. This claim has consistently polled well with working-class voters, particularly those who inhabit France's older industrial and urbanized regions, which also contain large numbers of immigrants from North Africa. These are the areas that have been hardest hit by economic crisis and where feelings of fear and insecurity are most acute.[78] The Front National's anti-immigrant platform was also compatible with its anti-European stance, as both positions hinged on a proclaimed need to strengthen and secure the territorial, as well as the cultural, boundaries of the French nation.

Recently, the Front National has turned its sights on "de-demonizing"[79] and "normalizing"[80] its political brand in order to expand its political base. One of the ways it has effected this transformation is by appointing a woman – Jean-Marie Le Pen's daughter, Marine Le Pen – to its top post. Elected party leader in 2011, after holding a prominent position in the FN since 2002, Marine Le Pen has appealed to voters by combining a kind of "familial charisma" inherited from her father with an ability to distinguish herself – partly through the fact that she is a woman – as an outsider to mainstream politics.[81] This unique combination affords Le Pen a highly distinctive status in the French electoral sphere. As Geva puts it, by being the "political daughter," she can "play the role of game-changer, distant from technocratic and ultraliberal political elites, and yet keeper of the FN tradition."[82] By providing the FN with a "softer, more domesticated and feminine" image, Marine Le Pen has made her party's message more palatable to a mainstream French audience.[83]

While seeking to "normalize" her party's brand, Marine Le Pen has not turned back on her father's commitment to destabilizing France's axis of competition by articulating a message that transcends traditional class cleavages. In addition to her working-class base, she has also reached out to skilled workers. While they "think of themselves as removed from the upper echelons of society," Wieviorka has argued that many such workers are "at pains to differentiate themselves from the lower reaches of society, which they conceive as a mix of immigrants who refuse to integrate and prefer to live on social welfare benefits, the poor who take advantage of state assistance, and young people who are nothing more than 'riff raff.'"[84] In order to link the concerns of skilled voters to her working-class base, Marine Le Pen has characterized these groups collectively as the "invisible" and the "forgotten," two terms that she also uses to interpolate farmers, the unemployed, and pensioners.[85]

By unifying disparate constituencies around a culturally and economically protectionist program, the Front National has succeeded in upsetting established voter-party alignments in France. In its early days, when it most directly threatened the ideological territory of the centre-right, the party was the object of intense debate over how best to limit its effect on the distribution of right-wing votes. During his tenure as RPR prime minister under Socialist president François Mitterrand from 1986 to 1988,[86] Jacques Chirac sought to appease the Front National by proposing a model of second-generation citizenship acquisition that made the attribution of nationality to those born in France to foreign-born parents dependent on a voluntary act. However, the political costs of this reform combined with opposition from the Conseil d'État (Council of State) forced Chirac to back away from the proposal.[87] Later, in his campaign for re-election as president in 2002, Chirac changed tack, dissociating himself more explicitly from his Front National rival, Jean-Marie Le Pen. Fearing that Le Pen had gained ground, Chirac sought to keep him from winning the presidency in the second round of voting (with the RPR pitted against the Front National, the Socialist Party having been knocked out in the first round) by joining forces with the left in a "republican front."[88] Although Chirac was easily re-elected in the second ballot with 82 per cent of the vote, this approach did not stem the long-term growth of the Front National's electoral base. In fact, in many ways, the coming together of left and right voters to secure Chirac's victory in the second round further entrenched what had become a key factor in Le Pen's growing electoral success: an impression that the ideological boundaries between left and right in France were eroding.

Debates over how to respond to the Front National's electoral rise continued to rage within the UMP, particularly in the aftermath of Le Pen's unexpected breakthrough to the second round of the 2002 presidential elections. While some advocated incorporating Front National themes into the UMP platform, others resisted this option, preferring to maintain a clear distance from the party. Vacillation between these alternatives has manifested itself in "contradictions and fluctuations" in the UMP rhetoric.[89] Former president Nicolas Sarkozy embodies this phenomenon. His discourse and action on immigration control diverged significantly from earlier centre-right handling of these issues,[90] earning him a reputation as a "neo-FN" right-wing politician.[91]

By focusing increasingly on globalization's displacement of French workers, and calling for the state to play a greater role in the economy, the Front National has also begun to tread on the territory of the French political left. In recent years, the party has "permeated" workers' organizations "from the ground up" and reconciled with teachers, a group with whom it previously shared a mutual antipathy.[92] Marine Le Pen's Front National has also broken with the party's past by explicitly embracing the state as "an essential component of the soul of France."[93] This strategic embrace of state intervention – linked to what others have referred to as the party's "state nationalism"[94] and "ethno-socialist" framing of inequality[95] – is part and parcel of the party's effort to attract an electorate perceived as "imbued with a culture of the left."[96]

The presence of the Front National has thus significantly destabilized the left-right ideological blocs that have traditionally constituted the main axis of competition in France. By forcing its rivals to engage – through either cooperation or outright opposition – with issues not historically relevant to their platforms, the party has redrawn the boundaries of French political space. Along with domestic and world events that heighten the public's concerns around immigration, it has made it nearly impossible for its rivals to run a political campaign in which newcomers' integration and "radical" Islam are not front and centre. The Front National has also made it difficult for the major parties to market themselves as diverging in their responses to this question. Indeed, Marine Le Pen is fond of portraying her main political rivals as essentially indistinguishable. For example, in the 2012 presidential election campaign, she spoke about the "Siamese-twins" Sarkozy (UMP) and Hollande (Socialist Party), whom she characterized as "two representatives of the UMPS (a combination of UMP and PS) system who stage a mock fight."[97]

With the Front National successfully manipulating popular unrest over immigration and diversity since the 1980s, the UMP and Socialists have found themselves in the position of having to decide between rejecting their rival's anti-immigrant stance outright and attempting to co-opt the Front National by adopting a tougher line on immigration and diversity issues. I will show below that, while both tactics have been employed at various times, pressure to appear tough on "radical" Islam has led the UMP and Socialists to embrace the restriction of religious signs. Moreover, in seeking to justify this move as consistent with French republicanism, both parties have articulated the boundaries of republican nationhood and politics in increasingly narrow and exclusionary terms.

DEMARCATING THE BOUNDARIES OF POLITICS DURING AND AFTER THE 1989 "HEADSCARF AFFAIR"

According to de Leon and colleagues, the characteristics of the existing social order critically shape parties' capacity to rearticulate the boundaries of electoral politics in a given period.[98] Because prior articulations can have lasting and constraining effects, periods of social transformation are more conducive to rearticulation. Such transformative circumstances were present in France at the time of the 1989 "headscarf affair." By that year, the growth of the French Muslim population had combined with global controversies – notably the fatwa against novelist Salman Rushdie for his portrayal of Mohammed in *The Satanic Verses* – to spark public debate over the place of Islam in France. That debate was further intensified by the mobilization of the "Beurs" generation,[99] whose members were beginning to demand their rights as full-fledged French citizens.[100]

These international and domestic shifts set the stage for rearticulating the "blocs"[101] that constitute the French electoral system. In particular, they enabled the Front National to mobilize previously apolitical constituencies around anti-immigrant and anti-Muslim positions, sending shockwaves through French politics in the process. In responding, the traditional parties – particularly the Socialists – found themselves constrained, both by their own historic programs and by their pre-existing positions vis-à-vis the axis of competition. These parties had to be creative in refashioning prior political articulations, which they did in large part by injecting aspects of the Front National's ethnic nationalism into their own more civic and republican discourses of French nationhood.

The "headscarf affair" of 1989 involved the expulsion of three Muslim girls by a school in Creil (northeast of Paris) for wearing the headscarf. Although the girls agreed, following negotiations with the school principal, to remove their scarves in the classroom, that event sparked a nation-wide debate over the meaning of French laïcité and the school's symbolic role as inculcator of republican values.[102] The UMP's eventual lead in this debate pushed the rhetoric around Muslim religious integration rightward, causing a deep crisis of legitimacy on the left, particularly among Socialists, who felt increasing pressure to demonstrate their dedication to preserving the secularity of public space.

When the "headscarf affair" initially broke out in 1989, the major political parties were reluctant to take a definitive stance on the issue. Hoping to lessen public concern while maintaining an arm's length approach, the Socialist minister of education, Lionel Jospin, referred the question to the Conseil d'État. Although its decisions are not binding, the Conseil provides a check on the administrative and executive powers of the French state. A historic defender of liberal and republican principles – mainly equality of individuals before the law – it continues to function as a mediator in state-individual relations in France. Governments have traditionally deferred to the Conseil in matters concerning the legality of state actions and the wording of bills, as well as in deciding whether a piece of legislation passes the test of French jurisprudence. Its elite status and historic legacy afford the Conseil a unique ability to deflect government efforts to restrict immigration. In this case, the Court's advice – that school principals should be allowed to determine on a case-by-case basis whether headscarf-wearing girls were engaging in propaganda – resolved the headscarf issue, but only temporarily.

In 1994, François Bayrou, the minister of education in an RPR-dominated National Assembly, resurrected the issue by announcing the prohibition of ostentatious religious signs in all schools. Although this second round of debate subsided when the Conseil d'État reaffirmed its initial ruling,[103] it was quickly revived by right-wing politicians who, under the banner of the newly formed UMP, sought to capture the religious signs issue for their own political gain. In 2003, Nicolas Sarkozy, then minister of the interior in President Jacques Chirac's government, introduced a policy to prohibit facial coverings in official identity photographs. When debate over this policy sparked a broader discussion of religious signs in schools, Chirac appointed Bernard Stasi, the French ombudsman and former government minister, to head an independent investigation – composed of twenty members from a wide variety of backgrounds, including teachers, academics, jurists, politicians, and school administrators – into the political and legal parameters of laïcité in France, focusing on the public school system. Between September and December of 2003, the Stasi commission board heard testimony from 140 teachers, intellectuals, politicians, and activists.[104] One of its twenty recommendations – that ostentatious religious signs should be prohibited in public schools – was instituted as law in October 2004.

Throughout his tenure as minister of the interior and later as the UMP's candidate in the 2007 presidential election, Nicolas Sarkozy continued to position himself as the most suitable candidate to defeat the Front National. In doing so, he adopted shifting and contradictory approaches to defining republicanism and its relationship to Islam, earning himself a reputation as a highly ambiguous figure in French politics. In his early years as minister of the interior, Sarkozy sought to institutionalize the role of Islam within France by establishing umbrella organizations under the supervision of the state. In 2003, he created the Conseil français du culte musulman (The French Council of the Muslim Faith, CFCM), bringing together France's three largest Muslim organizations – the Great Mosque of Paris, the Fédération nationale des musulmans de France (National Federation of French Muslims, FNMF), and the Union des organisations musulmanes de France (Union of Islamic Organizations of France, UOIF) – into a single and centralized body tasked with representing Muslim interests in policy discussions with the state. The first of the CFCM's constituent bodies – the Great Mosque of Paris – was then perceived by government elites as the strongest force for "moderation" in the French Muslim community.[105] Supported by the Algerian government, this institution is affiliated with numerous other mosques. The second organization to become part of the CFCM umbrella in 2003, the FNMF, was founded in 1985 as an alternative to the Great Mosque. With ties to Morocco, it has historically drawn the support of French converts to Islam. Finally, the UOIF is the most visible and politically controversial member of the CFCM. Founded in 1983, it represents local cultural and mosque-affiliated Muslim associations throughout France. The UOIF gained national significance in 1989, when it supported the girls expelled from school in the famous "headscarf affair."[106]

At the time of the CFCM's creation, many believed it would finally allow the French state to incorporate Islam into its republican compact. In its early days, the organization fulfilled these expectations, providing the government with a legitimate instrument with which to supervise key aspects of Muslim religious life in France, including the building and maintenance of mosques and the training of imams.[107] However, internal divisions and critical responses from the Muslim community subsequently rendered the CFCM an unstable and ineffective force in French politics on religious diversity. As I will explain in chapter 4, this organization nevertheless remains essential in granting legitimacy to the French state in matters tied to Islam and Islamic relations.

Although it secured him a reputation for being skilled in dealing with the French Muslim community, fraternization with Muslim groups like the UOIF also proved risky to Sarkozy's career and public image. When he failed to place himself squarely behind the ban on ostentatious religious signs in schools in 2003 – in a move that appealed to his new Muslim allies – both the Front National and his own colleagues in the UMP attacked Sarkozy as a weak defender of French values. Recognizing that he had a strategic interest in taking a firmer stance on religious signs, Sarkozy reversed his position. In a speech delivered to representatives of Muslim organizations in April 2003, he announced his intention to institute stricter laws requiring French residents to uncover their faces when having identity photographs taken.[108] Later that year, Sarkozy also publicly endorsed a prohibition of religious signs in schools. Crafting an image of laïcité as a sacred aspect of French republicanism – one that dictated much of his future discourse on the topic – he claimed in a speech that "when I enter a mosque, I remove my shoes. When a young Muslim girl enters school, she must remove her headscarf."[109] Both speeches, which shocked members of the Muslim community accustomed to seeing Sarkozy as an ally, helped place him ahead of Chirac as UMP candidate in the race for the presidency.

By adopting aspects of the Front National's anti-Muslim stance, Sarkozy succeeded in recapturing a significant proportion of the votes lost by Chirac to Le Pen in 2002. On the eve of the first wave of the 2007 presidential election, 26 per cent of those who supported Le Pen in 2002 reported that they intended to vote for Sarkozy. Of those voters – whom commentators referred to as "lepéno-sarkozystes" – 94 per cent agreed with the statement that "there are too many immigrants in France" and 86 per cent expressed a negative view of Islam.[110] Co-optation of FN themes also enabled Sarkozy to recapture geographic areas seized by Le Pen in 2002 – particularly in the north of France[111] – and to increase his support among Catholics, farmers, and voters over age fifty.[112]

Just as the UMP was increasing its share of the vote by co-opting Front National themes, the Socialists were falling behind in the battle to "own" the debate over religious signs. Rather than focusing her 2007 campaign for the presidency on this issue, the Socialist candidate, Ségolène Royal, stuck to a traditional leftist discourse centred on issues of education, violence, purchasing power, and the environment. Moreover, while she spoke to the questions of violence and threats to security in France, Royal maintained that social and economic marginalization were at the root of these problems. She thus refused, to a large extent, to adopt a negative tone in characterizing immigration to France.[113]

This campaign strategy proved unsuccessful for Royal, who lost the 2007 race for the presidency, earning 46.94 per cent of the vote in the second round. Unlike Sarkozy, the Socialist candidate also profited little from the FN's decline in that election, claiming only 6 per cent of Le Pen's 2002 voters.[114] Moreover, while she expanded the Socialists' reach among blue-collar workers in the Western regions of France – who traditionally vote "yes" to Europe and "no" to Le Pen – Royal lost ground in large city suburbs[115] and registered a far poorer showing than Sarkozy among Catholics, farmers, small-business owners, and artisans.[116]

Once elected president, Sarkozy strengthened his lead over the Socialists even further, by inviting religious Catholics – a key Front National constituency – to support him in establishing a renewed conception of laïcité, which embraces France's Christian roots. In his famous Latran speech delivered as president in December 2007, he asserted that "Laïcité does not have the power to cut France from its Christian roots ... To pull out the root is to erase the meaning [of laïcité], to weaken the cement of national identity, to further weaken those social relationships that crucially depend on symbols and memory. This is why we must hold together the two ends of the chain: assume the Christian roots of France – even develop them – while defending laïcité, which has finally matured."[117] By identifying Christianity (mainly Catholicism) as the cultural symbol that anchors the republican commitment to state secularism, Sarkozy sought to create a space for sympathizers of the Front National within the UMP, inviting them to endorse a discourse that he called *laïcité positive* ("positive secularism"). Recognizing the threat that this poses to her own electoral territory, Marine Le Pen has since responded by invoking a discourse of laïcité that similarly references the religion of the majority. In a section of its platform entitled *Laïcité: une valeur au coeur du projet républicain* ("Laïcité: a value at the heart of the republican project"), the Front National claimed that "Christianity was for a millennium and a half the religion of most, if not all, French people. It is normal that this fact should profoundly mark the French landscape and national culture. French traditions cannot be disregarded."[118] The fact that this statement appeared under the heading "laïcité" reveals a desire to demonstrate that, like Sarkozy's UMP, the Front National is committed to making republicanism – and laïcité – compatible with France's Christian roots. The effort to reconcile these two aspects of French national identity also speaks to the modern Front National's desire to be taken seriously by mainstream politics. While, like her father, Le Pen remains committed to promoting an ethno-religious conception of nationhood that overtly excludes new immigrants, she also recognizes the rewards to be reaped from embracing republican themes that resonate with voters. Her efforts in this area speak to the malleability of extant ideas – like republicanism – in French political discourse.

By rendering the secularity of public spaces (mainly schools) almost sacred and by linking laïcité to France's Catholic history, Sarkozy's UMP and Marine Le Pen's Front National transformed secularism from an organizing legal and institutional principle to a fundamental aspect of French national belonging. And in monopolizing the contours of laïcité, both parties also managed to discredit the Socialists as disloyal, elitist, and, in some cases, as collaborators in a Muslim ploy to denigrate French republican values and history.[119] This critique has since gained ground in left-wing activist groups that bemoan the right's "kidnapping" of laïcité for political gain. These groups have taken to blaming prior Socialist administrations for failing to take a firmer stance against "radical" Islamic practices, beginning with the "headscarf affair."[120] In numerous editorials, publications, and blog posts, those in this camp assert that, by giving in to a "political correctness" that feeds into the right's gross distortion of laïcité, "Socialists no longer know where they belong" on this question in French politics.[121]

This critique of the Socialist Party has also taken a firm hold in second wave feminist circles. Annie Sugier, who was president of the Ligue du droit international des femmes (International League for Women's Rights) at the height of the face veil debate, sees secularism as a "legacy of the left," which the right "poorly manipulates." However, she also believes that "criticisms tied to colonialism and conflict with the United States have altered the left," causing it to abandon the secular cause.[122] Likewise, Michéle Vianès, president of Regards de femmes (Women's Outlooks), maintains that she "quit the Socialist Party" in 1993 out of concern for the number of people who "supported the notion that, in the name of tolerance, we should allow the oppression of women."[123]

In the next section, I delve further into the role that feminists like Sugier and Vianès have played in demarcating the boundaries of political contention with respect to the religious signs issue in France. I show that while a pro-restriction feminist contingent has gained the attention of the French state by articulating a republican critique of veiling that aligns with the goals of pro-ban politicians, those on the anti-restriction side have been pushed to the margins of this debate.

CONTESTING THE BOUNDARIES OF FEMINISM: CONFRONTATIONS BETWEEN PRO- AND ANTI-RESTRICTION FEMINISTS IN FRANCE

Contestations over the boundaries of feminism are central to the French religious signs debate. Those contestations are informed by a historical dispute between two competing conceptions of gender (in)equality. The first – what many call "gender as sameness" – suggests that abstraction from difference is necessary for equal citizenship. Advocates of this approach thus reject recognition of the differences between men and women "as a precondition for equality."[124] An opposing conception – "gender as difference" – identifies difference and its recognition as a crucial facet of equality, and suggests that gender is a social position that cannot be abstracted.[125]

This dynamic has historically pitted materialist feminists like Christine Delphy, Monique Wittig, and Nicole-Claude Mathieu, who essentially adhere to the first view, against those who represent the *courant de la différence* ("the difference current"), notably Antoinette Fouque, Luce Irigaray, Hélène Cixous, and Julia Kristeva.[126] It has also been critical in shaping the contours of feminism through successive battles, namely the struggle for gender parity in the political arena, academia, and the media, which took place between 1992 and 2000. As Lépinard argues, parity activists "had to zigzag strategically between different meanings of difference and equality to make their claims compatible with the Republic's core doctrines and therefore acceptable to power holders."[127]

The unresolved tension between a conception of "gender as sameness" and "gender as difference" is among the key reasons why second wave feminism has, until recently, been relatively impervious to postcolonial themes in France.[128] Together with other factors – namely the delayed development of postcolonial and feminist studies in French academia – this continuing disagreement has thwarted the large-scale incorporation of issues of race and colonialism into the feminist discourse. This is in part because, whatever their differences, both the materialist approach and the *courant de la différence* overwhelmingly emphasize the "singular difference of sex," to the exclusion of other relations of power, including class, race, or sexuality.[129]

However, contemporary debates over (mainly Islamic) religious signs have brought these issues to the forefront. As we will see, colonial dynamics critically inform the contestations that have taken place among pro- and anti-restriction feminists, with important implications for the ways that activists envision the boundaries of feminism *and* French nationhood.

Like its counterparts elsewhere, France's pro-restriction feminist movement is composed of a "constellation"[130] of individuals and organizations that diverge in their relationships to key axes of difference, including national citizenship, ethnicity, and religious background. A first group consists of predominantly white second-wave feminists, whose actions in the 1960s and 1970s focused on access to employment, abortion rights, and combatting violence against women. Over the last several decades, many of these activists have become vocal spokespersons for state-led campaigns to curtail the visibility of Islam in the public sphere.[131] In the process, organizations that once viewed republicanism as an inherently sexist doctrine have mobilized republican themes to claim that the headscarf, niqab, and burqa violate the gender ideals of French nationhood.[132]

In articulating this "republican" opposition to veiling, pro-restriction feminists have sought the support of "authentic insiders":[133] that is, women of Arab-Muslim background who publicly condemn Islamic religious practices, attracting much media attention and political acclaim in the process. Because they are deemed to have unique insight into Muslim culture, these "insiders" help to sustain an image of the "Western woman" as the sole bearer of women's emancipation. By refusing the veil, moreover, they also serve as role models for "good Muslims," that is, "unveiled, enlightened Muslim women like themselves and secular, gentle Arab men who accompany them."[134]

Jeanette Bougrab is among the figures to embody the role of "authentic insider" in the feminist contestations around the French face veil debate. A lawyer of Harki[135] Algerian background, she gained notoriety for her 2013 book, *Ma République se meurt* (My republic dies), in which she laments what she regards as Muslim women's forced conformity to "antiquated" religious practices that limit their freedom to occupy the public space in France. During a launch hosted by the pro-restriction organization Regards de femmes (Women's Outlooks) in April 2013, a spokesperson for the group introduced Bougrab as the "illustration, the symbol even, of the struggle to defend freedom, equality, and secularism." By combining a consciousness of her own Islamic heritage with a refusal to submit to its "sexist" religious practices, the speaker maintained, Bougrab is both "Orient and Occident."[136]

Another Arab-Muslim feminist figure whose condemnation of the face veil has been incorporated into the pro-restriction feminist narrative is Sihem Habchi. Born in Algeria, Habchi moved as a child to Paris, and there developed a passionate dislike of traditional Islam and its treatment of women. Habchi became best known in French politics for her work as president of Ni putes, ni soumises (Neither Whores, Nor Submissive, NPNS), one of the first feminist groups to hinge its opposition to Muslim head and facial coverings on an idealized image of republican laïcité. NPNS came into being in 2002, when its founder Fadela Amara organized a demonstration for women demanding equality and an end to violence in immigrant neighbourhoods. At the time of its emergence, the movement centred on the story of Sohane, a young Arab woman who was burned alive by her boyfriend in the Parisian suburb of Virty sur Seine. The NPNS campaign portrayed this act as caused by the growing religious fanaticism of Muslim elements in France.[137]

In the script deployed by Habchi and her colleagues at NPNS, gender equality is a cornerstone of republicanism. Vividly recounting her personal memories and struggles, Habchi's 2013 book, *Toutes libres!* (All women free!), portrays republicanism as the birthplace of modern feminism. In one particularly poignant passage, she recalls being photographed along with thirteen other women of minority ethnic origins in a ceremony commemorating the iconic female republican figure, Marianne. Following a description of the day's events, which included a heartfelt tribute to republicanism by the president of the National Assembly, Nicolas Sarkozy, Habchi proclaims: "I am, and we are, the Republic."[138]

While they occupy different positions in the French feminist field, pro-restriction feminists in France have converged around a commitment to rooting out the face veil as a threat to women's equality, dignity, and agency. As I will show in chapter 4, the eagerness with which pro-ban politicians in France utilized this frame to validate their own antiveiling positions demonstrates the extent to which pro-restriction feminists have gained access to the "precincts of power."[139] It further serves to show how their framing of the face veil influenced hegemonic discourses in the legislative arena of French politics.

Like its pro-restriction counterpart, France's anti-restriction feminist movement includes an array of individuals and organizations. A first group consists of activists of Arab-Muslim origin who, whether or not they themselves wear the headscarf, niqab, or burqa, believe that these garments deserve protection under French law. This contingent includes the Mouvement des indigènes de la République (Movement of the Indigenous of the Republic, MIR), whose Algerian-born spokesperson and co-founder, Houria Bouteldja, has led a militant campaign to expose what she regards as the racist, colonial underpinnings of French republican culture. The group's 2005 manifesto called for a "decolonization of the Republic." Charging that "republican equality is a myth," it further demanded that France engage in a "radical and critical reflection on its colonial past-present."[140] These demands hinged on claims that, in refusing to grant full and equal rights to

Muslims, the French state was effectively carving an internal national boundary between ethnically French citizens and "foreign" – even if French-born – others.[141]

A small number of second wave feminists share this anti-colonial stance. For example, the sociologist, activist, and documentary filmmaker, Sylvie Tissot, has challenged attempts to disparage Islamic veiling as "anti-feminist" through her involvement in the Collectif des feministes pour l'égalité (Collective of Feminists for Equality, CFPE), a Paris-based organization that brings together Muslim and non-Muslim feminists who dispute measures to prohibit religious signs in the public sphere. Likewise, Christine Delphy, an established French feminist activist and author, has taken aim at the exclusionary foundations of restrictive laws through numerous written critiques, some of which appear in the journal *Nouvelles Questions Féministes* (New feminist questions), which she co-founded with Simone de Beauvoir in 1981.[142]

Anti-restriction feminists claim that their opponents subscribe to a colonial belief system in denying Muslim women an equal voice in French feminist politics. Describing this dynamic, Ismahane Chouder, who appeared before the Gerin commission as president of the Collectif des féministes pour l'égalité (Collective of Feminists for Equality, CFPE), told me in our interview: "There is a colonial way of thinking here. It is unavoidable, because we see that our feminist elders, thankfully not all, when they address us, it is always to say: 'it is we who will show you how to emancipate.' In other words, 'it is we who hold the tools of your liberation.' This approach is stunningly infantilizing and it reproduces the notion that the Western woman is the sole owner of the model of emancipation for all women in the world."[143] By attributing patronizing motivations to attempts to "liberate" veiled women, this statement echoes postcolonial scholars' assertions that the universalizing claims of "Western" feminists presuppose the subjugation of "non-Western" feminisms.[144]

This subjugation is further accomplished through acts of hostility toward anti-restriction feminists and their exclusion from the larger French feminist movement. In our interview, for instance, Christine Delphy recalled the sense of rejection she experienced at the hands of her former feminist colleagues when she publicly opposed the 2004 ban of religious signs in schools. During a particularly charged encounter, she explained, "these women I had known for forty years walked right past without looking at me. They cut me dead."[145] Such hostile interactions, Ndella Paye further claimed, appear to serve pro-restriction feminists' desire to delegitimize competing articulations of women's rights. In her words: "Established feminists responded to us with real violence [in 2004]. I remember that at different demonstrations and in the march for women's rights, they prevented us from speaking. They asked us: 'are you really feminists?' I do not understand feminists who work against other women. I do not understand what they mean by 'feminist.'"[146] This statement underscores the perception that hostility – enacted through a symbolic violence – serves as a mechanism by which pro-restriction feminists enforce a discursive opposition between "political Islam" and "Western liberal democracy."[147]

My interviews with anti-restriction feminists suggest that strategic imperatives tied to a desire for resonance in the French religious signs debate have made them reluctant to frame restrictive laws in primarily anti-colonial terms. The essayist and activist Pierre Tévanian described this reluctance in our interview, tying it to the difficulties he and others faced when trying to challenge the 2004 law on religious signs in schools. In his words: "We were working in an atmosphere in which the key goal was to score points and convince people ... For these reasons, we absolutely took at face value the secular and feminist assertions of our interlocutors. We would say things like, 'yes, but as a feminist, does it not bother you that girls [wearing the headscarf] will be excluded?' Or 'you talk about secularism, but you don't cite the legal definition of secularism,' etc. The arguments in our texts were extremely well constructed to demonstrate the facts."[148] This statement suggests that a desire to "demonstrate the facts" and "convince" the public of the illegitimacy of religious restrictions has driven anti-restriction feminists to focus on deploying a "legal definition of secularism" to invalidate such restrictions. Thus, Tévanian further explained, "although racism was always at issue, it was not immediately present in the debate. It was in the background. At most, we talked about exclusion, or the fact that the law would produce exclusion."[149]

The religious signs debate has thus brought about a new chapter in the French feminist struggle over what constitutes gender (in)equality, women's agency, and patriarchy. As in the debate between materialist feminists and those associated with the *courant de la différence*, this is a struggle for legitimacy, in which both sides claim the right to represent the feminist movement. Like the concurrent party political battle, it is also a struggle over boundaries, as pro- and anti-restriction feminists envision different ways of defining the contours of feminism and the feminist movement. In doing so, they interpret and articulate the meanings of extant republican ideals and legal frameworks in competing ways.

THE 2009 GERIN COMMISSION AND 2010 FACE VEIL BAN

So far, I have described how politicians and feminist activists strategically utilize the ideas and institutions inscribed in republicanism to proffer distinct understandings of Muslims' rights and belonging to the French nation. Regarding politicians, I argued that, in seeking to deflect the electoral threat posed by a shared political enemy – the Front National – the centre-right UMP and left-wing Socialists coalesced around an increasingly restrictive response to Islamic veiling. In this section, I consider how this jockeying for power in turn shaped politicians' positions in the 2009–10 face veil debate. I focus on the Gerin commission, the six-month government inquiry that preceded the 2010 law prohibiting facial coverings in public space.

The Gerin commission came into being following an incident in 2008, in which France's UMP president, Nicolas Sarkozy, denied citizenship to a French resident of Moroccan origin, on the basis that her wearing of the face veil signalled a "radical" practice of Islam. When reporting on this incident ignited a national debate over whether to legally ban this practice on the French territory, André Gerin, a Communist Party member of the National Assembly and mayor of Venissieux (a heavily immigrant suburb of Lyon), wrote an open letter to the prime minister, François Fillon, demanding government action. On 19 June 2009, fifty-eight members of the National Assembly ratified Gerin's proposal to launch a government inquiry into the face veil.[150]

Between June 2009 and January 2010, Gerin and thirty-one other members of the French National Assembly heard testimony from seventy-eight invited guests representing various organizations and social groups. The commission's 200-page report, which it submitted to the National Assembly in January 2010, outlined the moral and philosophical bases for condemning the face veil, a practice that it also proposed to tackle through restricted immigration policies. It also offered a series of recommendations, including: banning the face veil in public spaces; civic instruction as part of the integration contract for newcomers; inclusion of "the equality of men and women" among the values to be recognized by persons applying for a *visa de long séjour* ("long-stay visa") or family reunification; and refusal of residency cards to persons manifesting a "radical" practice of their religion.[151]

The Gerin commission was instrumental to the introduction in parliament of a bill to prohibit the "dissimulation of the face in public space." However, its proposals drew significant opposition from Socialists, a large majority of whom abstained from the National Assembly vote to pass this law. That abstention was motivated in part by a concern that the UMP was attempting to gain votes by strategically framing the face veil as a threat to national identity. This concern arose when, in November 2009, President Sarkozy launched a countrywide debate on "national identity," in which the purported threat of the niqab and burqa featured prominently. In introducing this debate, Sarkozy asserted that, in France, "there is no room for the burqa … there is no room for women's servitude, under any pretext, in any condition, or in any circumstance."[152] From the perspective of Socialist member Jean Glavany, the link thus drawn by Sarkozy between rejection of the burqa and the defence of French national identity produced an unacceptable image of immigrants as "suspect" or "dangerous."[153]

The Socialists' additional decision to boycott the Gerin commission's final vote also stemmed from anger toward Jean-François Copé, then a prominent UMP representative, for announcing his party's plan to legally ban the face veil even before the commission had finished deliberating.[154] In an article published by the newspaper *Figaro* in December 2009, Copé claimed ownership of this issue for the UMP by outlining the conclusions of a working group on the face veil sponsored by his party. "For six months," he wrote, "deputies in the UMP group questioned experts of various persuasions, including representatives of the Muslim community." Copé then explained that the UMP's position, which was to endorse a law to prohibit face coverings, stems from the party's "attachment to republican values."[155]

Despite their strong support for a ban, six UMP members voted against this recommendation in the context of the Gerin commission. They did so in protest against a proposal that would make a ban contingent on the advice of the Conseil d'État, voting "no" out of a concern that the Court would reject the law. This concern turned out to be well founded. In light of the commission's failure to present a unanimous front in favour of a ban, France's UMP-led National Assembly called on the Conseil d'État to render its opinion on the matter. In its consultative ruling released in March 2010, the Court maintained that a general ban would constitute a breach of non-discrimination and other fundamental rights, including the right to religious expression. Although limitations on these rights can in some cases be justified, the Court stated, the public order justification put forward by the Gerin report was found not to have any precedent in the French legal system. However, the Conseil d'État gave some hope to the pro-ban camp when it stated that it could conceive of a "partial" ban applicable to particular spaces and institutions in which covering one's face poses a security threat.[156]

Armed with this partial endorsement, the UMP pushed ahead with the face veil ban, making it a key promise of its campaign in the regional elections of March 2010. After those elections – in which the UMP claimed only 36 per cent of ballots, losing to the Socialist Party in all regions except Alsace[157] – the party brought a bill to the National Assembly that would prohibit "dissimulation of the face in public space." Even though the principles of equality, dignity, and laïcité had been resoundingly rejected by legal experts as insufficient bases for a complete ban, these appeared front and centre in Bill 2283, which identified veiling as "incompatible with the essential values of the French secular, democratic and social Republic, as with our social project, which rests on equal dignity."[158] In the vote registered on 13 July 2010, all but one of the 336 voting deputies in the National Assembly approved the bill. With the vast majority of left parliamentarians abstaining, including most Socialists,[159] the bill was subsequently approved by the Senate and came into effect in April 2011.

Although the Conseil d'État advised against a general ban of facial coverings in French public space, the 2010 law has since received the approval of the European Court of Human Rights (ECHR). In a case put before the Court in April 2011, the claimant – whose initials are S.A.S. – argued that the law contravenes article 8 (the right to respect for private and family life), article 9 (the right to freedom of thought, conscience, and religion), article 10 (the right to freedom of expression), article 11 (the right to freedom of peaceful assembly and association) and article 14 (the right to non-discrimination) of the European convention. The Court's initial report on the case heavily cited the Gerin report, indicating that the justifications provided in this document – and not just the actual law itself – would factor into its eventual decision. The Court also took into account the advice of European bodies, including the Council of Europe's Parliamentary Assembly on Islam, Islamism, and Islamophobia in Europe and the Council of Europe's Commissioner for Human Rights, both of which opposed the general ban.[160] In its final decision, in 2014, the ECHR rejected the claimant's assertion that the 2010 law violates her fundamental rights, stating that "the barrier raised against others by a veil concealing the face in public could undermine the notion of 'living together.'"[161]

Representations of the 2010 law as the result of an "established consensus" among French legislators contributed significantly to this judgment.[162] Adrian's 2016 analysis of recent ECHR decisions aptly demonstrates that, in adjudicating matters of religious freedom, the Court has increasingly deferred to state governments' subjective interpretations of their countries' secular policies and histories. For example, in two cases – *Refah Partisi v. Turkey* (2001) and *Sahin v. Turkey* (2005) – the Court gave a wide margin of appreciation to the Turkish state, allowing it to place limits on the right to religious freedom based on the then government's secular mandate.[163] A similar margin was granted to the French state in *S.A.S. v. France*. Despite expressing concerns that the 2010 law violated women's religious freedom, the Court accepted "the French government's claim that concealing the face makes living together more difficult."[164]

CONCLUSION

In this chapter, I analyzed party political and feminist articulations of republicanism – and laïcité – in the context of debates around immigrant (mainly Muslim) religious signs in France. Placing electoral politics at the centre of this analysis helped to reveal the extent to which the meanings attached to republican laïcité are contingent upon parties' strategic manipulation of this discourse for political gain. For reasons tied to positioning themselves against the ultra-right, France's two main traditional parties – the UMP and the Socialists – have converged around a program to target certain Islamic dress in the public sphere. This restrictive articulation of secularism has taken hold despite institutional mechanisms – mainly the 1905 law – which in theory guarantee individuals' religious freedom.

Two historical junctures were especially critical in producing this outcome. Coinciding with external events that sparked widespread fear of "radical" Islam, the 1989 "headscarf affair" brought the issue of Muslim religious covering to the forefront of French national politics. Highly mediatized portrayals of schoolgirls in headscarves aggravated a growing popular concern – encouraged by the Front National – that Islamic fundamentalism was gaining ground in the *banlieus* (suburbs) of France's largest cities. When the governing Socialists failed to take a hard stance on the issue, instead handing it over to the Conseil d'État, the party paid a hefty political price, gaining the reputation of being "lax" when it comes to protecting laïcité.

A second defining moment was the rise of Nicolas Sarkozy, first as minister of the interior (2002–04 and 2005–07) and later as president (2007–12). Like others in the UMP, Sarkozy was concerned that the Front National was winning over right-wing voters, particularly after the party's leader Jean-Marie Le Pen advanced to the second round of the 2002 presidential elections. In response, he sought to galvanize potential voters around a republican discourse that anchors laïcité in a decidedly Catholic conception of French nationhood.

These two events put pressure on leftist parties to engage in a kind of "nationalist one-upmanship"[165] by adopting an equally restrictive discourse of laïcité. As I will show in chapter 4, politicians and activists on the left have responded by shoring up the progressive roots of republican secularism, in part by relating it to other left-wing political projects, like strengthening the power of the state and bolstering the protection of universal rights. However, these efforts to construct a progressive secular project have not ultimately prevented left-wing politicians from portraying "radical" Islam as a threat to French republicanism. To the contrary, I will demonstrate that many leftists have employed the image of a strong state to justify narrowing the boundaries of inclusion in French nationhood.

The fact that French politics has been structured along a class-based axis of competition from the postwar period to the 2017 election has contributed to the ability of both traditional parties to portray their restrictive approach to religious signs as based in consensus. Because their political brands have historically emphasized diverging stances on the economy – rather than nationalism and identity – the Socialist and UMP parties have had some leeway in articulating the meanings of laïcité in ways that serve their shared electoral interests. As I'll show in the next chapter, this has not been the case in Quebec, where parties' electoral positioning is primarily defined by their positions on the "national question."

3

Which "Option for Quebec"?

Navigating Quebec's Nation-Centred Politics

This chapter utilizes secondary literature, government documents, media reports, and interviews to sketch the historic evolution of Quebec's politics of secularism. Highlighting successive nation-building periods, I underscore the ways that articulations of religion, secularism, and belonging map onto the structures of democratic debate in the province. From the 1960s Quiet Revolution until recently, two distinct national narratives have dominated Quebec politics. The first, which has been most prominently articulated by the federalist and centre-right Parti libéral du Québec (Liberal Party of Quebec, PLQ), envisions a Quebec that remains a part of Canada, albeit with significant autonomy, and that pursues immigration policies that further the province's economic interests. A second and competing narrative, offered by the pro-sovereignty and historically left-leaning Parti Québécois (Party of Quebec, PQ), associates the success of Quebec's nationalist project with the ability to safeguard and protect – through law-making if necessary – the province's language and culture.

In the recent debates over religious diversity, these narratives have become the bases of a no-holds-barred party political struggle over the meaning(s) of religion, secularism, and belonging. Whereas pressure from the ultra-right caused mainstream parties in France to accede to the restriction of religious signs, the major parties in Quebec have not attempted to proclaim consensus on this issue. The difference in these outcomes, I will argue in this chapter, stems to a large extent from the fact that Quebec's party system is structured by a nation-centred axis of competition, and that the province lacks a strong ultra-right political party. This prevents parties from desiring consensus on questions – like religious signs – that engage the themes of national identity and belonging.

I begin by situating Quebec's contemporary religious signs debate in the historical struggle to dismantle the Catholic Church's hold over the social, cultural, and political parameters of the province's identity. Next, I introduce the key features of – and players within – Quebec's modern political system. In a third section, I examine how the Parti libéral du Québec and the Parti Québécois have, in conjunction with other participants in the electoral field, engaged in a battle to "own" the religious signs issue, first in the context of the 2007–08 Bouchard Taylor Commission, and later in the debates surrounding the 2013 Charter of Values.

NATION-BUILDING IN QUEBEC: FROM FRENCH AND BRITISH COLONIAL RULE TO PROVINCIAL POLITICS

Nations' past experiences with religion and religious governance have been shown to impact the kinds of secular regimes that ultimately take shape. Catholic countries, in which the Church historically exercised a large degree of control over key areas of social, cultural, and political life, are especially susceptible to later adopting hard-line positions on secularism, in which the goal is to eradicate all signs of religion from the public sphere.[1] This is largely because of the way memories of subjection to clerical authority penetrate the national consciousness, causing strong distaste for public expressions of religion.

Negative memories of a society largely governed by Catholic authority have been central in shaping discourses of laïcité in contemporary Quebec. The use of terms like "theocracy," "Christian regime," "alliance of throne and altar," and the "Great Darkness" indicates just some of the ways that social and political actors convey the repressive power that the Church held prior to the Quiet Revolution.[2] These historical memories have significantly influenced the debate on religious signs in Quebec's public sphere.

Compared to the British colonial government that established itself in the 1760s, France was an arms-length colonial ruler in the territory now known as Quebec. Because they were embroiled in military engagements in Europe for much of the eighteenth century, the French had few resources to commit to defending their North American colony of New France, which they had sought mainly for its rich reservoir of furs. Yet, the French fact took cultural root in the region through the presence of priests and missionaries who gradually set up social institutions and acted as intermediaries between the colonial society and Versailles.[3]

Britain's conquest of New France in 1759 significantly restructured this relationship between church and state. Unlike their French adversaries, the British in North America were intent on erecting social and political institutions that mirrored those of Britain, with the aim of establishing an economically stable colony in North America. In order to secure the loyalty of their new francophone and Catholic subjects in New France, British colonial authorities created a system of cooperation between the Church and the British Crown. Two key measures secured this cooperation: the Treaty of Paris (1763) – which granted freedom of religion to Catholics – and the Quebec Act (1774) – which recognized the right of the clergy to collect tithes from the local population, thus affording the Catholic Church a distinct role in matters of education and social welfare.[4]

By defining the relationship between the Catholic Church and British Crown, these measures allowed clerical elites in New France to maintain their influence over the social and cultural mechanisms of nationhood, while British authorities dictated the terms of political governance.[5] Yet, popular support for this arrangement remained unstable. Although not opposed to the Church's influence in cultural and spiritual matters, a growing French-speaking professional elite began to criticize the alliance between clerical and British authorities, and the impact of this alliance in facilitating the latter's control over colonial government and the economy. Out of their struggle emerged the Patriote movement, which advocated a liberal nationalist vision centred on the goal of declericalizing the political institutions of New France and creating a representative state to serve the interests of the region's francophone majority.

The Patriotes' efforts culminated in the violent rebellions of 1837–38, during which hundreds of young radicals demanded a separate state. Their eventual defeat by British forces paved the way for the establishment in 1840 of a single unified and officially English-speaking colony – the Province of Canada – in which Lower Canada (now Quebec) would control only a limited share of the National

Assembly.[6] Since that period, the narratives of national identity formation in what is now Quebec have been shaped by the idea of minority nationhood.[7]

THE PERIOD OF *SURVIVANCE*

In the wake of the failed rebellions of 1837–38, the Catholic Church emerged as the pre-eminent driver of Quebec's nationalist discourse. Thanks to the support of Britain – which continued to delegate cultural matters to the Church in exchange for nearly uncontested control over politics and the economy – clerical figures were able to formulate that discourse around an explicitly cultural definition of the nation. Whereas the struggle of the Patriotes had focused on the political dimension of nationhood, the Church anchored its vision in a discourse of *survivance* ("survival"), which imagined Quebec's population as made up of rural Catholics who rejected British imperialism, industrialization, and urbanization.[8] This discourse framed Catholicism as the very raison d'être of the Québécois nation and the primary force in maintaining the boundary between French Canadians and other North American peoples.

To solidify survivance as the bedrock of Québécois nationhood, the Catholic clergy set about establishing a "retrospective messianic narrative of the French Canadians' historical destiny in North America."[9] Prominent clerical figures, such as Lionel Groulx, reinforced the proclaimed divinity of the nation by speaking to the bond between ancestry and territory in Quebec's national identity.[10] Over time, faith combined with language to become the "twin pillars" of the nation's collective imaginary. With Catholicism established as the "guardian" against linguistic assimilation – and the French language imagined as the "carrier" of Catholicism – "religion, language and ethnicity became increasingly fused, one reinforcing the other, resulting in the creation of a cohesive national identity."[11]

Print media were a prime vehicle in the dissemination of the Church's cultural definition of the nation during this period. In the 1843 issue of the journal *Les mélanges religieux* (Religious mixtures), Monsignor Bourget defined religion as Quebec's "primary national distinction." "It is because we are Catholic," he went on, "that we form a nation in this corner of North America."[12] The Church also conveyed an ethno-religious image of the national self through its role in administering the services usually provided by states, including education, health, and welfare.[13] After establishing a confessional school system in 1845, the clergy founded numerous colleges and seminaries between 1841 and 1875.[14]

Clerical authorities also ruled over marital affairs, thus playing a key part in establishing women's social and familial role in nineteenth-century Quebec. Virtually relegated to the status of minors, women during this period were subservient to their husbands in matters relating to children and their own civil rights. For instance, a woman could not form a contract or engage in commercial activity without her husband's approval.[15] The struggle for women's political rights – particularly for the provincial vote – also took shape under Catholic rule. In the 1920s, Catholic women's associations led the charge to grant women the vote. By the 1930s, the struggle shifted hands, becoming a key focus of feminist associations. Clerical authorities fought hard to prevent women's suffrage. When the project to institute the vote was announced in the Throne Speech of 1940, Cardinal Villeneuve opposed it, on the basis that "women's suffrage impinges upon familial unity and hierarchy" and threatens to "expose women to the passions and adventures of electoral politics."[16]

Although many increasingly opposed its conservative cultural views, the Church succeeded in institutionalizing its nationalist vision well into the twentieth century, in part due to the *laissez-faire* approach of Quebec's reigning political party of the time, the Union Nationale (National Union, UN).[17] A nationalist party that identified with the goal of maintaining Quebec's autonomy from the rest of Canada, the Union Nationale took an arm's length approach to governing, allowing the Catholic Church to maintain its hold over social and cultural affairs right into the 1950s. Founded during the Great Depression, the party held power from 1936–39, 1944–60 and 1966–70, during which time it advocated for a restricted role of government in the cultural affairs of the province.

The UN's pre-eminence during this period depended in part on its "non-aggression pact" with the Catholic Church and anglophone economic elites, as well as its *entente cordiale* with the federal Progressive Conservative Party, which agreed not to organize in Quebec.[18] Both sets of agreements prevented the Union Nationale from challenging the Catholic Church's role in public life. This party's close relationship with the Church is illustrated, for example, in the decision by its founding and long-time leader, Maurice Duplessis, to hang a crucifix on the wall of the National Assembly in 1936. To this day, that symbol serves as a reminder of the relationship between Catholicism and nation building in Quebec. In the context of contemporary debates over religious signs, it has also become viewed by many as emblematic of the dangers of allowing religion to permeate the political and public realms.

NAVIGATING A NATION-CENTRED POLITICS: THE PARTI LIBÉRAL DU QUÉBEC AND PARTI QUÉBÉCOIS

Before turning to an examination of political parties' role in contemporary debates over religious signs in Quebec, it is necessary to lay out the institutional structures, main players, and key voter constituencies that shape the dynamics of electoral contention in the province. I build on secondary literature to suggest that, unlike France, where the economy has traditionally served as the major axis of competition, Quebec's political system is structured along numerous cross-cutting dimensions, the most salient of which is nationhood.[19] I will later argue that the centrality of nationhood to electoral politics helps explain why politicians in Quebec are less inclined than their French counterparts to proclaim "consensus" on the matter of religious signs.

As in the rest of Canada, provincial-level voting in Quebec takes place according to a first-past-the-post system, in which the candidate with the largest number of votes wins a seat in the 125-member Assemblée Nationale (National Assembly), located in Quebec City. This system is apt to produce large disparities in the number of seats a party obtains compared to its share of the popular vote. In elections, which since 2013 are mandated to occur every four years, the leader of the political party with the largest number of *députés*, or members of the National Assembly (MNAs), is asked by the Lieutenant-Governor of Quebec to form the government as premier.

Quebec's party system also mirrors Canada's in that voter-party alignments are only weakly influenced by class.[20] The limited impact of class at the federal level derives from cross-cutting cleavages associated with region, language, and religion, which diminish the salience of class for the average voter. Canada's vast geographic size, combined with its relatively small population, has resulted in the emergence – and persistence – of distinct political cultures that often emphasize regional over economic concerns.[21] Class identities in

Canada are also diminished by religious divisions, which, for historical reasons, are inscribed into the Canadian party political system.[22] For example, the Progressive Conservative Party (since incorporated into the Conservative Party of Canada), which arguably has the strongest ties to Canada's British colonial legacy, receives disproportionate support from Protestant voters. By contrast, the Liberal Party of Canada, which held power during periods of large-scale immigration from Catholic countries, has long been the pre-eminent party in Catholic communities. The New Democratic Party has evolved into one that garners support from liberal Protestant and non-religious voters.[23]

Voting at the provincial level in Quebec is very much shaped by similar dynamics. Although conservative in outlook, the Union Nationale was able to secure the working-class vote in Quebec into the 1960s, with its main opponent – the Parti libéral du Québec – holding sway over the middle class. This dynamic, which defied traditional expectations about the relationship between class consciousness and vote choice, was described in 1960 by Lipset as "one of the most striking cases of deviation from leftist voting within the lower-income group."[24] Picking up this issue a decade later, Pinard drew renewed attention to the question of why Quebec "has had no leftist politics."[25] At the time of his research, the prevailing theory held that the predominance of religiously based and conservative values, as well as a high degree of ethnic consciousness among the French Canadian lower classes, prevented the emergence of strong class affiliations in Quebec. This set of factors, it was argued, reinforced "the triumph of the politics of nationalism and conservatism."[26] Yet, Pinard's studies pointed to a different explanation, which is that relationships among established elites, whose interests were well served by existing political arrangements, obstructed the emergence of class as a principal driver of electoral politics in Quebec.[27]

The disappearance of the Union Nationale from provincial politics in 1970, which paved the way for a party system centred on competition between the established Parti libéral du Québec and the nascent Parti Québécois, did not disrupt the weak relationship between class and voter alignment in Quebec. Indeed, the alternation of power between these parties from the 1970s to 2018 solidified a tradition of electoral competition in which the main competitors would distinguish themselves mainly via their opposing visions of Quebec's national future and political status.[28] With the exception of the 1976 election, which brought the PQ to power for the first time, these two parties jointly obtained at least 85 per cent of the popular vote in every provincial election between 1973 and 2001.[29] While both parties have shared a commitment to modernizing Quebec society, to transferring authority over the social, economic, and political dimensions of nationhood from the church to the state, and to creating a protected space for the French language, the PLQ and PQ have, over the decades, presented Quebec's electorate with starkly different visions of the province's national future.

Unlike its counterparts in other provinces, the PLQ enjoys significant autonomy from the federal Liberal Party of Canada (LPC). Tracing its roots back to the Parti Rouge (Red Party), which fought for responsible government and against the authority of the Catholic Church in Lower Canada between 1847 and 1867, the party disaffiliated from the Liberal Federation in 1955, and formed a separate infrastructure, personnel, and membership.[30] This institutional separation has been critical in allowing the PLQ to pursue a federalist conception of Quebec's relationship to Canada without binding itself to the interests of the LPC. Such an arrangement was especially vital during Pierre Trudeau's prime ministership, as his multicultural citizenship agenda conflicted with the PLQ's commitment to preserving Quebec's status as a "distinct society."[31]

The Parti libéral du Québec is regarded as the party of dominant business and financial interests in Quebec.[32] Over the decades, it has tended to draw support from voters whose mother tongue is not French, who live in the Montreal region, and who are wealthier relative to those who vote for the PQ.[33] PLQ voters are also distinguished by their greater concern, compared to supporters of other parties, with economic questions versus issues tied to identity and to Quebec's position within Canada.[34]

The PLQ's main opponent for the last fifty years, the Parti Québécois, owes its origins to the same modernist national project that has defined Quebec politics since the 1960s. The party itself sprouted from the PLQ, when its founding leader, René Lévesque, resigned in 1967, but not before playing a significant role in establishing the major economic and social institutions that would shape the governance of Quebec society in the decades to come. Lévesque exited the PLQ after the party turned down his proposal to forge a sovereign association between Quebec and the rest of Canada. In 1968, the Mouvement souveraineté-association (Movement for Sovereignty-Association, MSA), which he formed in the aftermath of his resignation, merged with the Ralliement national (National Rally, RN), a political party advocating Quebec's independence from Canada, to form the Parti Québécois. By 1970, the party received a significant enough vote share to surpass the Union Nationale as the province's "second party."[35] The election of 1976 led to a strong "bipolarization of the electorate" between the PQ and PLQ,[36] which shaped the dynamics and discursive content of Quebec's electoral politics for the remainder of the twentieth century and into the twenty-first.

Until recently, the Parti Québécois has campaigned on a left-leaning and *étatiste* (statist) program, which advocates positive labour conditions and public ownership of resources and industries. During its first year in power beginning in 1976, the party nationalized the province's automobile insurance industry and revised the Labour Code, strengthening union finances, prohibiting the use of replacement workers or "scabs" during strikes, and facilitating union certification. It also responded to explosive labour strikes by purchasing the American-owned Asbestos Corporation in an attempt to create manufacturing jobs.[37]

The PQ has also been the leading political force in establishing French as Quebec's sole official language. In 1974, the PLQ government under Robert Bourassa sponsored the Official Languages Act – or Bill 22 – which made French the language of civic administration and services, and of the workplace. Only children demonstrating sufficient knowledge of another language would be exempted from attending school in French. When it first formed the government in 1976, the PQ made it a priority to further restrict the language of instruction. Adopted in 1977, its Bill 101 identified French as the language of instruction from kindergarten to secondary school, with exceptions allowed for children whose mother or father is a Canadian citizen who received elementary instruction in English anywhere in Canada.[38] The bill also contained articles to ensure that French is the predominant language in business and advertising, with specific provisions regarding labour relations and signage.

The Parti Québécois has traditionally fared best with younger, well-educated francophones, who work in professional occupations in which there is some direct contact with English Canadians.[39] Support for the PQ also overlaps, although not perfectly, with support for independence. However, ambivalence regarding the independence project, which fluctuates over time and across constituencies, also complicates the PQ's relationship to voters. During periods of high ambivalence – that is, when a high percentage of voters do not state their intentions ahead of time – pollsters have been apt to underestimate support for the PLQ, since a higher than expected number of voters end up shying away from the sovereigntist option in the actual vote.[40]

Over the decades, the association established by the PQ between the project to secure sovereignty from Canada and a left-leaning approach to economic policy has waned. Social democratic voters who historically hitched their electoral wagons to the party found it increasingly difficult to support its gradual embrace of market principles and a budget-cutting agenda.[41] As I will show later on, this discomfort with the PQ's rightward shift, and the wedge it has drawn between progressive ideology and the sovereigntist project, has played a role in the proliferation of alternative parties in Quebec's political system. It has been especially important to the growth of Québec solidaire (QS), a pro-sovereignty party whose mandate since it was created in 2006 has been to provide an egalitarian, feminist, anti-racist, and social democratic voice in Quebec politics.[42]

Thus, from the postwar era until very recently, voters in Quebec have had two distinct choices at the provincial ballot box: a centre-right, pro-business party whose vision of the province's national future is bound up with federalism, and a left-leaning, pro-labour party whose message – and indeed very raison d'être – centres on a program to secure Quebec's independence from Canada. As we will see, the recent emergence of new opposition parties has begun to disrupt this established linkage between economic policy and two very distinct articulations of Quebec's national project. Yet, as the next section demonstrates, the prevalence of nationalism as the basis for party alignment has been essential in shaping the development of Quebec's modern secular regime.

FORGING A "DISTINCT SOCIETY": NATIONALISM AND IMMIGRATION POLICY DURING THE QUIET REVOLUTION AND BEYOND

The Quiet Revolution of the 1960s was a period of rapid urbanization and industrialization in Quebec. During this period, a growing francophone middle-class became conscious of the damaging effects of clerical influence on education and the economy, as well as of the continued economic and political dominance of Quebec's anglophone minority.[43] With allies in the arts and academia, this group steered a shift in perceptions of nationhood, expressed in publications such as *Cité Libre*[44] and *Le Devoir*.[45] The discourse of survivance was overtaken by that of *rattrapage* ("catching up"), which portrayed the state as the most suitable vehicle for achieving nationalist goals and reimagining Quebec as a secular, urban, and industrialized nation. Unlike the French-Canadian identity that prevailed prior to the Quiet Revolution, this nation would have clear territorial boundaries, with lasting impact on the relations between the Québécois and francophones elsewhere in Canada.[46]

Along with the realignment of politics, religion, economy, and culture that the Quiet Revolution entailed also came the massive expansion of scientific research and universities in Quebec.[47] These universities in turn became sites in which to study the "national question," particularly in budding Sociology departments.[48] This has resulted in a large and comprehensive body of research into several facets of the Quiet Revolution, including, but not limited to, the role of clerical organizations,[49] the long-term implications for collective identity,[50] and the impact of the Quiet Revolution on the cultural significance of Catholicism.[51]

The Quiet Revolution also bridged the gap between Post-Revolution France and Catholic Quebec, thus marking a shift in the relationship between the two nations. Since the 1960s, provincial governments have sought collaboration with France and other francophone countries to gain support for culture and language promotion.[52] French authorities have reciprocated, entering into agreements with Quebec in matters of culture and education, often without the support of the Canadian federal government.[53] French interest in, and support for, Québécois nationalism is also evident in the views expressed by politicians. In a speech given during a visit to Quebec in 1960s, President Charles de Gaulle said: "You can count on France, Canadians and French Canadians. You can count on her in the debate that is about to take place. She counts on you to think of her, follow her, and support her by all means, direct or indirect, that free men now have at their disposal to communicate their ideas."[54]

These institutional and political linkages have nurtured the creation of a Québécois national identity, which occasionally draws on French themes. Indeed, many of the intellectuals responsible for Quebec's modern nationalist discourse either spent time in France or explicitly relied on French philosophy in developing their perspectives. André Laurendeau, once editor-in-chief of the newspaper *Le Devoir* and co-chair of the Royal Commission on Bilingualism and Biculturalism (1963),[55] advocated a universalist and egalitarian approach to Québécois nationalism, which he developed after attending lectures by leading French intellectuals at the Sorbonne and other Parisian institutions, between 1935 and 1937. Charles Taylor, the leading Canadian philosopher, has drawn heavily on the Rousseauist tradition to craft a vision of Quebec's place within Canada that reconciles individual freedom and community.[56]

Frameworks developed in connection with French thinkers and institutions contributed to the forging of two distinct visions of Quebec's national future during and after the Quiet Revolution. The first, which was principally articulated by Pierre Trudeau, who was prime minister of Canada from 1968–79 and again from 1980–84, sought to integrate Quebec into a pan-Canadian nationalism centred on a liberal understanding of the nation-state as a political compact intended to protect individual rights and freedoms. This resulted in the federal multiculturalism policy in 1971 and enactment of the Charter of Rights and Freedoms in 1982 (to which Quebec is not a signatory).

Many Quebec nationalists perceived Trudeau's program as a ploy to dilute the province's claims to distinctiveness by equating national (Québécois) and immigrant minorities.[57] In response, they set about elaborating a nationalist discourse that portrayed Quebec as a distinct historical, linguistic, and cultural society. This approach took shape under the leadership of René Lévesque, founding leader of the Parti Québécois. Beginning in his role as Minister of Natural Resources in the Lesage Liberal government (1960–66), and later as PQ leader, Lévesque mobilized state resources to solidify francophone business and cultural interests in Quebec through the creation of public ministries, the nationalization of public resources, and the introduction of language legislation entrenching French as Quebec's sole official language. Lévesque later drew upon the strengthened cultural dimension of Québécois identity to bolster Quebec's claims to political independence, organizing the province's (failed) first referendum to achieve political sovereignty while maintaining close economic ties to Canada in 1980.

Both Trudeau and Lévesque saw state power as a key mechanism for setting the boundaries of Québécois nationhood. Yet, the significance of culture and ethnicity to these boundaries differed markedly in the nationalist discourses advocated by the two leaders. For Trudeau, cultural nationalism was a superfluous and potentially damaging feature of nation-statehood. Rather than strengthening national cohesion, he believed recognition of sub-national communities reduces states' ability to govern effectively.[58] By contrast, in his treatise entitled *An Option for Québec*, Lévesque portrayed cultural distinctiveness as foundational to Quebec's state-building project.[59]

The tensions between these distinct visions came to a head when two rounds of attempted constitutional amendment – the Meech Lake (1987) and Charlottetown (1992) Accords[60] – failed to make Quebec a signatory of the Canadian constitution. The perceived unwillingness of English Canada to meet the province's demands, the most important of which was its recognition as a distinct society, increased support for independence. In 1995, the Québécois were summoned to vote in a second referendum, this time on the question of whether Quebec "should become sovereign after having made a formal offer to Canada for a new economic and political partnership." When the pro-sovereignty side failed by a margin of 1 per cent, then premier Jacques Parizeau famously blamed the defeat on "money and the ethnic vote."

In lieu of independence, policy-makers and intellectuals in Quebec then set about elaborating a discourse of citizenship and integration that would foster a rapprochement between the French-speaking majority and immigrant minorities.[61] In its 1981 action plan, the Parti Québécois government advocated a model of "convergence," based on a dialogue between the province's "core" francophone population and incoming minorities, in which the former takes precedence. Three goals oriented this approach, according to the 1981 report: to assure the maintenance of cultural communities,[62] to sensitize Quebec's francophone majority to the place of these minority communities in Quebec's patrimony, and to promote immigrant communities' entry into fields in which they had previously been relatively absent, including the public service.[63]

The notion that "convergence" serves to promote the values of an emerging Quebec state is palpable in the 1981 report. Its authors describe the Quiet Revolution as a key transformative event in the province's history, one that marked the transition from an isolationist and insecure past to a modern and cosmopolitan nation-building project. Crucial to the success of this project is the recognition that incoming minorities strengthen the province's "cosmopolitan character" and "contribute greatly to a Québec that is open to the world's diverse cultural traditions."[64] This expansion of the boundaries of nationhood to include immigrants' contributions was described by the report as reflective of Quebec's "cultural maturity."[65]

In 1991, the PLQ-led provincial government adopted a revised action plan in the field of immigration. Entitled *Au Québec pour bâtir ensemble: Énoncé de politique en matière d'immigration d'intégration* (Building Quebec Together: Policy Statement on Immigrant Integration), the document provides additional details on how to approach citizenship and integration by outlining three parameters of belonging to Quebec society: French as the language of public life, the engagement of all citizens in the democratic process, and intercommunity exchange.[66] These parameters amount to a vision of integration as a "contract" between immigrants and the host community, the aim of which is to establish a "common public culture."[67] Where conflicts arise over the accommodation of particular cultural practices, they are to be dealt with on a case-by-case basis, with recourse to judicial solutions only where absolutely necessary.[68] As in the PQ's 1981 document, "openness to the world" is an orienting feature of this approach. Indeed, the document states that "in a context of the interdependence and globalization of economic, ecological and social phenomena, Québec's population attaches great importance to openness to the world. Indeed, just as the early exchanges gave rise to human civilization, it sees contact with all peoples and nations of the earth as essential factors of development."[69]

The parameters of integration set by the 1981 and 1991 government reports exemplify a shift in dominant ways of defining nationhood in post–Quiet Revolution Quebec. The emphasis on democratic values, cosmopolitanism, and openness to the world suggests a growing interest in gaining legitimacy as a quasi-nation state in the global political field. Efforts to reconcile the struggle for cultural survival with the quest for recognition have produced a unique brand of pluralism in Quebec, one in which acceptance of diversity is predicated on a commitment to reinforcing cultural characteristics – primarily the French language – that delineate the majority group. Recent conflicts over the regulation of minority religious practices have brought to the fore remaining tensions around ways to interpret and promote this approach.

Since signing an accord with Canada's federal government in 1991, Quebec has had sole jurisdiction over the selection and integration of immigrants arriving through the points system (which does not include those being admitted through family reunification or as refugees). The huge emphasis placed on French proficiency in the province's selection policy has increased the number of immigrants arriving from former French colonies, many of which have large Muslim populations. The 2011 Canadian National Households Survey reports that Muslims account for nearly 20 per cent of immigrants to Quebec. Of this group, over 60 per cent originate from North Africa and the Middle East, 10 per cent come from South Asia, and 8 per cent are of West and Central Asian origins.[70] These Muslim populations have become the principal targets of contemporary efforts to tighten the boundaries of secularism in Quebec, in some cases through law.

HEADSCARVES, KIPPAS, AND KIRPANS: PARTY POLITICAL STRUGGLES OVER RELIGIOUS PRACTICES AND REASONABLE ACCOMMODATION

As I mentioned above, the dismantling of the Catholic Church's institutional hold over Quebec society was chief among the transformative effects of the Quiet Revolution. In 1964, the governing PLQ transferred authority over education from the Church to the state by creating a public school board. However, public education continued to be run by confessional boards – Roman Catholic and Protestant – since the position of the boards was enshrined under Section 93 of the *Constitution Act, 1867*. This only changed in 1997, when Quebec's PQ premier Lucien Bouchard and Canada's Liberal prime minister amended the constitution to exempt Quebec from Section 93.[71] The secularization of education was completed in 2008 when public school boards replaced religion courses with an ethics and religious culture curriculum now mandatory in all schools.[72]

When the Church lost its hold over the institutions – including education – that define Quebec's national identity, it also lost some of its purchase over the cultural systems of identity formation. As Zubrzycki shows, the rapid decline in religious affiliation and practice that accompanied the Quiet Revolution was manifested in a series of "aesthetic revolts," in which a new generation of Québécois publicly repudiated iconic Catholic symbols – including Jean-Baptiste the Saint – as defining elements of the province's visual and material culture.[73] This symbolic process of secularization also soon manifested itself in declining fertility rates. Between 1959 and 1972, the birth rate in Quebec declined by nearly half, to 2.09 children per woman, causing it to become the province with the lowest fertility rate in Canada.[74]

Despite a steep decline in its institutional and cultural significance, Catholicism continues to operate as a source of identity for most Québécois. Although less than 10 per cent regularly attend church, 75 per cent of Quebec residents declared themselves Catholic in the 2011 National Households Survey by Statistics Canada.[75] (This compares to only 43 per cent of French residents between the ages of eighteen and fifty-one.[76])

The increasing number of Muslim residents has put pressure on this fragile and unstable relationship between secularism and religiosity in Quebec. In 1994, controversy broke out when a student who had converted to Islam was expelled from school for wearing a headscarf. Although the matter was resolved in 1995 when the provincial Commission des droits de la personne et des droits de la jeunesse (Human Rights and Youth Rights Commission, CDPDJ) proposed guidelines to protect religious freedom in schools, the issue continued to attract public attention.

Subsequent controversies around the religious practices of the Muslim, Jewish, and Sikh communities triggered a new series of legal challenges, in which the Supreme Court of Canada overturned key denials of accommodation by the Quebec Court of Appeal. For instance, in 2004, the Supreme Court cited freedom of religion in reversing a judgment prohibiting Orthodox Jewish condo-owners from erecting sukkahs – temporary wood and canvas shelters built for the Sukkoth festival – on their balconies.[77] Two years later, the Court reversed another decision by Quebec's Court of Appeal, this time involving the right of Sikh students to wear a kirpan – the Sikh ceremonial dagger – to school.[78] In reaching this decision, the Court relied on the principle of "reasonable accommodation," which refers to the duty that arises to accommodate individuals when they encounter rules that, while neutral on the surface, have a discriminatory effect.

Popular discontent over these court decisions and over public expressions of religion, particularly Islam, became the central focus of party political contention when in 2006 the rural town of Hérouxville (which lacks a visible Muslim population) instituted a town charter forbidding activities deemed incompatible with Québécois culture, including the public beating or stoning of women, the use of facial covering, and any accommodation of religious practices in schools, health care, and other public institutions. The publication of this charter sparked a sustained political debate around religious accommodation in Quebec. In the provincial election that followed the incident in 2007, the right-wing populist Action démocratique du Québec (Democratic Action of Quebec, ADQ) shot up in the polls, replacing the Parti Québécois as official opposition and reducing the PLQ to a minority government. Although it offered no clear stance on sovereignty, opting to brand itself as "autonomist" rather than sovereigntist or federalist, the ADQ was a vocal critic of religious accommodation. Indeed, its leader Mario Dumont described the accommodation of minority religious practices as a kind of "groveling" that undermines Quebec's own "right to exist, to have traditions, to have a way of doing things."[79] This line of argument, combined with an appeal to voters' mistrust of current office holders, taxpayer frustration, and fatigue with the constitutional question, drew support for the party in largely francophone and rural parts of Quebec, areas in which the Union Nationale had managed to hold sway even as it was defeated in the election of 1976.

In 2007, Jean Charest's Liberal government sought to damp down the public controversy around religious accommodation by appointing two well-known figures, sociologist and historian Gérard Bouchard and philosopher Charles Taylor, to conduct a province-wide investigation into the incorporation of minority religious signs and practices in Quebec. Between February 2007 and March 2008, over 900 briefs were submitted and almost 250 individuals testified before the Bouchard-Taylor commission in more than fifteen of the province's urban and rural communities. The resulting report, entitled *Building the Future: A Time for Reconciliation*, begins by denying the media's claims that Quebec is in the throes of an accommodation "crisis." Although religious minorities occasionally make requests for accommodation, it argues, these requests are rare and usually granted with little or no inconvenience to the institutions in question.[80] Thus, the report recommends that public and private enterprises continue to treat accommodation requests on a case-by-case basis, with two orienting principles in mind. First, it proposes a model of *laïcité ouverte* ("open secularism") to guide religious incorporation in Quebec. According to the authors of the report, this pragmatic approach distinguishes itself from France's more ideological model of laïcité by prioritizing religious freedom and church-state separation over the achievement of a religiously neutral society.[81] *Laïcité ouverte* is then couched in a second and broader project of clarifying the parameters of Quebec's developing integration model: interculturalism. This model seeks to reconcile tolerance of diversity with the protection of Québécois identity, through a process that the report defines as "integrative pluralism."[82]

However, the Bouchard-Taylor report did take a more restrictive stance on expressions of religiosity in *certain* arenas of government. It proposed, for example, that religious signs be prohibited by individuals whose roles represent the authority of the Quebec state, including judges and police officers. The co-chairs of the commission further recommended that facial coverings – including the Islamic niqab and burqa – be disallowed among individuals providing or receiving public services in Quebec. The restrictions recommended by the Bouchard-Taylor report were not limited to individual citizens, however. Indeed, in order to ensure a balanced approach, one that would apply equally to visibly Catholic symbols in Quebec's governing institutions, the co-chairs of the commission proposed that the crucifix on the wall of the National Assembly also be removed and that prayers at municipal council meetings in various parts of the province be discontinued.[83]

According to the Bouchard-Taylor report, these proposals derive their legitimacy from the norms of collective life in Quebec. The first norm has to do with Quebec's position as a minority nation. Indeed, the report consistently frames the issue of religious incorporation in relation to a larger concern for the perpetuation of francophone culture in Quebec. The perceived need for vigilance in this matter underlies a strong opposition to multiculturalism in the province. According to Bouchard and Taylor, multiculturalism is not suited to Quebec, where the presence of a "core culture" and concern for language preservation justify a different approach to integration.

Although it regards Quebec's position as a minority nation as demanding the prioritization of the dominant culture in matters of integration, the Bouchard-Taylor report openly rejects the notion of a hierarchy of rights. This rejection is based on a second purportedly fundamental norm of collective life in Quebec: liberal democracy. In numerous sections of their report, Bouchard and Taylor refer to Quebec as belonging to a community of "liberal" and "modern liberal" nations. Its membership in this community hinges on the province's ongoing commitment to individual and collective rights, embodied in both the Québécois (1975) and Canadian (1982) Charters.

Another central and recurring theme in the Bouchard-Taylor report is the need to strike a balance between opposite "poles" in Quebec's national consciousness: French-English, separatist-federalist, majority-minority, past-future, et cetera. The report seeks a balance between these distinct "poles" by advocating state religious neutrality as necessary to protect individual freedom and equality,[84] while insisting on the need to recognize group-based characteristics, whether they pertain to the majority society or minorities. In a section entitled "The Legacy of the Quiet Revolution," the report describes "the two poles that have constantly guided changes in intercultural thinking in Québec, i.e. the constant tension between the concern for openness and anxiety for the future of the French-speaking community. In other words, we have liberalism and pluralism on one side, and hesitation and restraint on the other."[85] This passage explicitly recognizes the particular and universal aspects of Québécois nationhood and grounds these in the Quiet Revolution. However, by using the term "poles," the report makes clear that these are separate, even competing features of the national consciousness. The embrace of one threatens a commitment to the other. For that reason, a conscious effort should be made to ensure that both are equally recognized and respected.

In order to strike the proposed balance between particularity and universalism, the Bouchard-Taylor report dedicates full sections to recognizing the unique aspects of Québécois national identity. For instance, it makes repeated reference to the challenge facing francophone Quebec in its struggle to achieve recognition as a distinct society.[86] Its authors are also sympathetic to the need to specify the content of Quebec's "common public culture."[87] In our interview, the commission's co-chair, Gérard Bouchard, explained that:

> Approximately 75 per cent of francophones in Québec are descended from the foundational culture of the seventeenth century and they remain attached to the memory of this culture … One of the

> founding myths of francophone Québec is that this population is a fragile and threatened minority in need of protection. This is a deeply rooted sentiment. If we ignore this fact, if we rely simply on a legal discourse, it will not work, it cannot work, because this majority culture, that is also a minority, will react forcefully and negatively. We saw this in the period following the report. Our preoccupation, Taylor and I, was precisely to establish a balance … To me, it seems we succeeded in achieving this balance.[88]

According to the report, this "balance" is best achieved through a recasting of Québécois nationhood as consistent with the criteria of modern liberal democracies: "From this past has nonetheless emerged a taste for the future, a desire for affirmation and development at the same pace as other Western nations, a determination to engage in self-assertion and openness expressed in numerous ways, and a vitality that draws international attention to this unusual, improbably French-speaking community."[89] Evidently, the juxtaposition between the particular and the universal that the Bouchard-Taylor report endorses relies in part on separating the past from the present. The above passage does this by associating Quebec's history with a more narrow conception of nationhood and visualizing the future as broadening that conception, by transforming Quebec into a modern, liberal quasi nation-state.

Reactions to the Bouchard-Taylor report attest to a deep ambivalence regarding its portrayal of the balance between Québécois nationhood's particular and universal elements. Newspaper reports resoundingly rejected the report, claiming its recommendations contained a multicultural bias.[90] One member of the commission's own advisory board concurred. Jacques Beauchemin is professor of sociology at the Université du Québec à Montréal (UQAM), and has written extensively on the role of politics, identity, and memory in Québec's nationalist movement.[91] A dissident member of the Bouchard-Taylor commission board, he publicly dissociated himself from the report's main recommendations.[92] His criticism centred on the claim that the co-chairs attempted to prescribe a vision of Québécois national identity that overemphasizes its universal features to the detriment of its particularity. In our interview, Beauchemin stated that:

> The only thing that stunned me when reading the final report [of the Bouchard-Taylor commission] was that its positive orientation

> toward interculturalism – and Québec pluralism in general – was even more marked than I could have imagined ... In essence, the report portrays Québec as a diverse and pluralist society. At the same time, it says, Québec also contains a historical majority, one that must be open to diversity. This is shocking to read. One would expect the work of a nationalist intellectual [Gérard Bouchard] to approach the question from the opposite direction. It would first assert the presence of a francophone majority and then ask: "how can we integrate the immigrants with whom we live?"[93]

This statement rejects the Bouchard-Taylor report, not so much because it advocates pluralism, but rather because of the way it connects pluralism to nationhood. For Beauchemin, pluralism is a second-order priority of the nationalist movement; it is necessary only insofar as it strengthens the national project. In his words,

> The report buries all of this by saying that being Québécois can mean being old stock French Canadian, but it can also mean being a Vietnamese immigrant of six months ... it's everyone. And of course, this is true. But that is how it's framed. And so I said to myself: "where is the nationalist Bouchard in all of this?" To be blunt, there was no longer this idea that the francophone majority enjoyed a certain sociological pre-eminence. I don't mean pre-eminence in the sense that members of this majority should be given more rights than others, but in the sense that its historical rootedness in Québec is obviously deeper. That is hard to deny. It's not that the report denied it entirely, but it was drowned out. And what we had instead was a representation of contemporary Québec as part of Canada's mosaic of identities. Again, it's not that this is a false interpretation, but the point of view reflected is still quite shocking.[94]

Once again, Beauchemin does not directly deny the significance of universal values, such as pluralism, here. Rather, his critique focuses on at what point, and how, pluralism is discussed and tied to the national project.

Both of the Liberals' key political adversaries, the Parti Québécois and the (since dismantled) Action démocratique du Québec, denounced the Bouchard-Taylor commission, echoing media reports' claims that its co-chairs had tried to insert a multicultural discourse into Quebec's accommodation debates.[95] Aware of the political repercussions of appearing onside with the commissioners, Premier Charest shelved the Bouchard-Taylor report, but not before publicly refusing one of its key proposals: to remove the crucifix from Quebec's National Assembly. Drawing on a widespread perception of the crucifix as part of Quebec's "cultural patrimony,"[96] Charest claimed that its presence does not violate the principle of state religious neutrality.[97] However, in 2010, Charest's Liberals did seek to implement a key recommendation of the Bouchard-Taylor report by proposing Bill 94, which would also prohibit providers and receivers of public services from wearing facial coverings. The bill never made it to final reading.

Seeking a clear mandate in the aftermath of the Bouchard-Taylor commission, Charest's Liberals called a snap provincial election to be held in December 2008. Unable to maintain its second-place position, the ADQ faded from the political landscape until 2012, when it merged with the newly formed Coalition avenir Québec party (Coalition for Quebec's Future, CAQ). Partly made up of former PQ members of the National Assembly and members of the ADQ, the CAQ is a centre-right party that advocates conservative economic policies while favouring a largely liberal discourse on social issues. Like its partial predecessor, the ADQ, the party advocates Quebec nationalism without independence. In recent years, it has increasingly supported reducing immigration levels and restricting religious practices in various public spaces and institutions.

Part of the raison d'être of the CAQ, and the ADQ before it, is to challenge the prevailing ways that issues of class and national identity traditionally intersect in Quebec politics. In its 2015 manifesto entitled *A New Agenda for Québec Nationalists*, the party asserts that: "For too long, the PQ has claimed to be the lone voice of national pride, while the Liberal party has claimed to be the champion of prosperity." "These illusions," the document further suggests, "have been shattered, as both parties have proven their respective inability to move Québec out of its constitutional impasse and overcome its slow economic growth."[98] This excerpt suggests that a prosperous future for Quebec will require uncoupling the nationalist project from its (historically) leftist roots in the Parti Québécois and taking a "pragmatic" approach to surmounting the obstacles to the province's autonomy within Canada. As we will see, this uncoupling appeals to voters, in part because it offers a new way of envisioning the relationship between economic objectives and the promotion of Quebec's national culture and identity.

A second, newer opposition party – Québec solidaire – also defies the traditional axis of competition in Quebec, but in a different way. This party came into being in 2006, as a result of a merger between the left-wing Union des forces progressistes (Union of Progressive Forces, UFP) party and the Option citoyenne (Citizens' Option, OC) political movement. QS was led by Françoise David, who was also president of the Fédération des femmes du Québec (Quebec Women's Federation, FFQ) from 1994 to 2001. Until her retirement from politics in January 2017, David personified and gave voice to the growing dissatisfaction of many voters with "politics as usual" in Quebec, particularly with the perceived decline in office-holders' commitment to progressive policies. In founding Québec solidaire along with her co-spokesperson, Amir Khadir,[99] in 2006, David opened the way for other activists reluctant to engage in partisan action and institutional politics to begin making a mark on Quebec's electoral discourse.[100] From that point forward, the party's platform would be underlined by commitments to the environment, social justice, feminism, and anti-racism.

Although it has occupied an important symbolic role in Quebec politics, being deemed the missing voice "for the disenfranchised,"[101] QS has struggled to make inroads at the ballot box. In 2008, voters elected the party's first candidate, Amir Khadir. Khadir was then joined by David in 2012, and Manon Massé became the party's third elected candidate in the provincial election of 2014. The 2018 election marked a major turning point for QS. In that election, which saw the sharp decline of the traditional parties, QS earned an unprecedented ten seats in the National Assembly, surpassing the PQ's nine elected representatives.

Like the CAQ, therefore, Québec Solidaire's founding ambition was to disrupt the established alignment between economic and national interests in Quebec's party political system. In QS's case, that disruption would take the form of attempts to suture back together the link that had once, under the stewardship of the PQ, existed between social democracy and independence. Yet, the pre-eminence of sovereignty as the main question around which political parties organize themselves has continued to manifest itself through periodic calls to merge the PQ and QS in order to strengthen the mandate for another referendum.

CONTESTING THE BOUNDARIES OF FEMINISM: CONFRONTATIONS BETWEEN PRO- AND ANTI-RESTRICTION FEMINISTS IN QUEBEC

Chapter 2 showed that, in France, there exists a clear dividing line between pro-restriction feminists – who have gained the attention of the state by mobilizing a "republican" discourse of gender (in)equality – and anti-restriction feminists – who view state legislators and their feminist allies as reproducing Muslims' colonial subjugation. In Quebec, the association between a particular feminist outlook and the state's agenda with respect to religious signs is somewhat less clear-cut. This is partly due to the fact that, because of the province's complex colonial history, feminists on both sides of this debate have been able to stake their claims in different conceptions of anti-colonialism: one that condemns "Western" feminists' attempts to suppress their "Third World" counterparts, and another that represents the Québécois themselves as victims of colonial domination.[102] These two conceptions have intersected in complex ways in Quebec's contemporary religious signs debate.

Originating in the suffrage movement that demanded the right of women to vote in the early 1900s, Quebec's women's movement has existed for over a century. Once women obtained the right to vote – at the federal level in 1918 and provincially in 1940 – the movement's "first wave" disintegrated, opening the way for more "radical" feminist associations, such as the Front de libération des femmes (Women's Liberation Front, FLF), whose goals were to raise collective awareness of patriarchal oppression and to assert women's economic equality. Since the Quiet Revolution, organizations like the FLF have been integrated into the administration of public policy in Quebec, with some being assigned responsibility over the governance and expression of women's demands. This state of affairs has led the women's movement to gain a "certain monopoly over the representation of women's interests" and to become "recognized as an authorized and legitimate representative of women in general."[103]

The two largest women's organizations in Quebec today – the Fédération des femmes du Québec (Quebec Women's Federation, FFQ) and the Association féminine d'éducation et d'action sociale (Women's Association for Education and Social Action, AFEAS) – can be situated along the continuum of two major streams of feminism mentioned in chapter 2: "gender as equality" and "gender as difference." The AFEAS was founded through a merger of rural women's and farmers' organizations in 1966. Its approach to women's rights is closely associated with the "difference" stream, and with the emphasis on home economics that swept through North America at the beginning of the twentieth century.[104] By contrast, the FFQ, also founded in 1966, supports an egalitarian ideology that centres on women's access to affordable daycare, pay equity, and other employment rights. Its dedication to achieving solidarity among women of diverse class, racial, and religious backgrounds has led the group to both embrace intersectional feminist discourses and stress concerns about race discrimination wrought by neo-liberal capitalism, imperialism, and neo-colonialism.[105] The FFQ was also instrumental to the 1973 creation of Quebec's second major feminist organization: the Conseil du statut de la femme (Council for the Status of Women, CSF), a consultative body tasked with issuing recommendations concerning legislation, policies, and programs to the Quebec minister responsible for the status of women. The council's eleven members, including its president, are appointed by the Quebec government.

The FFQ and the CSF have fluctuated in their stances on the question of religious signs. In the debates that surrounded the Bouchard-Taylor commission in 2007–08, the FFQ criticized the then Liberal government and the commission's co-chairs for failing to take a tougher stance on religious threats to gender equality.[106] Yet, when the Parti Québécois took up the gender equality discourse to validate its Charter of Values in 2013, the organization turned against the proposal, citing its anti-racist concerns with greater fervor. In its brief before the parliamentary hearings on the Charter, the FFQ denounced the proposed restriction of religious signs in public sector employment as discriminatory and detrimental to women's emancipation. Instead it called for an approach to gender equality constructed around the principles of "non-domination," "self-determination," and respect for women's equal right to fundamental freedoms, including freedom of religion.[107]

Although state-appointed, the CSF has also maintained an arms-length relationship to the religious signs discourses adopted by governments in power. In its 2007 brief to the Bouchard-Taylor commission, the organization recommended that public sector employees be prohibited from wearing religious signs on the job,[108] thus contradicting the position of the Liberal government at the time. Yet, during the 2013 Charter debate, the organization reversed its position.

Asserting its independence once again, the CSF opposed the blanket prohibition of religious signs for public sector employees; although adopting the Bouchard-Taylor report's recommendation, it conceded that restrictions might be needed to ensure the religious neutrality of teachers and civil servants in positions of authority (mainly judges, police officers, and prison guards).[109]

The positions taken by the FFQ and CSF on the question of religious signs have garnered competing reactions from feminists in Quebec. Those who support restricting – or at least limiting – religious accommodations maintain that these organizations serve the interests of an "elite intellectual" class[110] that controls the public discourse through its "monopoly" of the media and the "domination of progressive left-wing and feminist politics."[111] By contrast, anti-restriction feminists have praised the FFQ and CSF for having the "courage" necessary to contest legislative proposals that curtail women's rights.[112] In chapter 5, I will show that, in the context of the Charter of Values, debate between these two camps centred on the significance of multiculturalism to Quebec's political discourse, thus demonstrating the role of politics – in this case feminist politics – in shaping the way actors interpreted and mobilized extant ideas in Quebec's religious signs debate.

NEW RUPTURES: PAULINE MAROIS AND THE CHARTER OF VALUES

The Bouchard-Taylor commission and its aftermath produced a shift in the PQ's approach to framing Quebec's national identity. Overtaken by the ADQ in the 2007 provincial election, the party needed a new strategy for reaching its political base. Forging that strategy was made even more difficult by the fact that support for sovereignty – the chief raison d'être of the PQ – had steadily declined since the second referendum in 1995. Pollsters and analysts have attributed that decline to a variety of factors. One of these is generational. The two main groups to support sovereignty in 1995 were the "baby boomers" born between 1945 and 1962, and voters born between 1962 and 1977. Subsequent generations did not pick up the mantle of independence with nearly as much enthusiasm.[113] Especially among the young, there has been significant demobilization around the questions of sovereignty and Quebec's role within Canada. Among these younger voters, moreover, the "grievances" that once drove the sovereigntist project are far less resonant today than in the past. This is exacerbated by the fact that, while the Québécois remain more progressive on social and economic issues than the rest of Canada, they have less confidence in the state, taxation, and unionization as cornerstones of solidarity.[114]

In responding to voters' declining interest in sovereignty, the Parti Québécois sought to rebrand its nationalist project in terms of a commitment to curbing the infiltration of religion into the public sphere. This strategy was central to Pauline Marois's tenure as party leader from 2007 to 2014. Soon after taking the helm, she enlisted the help of dissident Bouchard-Taylor commission member Jacques Beauchemin. In our interview, he explained that:

> When Pauline Marois first contacted me, the Parti Québécois was in disarray. She knew it. And the ADQ was the official opposition. I told her – it was my opinion – that the Parti Québécois was off course because it no longer spoke to anyone. I told her: "If you are not able to speak to the French majority – in other words, if you talk like Bouchard and Taylor – you aren't speaking to anyone." Because if you tell the Québécois that we are a big open and pluralistic society, they will agree with you. But then why vote for the Parti Québécois? The Liberal Party says the same thing. You need to be able to say that we are an open and pluralistic society, but one that has long been fighting to assert its national identity. You have to say that to people, to francophones. They are not all separatists. But they are nationalists. If you address them with that kind of [pluralist] language, you lose them.[115]

This statement sets out in remarkably candid terms the way a nation-centred axis of competition circumscribes party decision-making with respect to religious diversity in Quebec. In particular, it underlines the perception that attracting voters to the PQ in the current political climate requires the willingness to project a more starkly nationalist vision, one that prioritizes language and identity over pluralism and diversity.

Marois ultimately took the advice offered by Beauchemin and others in this regard. Under her leadership, the PQ adopted a stronger nationalist rhetoric and made restrictive secularism central to its political platform. The deepening crisis of legitimacy in the PLQ government of Premier Jean Charest gave Marois's Parti Québécois the chance to test this revised strategy on a province-wide scale. In 2011, a number of Liberal officials were charged with corruption in their provision and management of public construction contracts. Detailed and high profile investigations into these corruption charges by the Charbonneau commission reinforced the public's distrust in the PLQ premier and his party. The mass student protests of 2012 added to the unease. Launched in objection to tuition hikes introduced by the Liberals, the protests grew into a province-wide anti-government movement, in which the PQ positioned itself as the ally of the students. In the campaign leading up to the election of fall 2012, the party capitalized on the public's distrust of the Liberals to portray itself as the voice of honest social change. With a platform that focused on the need to assert Québécois values, the party obtained a minority government, winning 54 of the 125 seats in Quebec's National Assembly. With 50 seats, the Liberals formed the official opposition.

With only a four-seat lead over the Liberals, the PQ struggled to assert a clear leadership role in the early months of its administration. Combined with the fact that independence from Canada – article 1 of the party's manifesto – was unpopular among many Québécois, the province's poor economic performance weakened public confidence. By June 2013, only 27 per cent of those polled said they would vote for the PQ in a future election.[116]

However, the PQ's chances of re-election dramatically improved in August 2013, when the press leaked the contents of its promised Charter of Values. The purported purpose of the Charter was to implement a series of proposals developed by civil society actors and by the Parti Québécois. In 2007, when the PLQ were still in power, the PQ proposed that article 50.1 be added to Quebec's Charter of Human Rights and Freedoms so as to entrench the principle of laïcité in public sector institutions.[117] Later, in 2009, the party amended its proposal, expanding its definition of laïcité to the "separation of the state and religion." Several civil society organizations approved this approach. In the debates around the Liberals' Bill 94 in 2010, the Mouvement laique québécois (Secular Movement of Quebec, MLQ) proposed that the preamble to Quebec's Charter of Human Rights and Freedoms cite laïcité as a "public value and source of social cohesion" as well as proposing the addition of article 9.2 to prohibit practices and behaviours that contravene the neutrality of the state, its institutions, and services.[118]

Based on these proposals, the PQ and other civil society organizations began to advocate more elaborate measures to entrench the principle of state neutrality, calling on the government to institute a Charter of laïcité. During the PQ's 2011 national congress, Marois specified that such a Charter would affirm "that Québec is a secular state, which is neutral in relation to the religious beliefs or non-beliefs of individuals; that freedom of religion cannot be invoked to contravene either the right to equality between the sexes or the proper functioning of public and semi-public institutions; that public and semi-public service agents must abstain, when exercising their functions, from wearing all ostensible religious signs."[119] The proposal to institute such a Charter featured centrally in the PQ's election platform of September 2012.

By September 2013, one year into its mandate, the PQ had generated a website outlining its draft Charter of Values. Put before the National Assembly in November 2013, Bill 60 – which proposed to make the Charter into law – recommended legislation that would prohibit public sector employees from wearing religious signs on the job,[120] establish a duty of neutrality and reserve for all state employees, and make it mandatory to uncover one's face when providing or receiving public services.[121] It also proposed to entrench state religious neutrality and the secularity of state institutions in Quebec's Charter of Human Rights and Freedoms and implement a government policy to regulate demands for accommodation in state organizations. Meanwhile, however, the Charter specified that the crucifix in Quebec's National Assembly and the cross on Mount Royal in Montreal would *not* be removed, as they commemorate Quebec's Catholic heritage as a key element of the province's history and culture.

All three opposition parties – including the centre-right and federalist Parti libéral du Québec, the centre-right and autonomist (but not pro-sovereignty) Coalition avenir Québec, and the left-wing sovereigntist Québec solidaire – opposed the Charter's proposed restriction of religious signs in public sector employment. As chapter 5 will demonstrate, their precise responses reveal the significance of a nation-centred axis of electoral competition in determining parties' strategies for gaining ownership of the religious signs issue in Quebec.

Although he opposed the restrictions on religious expression among public sector employees, Liberal leader Phillippe Couillard supported the PQ's commitment to maintaining the crucifix in the National Assembly,[122] as well as the requirement that employees and clients remove facial coverings in public service encounters (a recommendation of the Bouchard-Taylor report).[123] The Coalition avenir Québec (CAQ) took a somewhat different stance. While it supported the prohibition of religious signs for civil servants who represent the state's authority, including teachers, the party feared that the application of this requirement to all public sector employees was too radical.[124] Quebec's third opposition party, Québec solidaire, declared that it broadly supported the Charter's commitment to strengthening state religious neutrality and protecting the French language, but it opposed both the restriction of religious signs and the maintenance of the crucifix in the National Assembly.[125]

The Charter of Values received mixed support from Quebec's public. Residents of the province split in two, with a majority of rural francophones supporting its proposed ban of religious signs in public sector employment, compared to just 15 per cent of anglophones.[126] Moreover, the fact that anglophone voters – and other groups unlikely to support the Charter, such as immigrants – concentrate in urban areas meant that all of the mayoral candidates in Montreal's fall 2013 municipal election denounced the Charter's key recommendations, promising to request exemptions for the city's public employees.[127]

Not only did Quebec's population respond strongly to the Charter of Values, suggesting this was indeed a very salient political issue around which parties could distinguish themselves, the debate over the Charter also brought Canadian national politics into Quebec. Shortly after the press leaked the Charter's contents in August 2013, all of Canada's federal parties (with the exception of the pro-sovereignty Bloc Québécois) condemned its recommended ban on religious signs. The ruling federal Conservative Party went even further, promising to take the Province of Quebec to court if its ban of religious signs in public sector employment were to pass a vote in the National Assembly.[128] This disturbed the carefully maintained sense of Quebec's political independence, bringing the issue of the province's lack of autonomy back on the table and rallying support for the PQ amongst those who continue to favour sovereignty.

The division between those for and against the Charter of Values did not cleanly map onto support for the PQ versus the PLQ. The Charter pitted progressive, pro-diversity factions of the sovereigntist movement against those who sought to narrow the requirements for participation in Quebec's public sphere. In his numerous media appearances and newspaper contributions, for example, the co-chair of the Bouchard-Taylor commission, Gérard Bouchard, warned that, if adopted, article 5 of the Charter would derail Quebec's independence project, by reviving defensive and exclusionary discourses of nationhood.[129] Prominent political leaders in the sovereigntist movement echoed those concerns, including former Parti Québécois premiers Bernard Landry, Lucien Bouchard, and Jacques Parizeau, and former leader of the Bloc Québécois (Quebec Bloc, BQ) Gilles Duceppe, all of whom opposed a ban on religious signs in public sector employment.[130]

These strong voices of opposition did not significantly dampen popular support for the Charter of Values, however. In fact, polls indicating a high approval rating for the bill – mostly among francophones, who in 2011 made up nearly 80 per cent of Quebec's population[131] – encouraged the PQ government to strengthen its mandate by scheduling a provincial election to take place on 7 April 2014. But this would turn out to be a grave strategic error. Despite its effort to avoid losing votes over sovereignty, which as I mentioned has declined in popularity,[132] the PQ became hostage to the issue when in mid-campaign its newest candidate, media mogul Pierre Karl Péladeau, raised a clenched fist while proclaiming his commitment to making Quebec "a country" at a press conference on 9 March 2014.[133] This announcement caused Marois herself to go off message and veer away from the party's plan of representing itself as the choice for "good government," by musing about what a sovereign Quebec might look like – what kind of currency it would adopt, dual citizenship, and so on.

When they raised the spectre of a third referendum in an ill-advised series of public speeches and appearances, the PQ made a political misstep that brought to light a lack of internal cohesion and a splintered message. In response, the PLQ was able to position itself as the party of stability and economic growth. As the PQ struggled to defend itself, the main feature of the party's platform that had resonated with the electorate – the Charter of Values – receded into the background. Incapable of generating enough support in the face of accusations that it would destabilize Quebec by calling a third referendum on sovereignty, the PQ lost the election of 7 April, allowing a majority PLQ government to take office.

CONCLUSION

As is the case in other societies, the process of secularization in Quebec has evolved through numerous transformative phases, each characterized by heavily politicized debates about the relationship between religion, the state, and the nation. Once aided by a British colonial government seeking to secure the loyalty of its religiously and linguistically distinct subjects, the Catholic Church no longer holds significant influence over governance in Quebec. Yet, its former influence remains apparent, both in Quebec's visual landscape and in the discourses deployed in contemporary debates around religious covering.

The nationalist project has crucially shaped Quebec's secularization process throughout its evolution. From the Patriote movement of the 1830s through the massive popular abandonment of Catholicism in the 1950s and '60s to the recent debates over religious accommodation, the question of how to assert Quebec's national distinctiveness and claim autonomy has been at the forefront. In each period, political actors in the province have had to reconcile a desire to safeguard Quebec's cultural, linguistic, and (sometimes) religious heritage, with the more long-term goal of establishing a modern quasi-nation-state that is open to the world. As in France, these efforts have raised questions about how a commitment to universal values intersects with, and indeed may strengthen, claims to national particularism.

However, unlike the French political system, where class conflicts have until recently defined the central axis of competition, party political contention in Quebec is heavily dictated by the national identity debate. Although distinctive economic visions also orient parties' platforms, these are entangled with the "national question" in ways that reduce their independent effects on voter alignment or party cleavage structures. Broadly neo-liberal in its approach to taxation and the size of government, the PLQ's economic policy reflects its ties to big business, by rejecting sovereignty – even a referendum – as detrimental to trade and growth. By contrast, the PQ's broadly social democratic approach to governance has historically aligned with the party's goal of positioning Quebec as a society that harbours distinctive social values from the rest of Canada. This interconnection between nationalism and economic policy has made distinguishing the PLQ and PQ on purely economic grounds periodically difficult.

Parties' positions along a nation-centred axis of competition have strongly influenced their articulation strategies in the contemporary religious signs debate. Committed to maintaining a strong record of tolerance for minorities – one that resembles that of Canada as a whole – the PLQ has struggled to put forward a coherent agenda regarding religious accommodation. Its leadership has fluctuated between outright refusal to legislate and a series of ambiguous proposals intended to reconcile a restrictive secularism with commitment to freedom of religion. By contrast, the PQ has sought to re-energize the independence movement by conceptualizing the rights of religious minorities in ways that "fit" with Quebec's unique value system. This values-based approach in turn validates an understanding of nationhood that requires minorities to shed visible signs of difference.

As I will show in chapter 5, legal principles enshrined in the Québécois (1975) and Canadian (1982) Charters inform but do not dictate the conflict among parties over these distinct articulations of secularism. While legal experts and practitioners brought forth significant objections to the 2013 Charter of Values, these did not prevent the PQ from forging ahead with its proposals. Instead, the party proffered an interpretation of the rights constituting belonging to the Québécois nation that in many ways conflicts with Quebec's – and Canada's – legal institutional framework. By reinscribing the "rights" associated with national membership as "values," the PQ reinforced its ownership of the religious signs debate, causing dismay among its rivals.

PART TWO

Demarcating the Boundaries of the Nation

4

"We Are All Republicans"

Sharing Ownership of the Nation in France's Face Veil Debate

Chapter 2 traced the structures of partisan conflict that I argue encouraged France's major political parties to converge around the claim that republican laïcité requires restricting Islamic veiling in certain public spaces and institutions. I showed that, in seeking ownership of this issue for political gain, the right-wing UMP and left-wing Socialists advanced an increasingly narrow conception of the boundaries of French nationhood. This chapter addresses two different, but related, substantive questions. First, how is the alleged consensus around this interpretation of laïcité articulated, and thus reaffirmed, in periods of contestation over religious symbols and practices, in particular the Islamic face veil? Second, what are the implications of that consensus for the ways in which politicians and civil society actors constitute the meaning(s) of national belonging?

To answer these questions, I analyze the Gerin commission – the six-month government inquiry that preceded the 2010 ban of facial coverings in French public space – and its surrounding debates. Between June and December 2009, the commission's president, André Gerin, and thirty-one other members of the French National Assembly heard testimony from seventy-eight invited guests representing various organizations and social groups in France. They also questioned representatives of other EU countries, the United States, Canada, Turkey, and some Arab nations, and received submissions from all political parties represented in the French National Assembly and Senate. The commission's stated objective was to "review the practice of wearing the burqa and the niqab by certain Muslim women" in order to "better understand the problem and to find ways to fight against this affront to individual freedom."[1]

Although they could not reach unanimous agreement on a complete ban – for reasons I detailed in chapter 2 – the Gerin commission's members broadly agreed that the face veil violates the philosophical tenets of French republicanism and should thus be curtailed on French soil. I argue in this chapter that framing these conclusions as deriving from a widely shared consensus was a key objective of the major figures involved in the Gerin commission, one that required a careful formulation of the commission's mandate, as well as a highly strategic solicitation and framing of the views of its participating groups. In order to buttress this alleged consensus, those responsible for establishing and administering the Gerin commission took a remarkably top-down approach, one that reveals a pre-existing desire to invoke the need to ban the face veil. Not only did the commission's mandate proclaim the need to fight against the face veil, but its members also consisted of many politicians active in the National Assembly who had expressed strong positions on veiling prior to the commission. Those politicians were then responsible for deciding who would appear as experts before the commission, a fact that resulted in the selective omission or under-representation of certain key groups.

I further suggest that, as they struggled to offset the ultra-right's monopolization of the question of diversity for political gain, politicians on the mainstream right and left converged around a narrowed conception of nationhood, in which full belonging depends on commitment to a particular interpretation of French republicanism. Members of the UMP conveyed that interpretation through references to a "clash" between Muslim and republican values; through allegations that North Africans in France pose an economic threat; and through representations of the face veil as violating the universal values that define French national particularity on the world stage. On the left side of the spectrum, and especially within the Socialist Party, I argue that there was greater disagreement over the implications of veiling for the meaning(s) of religion, secularism, and national belonging, manifested through three main discursive strategies. First, those aiming to "rescue" laïcité sought to delegitimize right and ultra-right manipulations of the term. Driven mainly by the quest for issue ownership, the resulting discourses emphasized partisanship over shared nationhood. Second, discourses aimed at "reclaiming" laïcité as a principle enshrined mainly by left-wing politicians – such as in the 1905 law – focused on tying the concept to issues theoretically "owned" by the left, such as the fight for equality and the emancipatory role of the state. Though they aimed to re-establish the universal aspects of national belonging, these discourses ran up against the challenge of reconciling universalism with the perceived political rewards associated with more particularistic accounts of French politics and culture. A third and final discourse of "rejection" dismissed the dominant secular vision, bringing to the fore the racist undertones of its use in both right and left political discourse. As I will demonstrate, dilemmas stemming from the competition for issue ownership, at least until recently, have caused the former two strategies to prevail.

THE GERIN COMMISSION (2009): MANDATE AND COMPOSITION

Although its deliberations largely took place in central Paris, in the Bourbon Palace that houses the French National Assembly, the confrontations that sparked the 2009 Gerin commission and subsequent face veil ban have their roots outside the French capital, in Vénissieux, a suburb of Lyon. Once a small agricultural town, Vénissieux underwent significant population expansion during the 1950s economic boom. Over the ensuing decades, the town became a key destination for North African migrant men – mainly from Algeria – who came to seek work in its thriving industrial sector, their spouses and children joining them a decade or so later. The initial prosperity brought on by industrialization was short-lived, however, as the oil crisis of the 1970s hit the region hard, causing unemployment to spike. Residents with sufficient means fled Vénissieux for surrounding areas, leaving behind a large North African community with limited work opportunities and deteriorated housing.[2]

Born and raised in a nearby farming community, André Gerin began working at age eighteen in an automotive plant, where daily mistreatment by factory managers drew him into communist activism. By the late 1970s, after he had scaled the ranks of the company, Gerin joined the Communist Party of France. But it was his experience as municipal councillor and later mayor of Vénissieux that solidified Gerin's political vision. When he won the mayoralty race in 1985, Gerin's stated goal was to bring national attention to Vénissieux's unemployment crisis, which at the time he blamed on the deindustrializing and housing policies of the French state. However, as residents affected by poverty increasingly took to rioting in the streets of Vénisseux in the late 1980s and early 1990s, Gerin shifted the blame to the local Imams, whom he claimed were taking advantage of North African residents' desperation to promote violence and Islamic radicalism.[3]

By the time he was appointed to chair the infamous "Burqa commission" (a popular nickname for the Gerin commission) in 2009, Gerin had come to embody an amalgamation of the disparate ideological streams that constitute the professed consensus around religious signs in France. The fact that he deplored the Front National's opportunistic use of the French identity "crisis" to promote racism, and saw "radical" Islam as a by-product of capitalism, testified to his left-wing roots. Yet, Gerin also subscribed to predominantly right-wing claims that Islamic culture clashes with that of Judeo-Christian societies[4] and that immigration to France should be curtailed.[5] These seeming contradictions earned Gerin the reputation as a *maire sécuritaire* ("security mayor") and a *Sarkozy de gauche* ("Sarkozy of the left") among many leftists.

In June 2009, Gerin approached the National Assembly with a proposal for a government-led inquiry into the advisability of legally banning the face veil in France's public spaces. Although his fellow deputies initially rejected the proposal, Gerin's lobbying efforts, including his use of the media to draw public attention to the issue, eventually resulted in a petition in support of a government inquiry signed by fifty-eight deputies of all political stripes.[6] In my interview with him, Gerin claimed that this petition "made a huge splash, in the media, in the government, even for the president." "That was a Wednesday," he explained, "By Friday the president of the Republic had made a statement in which he indicated that we must absolutely address this problem. The following Tuesday morning, the president of the National Assembly announced a decision to put in place a commission of information on the face veil."[7]

Throughout the commission's proceedings, and again in our interview, Gerin declared himself neutral on the question of whether to legally ban the face veil. Yet, he expressed strong negative sentiments about this garment well prior to the start of the commission's proceedings. For example, in a statement published by the newspaper *Le Point* on 19 June 2009, Gerin described the wearing of face veils as both "worrying and shocking." He added that "to see ghosts and mobile prisons walking in the streets creates a real discomfort among the population."[8] In the same interview, Gerin then called for a "republican battle" to forge an "Islam of the Enlightenment."[9]

Gerin's evident opposition to the face veil did not prevent him from being nominated to chair the commission. On the contrary, it likely helped his case. As a leftist – indeed a Communist – who favours a strong response to "radical" Islam, Gerin was regarded as uniquely capable of ensuring that the commission's findings would reflect a cross-party consensus on the face veil. Gerin himself saw his nomination as part of a conscious effort to foster bipartisanship in the commission. In our interview, he proposed that "had a Communist not initiated it, this project would not have taken place. There would have been indecision in the Assembly. If the right takes the initiative, everyone on the left refuses to participate."[10] Forging a cross-party alliance on the face veil issue thus appeared to be foremost in the minds of the commission organizers.

Not only had Gerin personally declared himself hostile to the face veil prior to the commission's proceedings, but this position was front and centre in the commission's own official mandate. In the seven-page document registered with the National Assembly on 9 June 2009, the signatories of the resolution to launch the commission stated in no uncertain terms that the practice of face veiling must be put to an end, as it represents a "communalist affront that contradicts our principles of laïcité, our values of freedom, equality, and human dignity."[11] The document further suggested that, although "useful," existing measures aimed at curtailing the practice of covering one's face "are insufficient to address these practices, which we cannot tolerate in France."[12]

On the dangers of the face veil, therefore, it was assumed that all participants in the Gerin commission would be in agreement before the deliberations began. The only real question left for commissioners to consider was which precise measure – a parliamentary resolution or a law – would be most effective in restricting the presence of the face veil in France's public spaces. As we will see, commission members favouring the latter solution balked at the objections raised in legal experts' testimonies.

With the Gerin commission's mandate established, the question of its composition was then addressed. Significantly, it was to be made up exclusively of members of the National Assembly. This approach to representation was far different from that adopted by the 2003 Stasi commission, which was mostly led by academics, legal experts, and former politicians. Instead of being removed from the process of governing, members of the Gerin commission *were* the government of

France at the time. Every political "group"[13] was invited to send a specified number of delegates – proportional to its representation in the Assembly – to serve as members of the commission board.[14] Ultimately, thirty-two members of the National Assembly formed the commission's membership: seventeen representatives of the UMP, eleven Socialists, one Communist, two members of the right-of-centre New Centre Party, and one Green Party representative.

The composition of the Gerin commission thus decided, the next question was who would appear before it as experts. No precise method for selecting the Gerin commission's seventy-eight invited participants was officially stated. However, my interviews with commission members and organizers revealed that, for the most part, these participants were either solicited directly by individual commissioners or were identified as persons or groups of interest during weekly meetings attended by Gerin and his team of administrators.[15]

Close examination of the roster of participants – among them feminists, pro-secularism activists, representatives of the French Muslim community, academics, journalists, public intellectuals, legal experts, Freemasons, and government actors[16] – suggests that important strategic choices were made, resulting in two significant omissions. First, at seven out of seventy-eight[17] – five of them from the same organization – the number of participants representing the French Muslim community was remarkably low, given that the issue before the commission directly involved and impacted that community. Moreover, of those who did appear, only one woman who wears the face veil – the very practice whose legality was before the commission – was heard. Second, nearly all of the fourteen feminists to appear before the Gerin commission supported a legal ban of face veils. The commission thus failed to consult a significant number of feminist organizations that oppose restrictions on Islamic religious signs in France.

Besides being highly selective in its choice of participants, the Gerin commission was also unabashed in claiming that the testimonies of its participating groups supported the assertion of consensus around the need to restrict facial coverings in France. In fact, the report used the term "consensus" to describe participants' opinions on a number of specific issues, including: that national Muslim organizations widely approve of the ban,[18] that the 2004 law banning ostentatious religious signs in schools was a clear success,[19] that the face veil poses a threat to women's dignity,[20] and that French society is founded on shared "implicit values," which facial coverings clearly violate.[21] The

Gerin report even used the term "consensus" to characterize its overall conclusions, stating that "the quasi-totality of propositions formulated by the commission form the basis of a consensus. They are founded upon the conviction that it is necessary to convince, educate, and protect, that we must confront public agents with a single objective: to eliminate a practice that contravenes our republican values."[22]

The strong desire to portray the Gerin commission's findings as deriving from a "consensus" was also evident in my interviews with commission members. For example, when I asked whether he observed any fractures along party lines, UMP member Georges Mothron answered: "not at all, it was really bipartisan." He added that "the vast majority of the commission's members opposed the veil." Mothron even claimed that the "reasons" for opposing the veil overlapped by "99 per cent" across parties.[23] Mothron's colleague in the UMP, Nicole Ameline, also revealed, albeit less directly, a desire to show a consensus when she credited André Gerin – who she noted was a representative of a competing and strongly divergent political party – with bringing the issue of the veil to the public's attention. In her words: "I visited Les Minguettes [a neighbourhood outside Lyon which houses a large number of immigrant families from North Africa] with André Gerin and we were very much accomplices and allied in our reflection. He is the one who informed us that, more and more, women were wearing the burqa."[24] Although they sat on opposite sides of the aisle, Ameline had come to regard Gerin as a close ally in the project to ban the face veil in the French public sphere.

Left-wing members of the Gerin commission were similarly intent on emphasizing the agreement among commissioners over the need to curb the face veil. In our interview, Socialist member Christian Bataille insisted that "we cannot say there is a right-left cleavage" on this question.[25] Bataille's colleague, Socialist commission member Jean Glavany, also promoted this image of a cross-party alignment when he told me that "we are all republicans, each and every one of us, with some exceptions on the extreme left and extreme right. We are all republicans with the same set of values."[26] These two statements illustrate the degree to which politicians involved in the Gerin commission were willing to downplay partisan differences in the interest of projecting an image of consensus.

When it came to claiming unanimity in politicians' outlooks on the face veil, the position of the Front National was conspicuously left out. At the time of the Gerin commission, Jean-Marie Le Pen was still party leader. Appealing to his Catholic supporters, he was highly reticent to support the outlawing of face veils, for fear that it might have repercussions for religious expression more generally. However, Marine Le Pen – who by 2009 was a prominent figure in the FN and soon-to-be leader – took a much stronger anti-veil stance. From her perspective, the 2010 face veil ban did not go far enough. Indeed, in an interview conducted before the law was passed, she proclaimed that the face veil "is merely the tip of the iceberg." "In reality," Le Pen continued, "what we need is an integral law that condemns all communalisms, and to inscribe in the constitution that the Republic recognizes no community."[27]

By the time of my interviews – which took place in 2012–13 – politicians saw Marine Le Pen – and not her father – as the main voice of the Front National. When they mentioned her name, it was usually to show that mainstream condemnations of the face veil were grounded in reasonable and legitimate concerns around women's equality and dignity, not in the exclusionary anti-immigrant discourse of the ultra-right. For instance, the UMP's Nicole Ameline claimed that "it is people like Marine Le Pen who create communalism, by causing people to retreat back to their identities." "What we need to do," Ameline continued, "is the opposite, that is, to be inclusive."[28] By using the term "inclusive" to justify a rejection of face veils, Ameline was able to simultaneously exclude two points of view: that of veiled women from the boundaries of French nationhood, belonging, and citizenship, and that of the Front National from the boundaries of legitimate politics.

Thus, whereas many politicians in the Gerin commission portrayed consensus as a source of legitimacy, that consensus did not embrace the ultra-right. Even though the Front National has been responsible for much of the vilification of Islamic veiling that was the impetus for the ban, the party's fringe and threatening position makes it ineligible for membership in a narrative, however contrived, of cross-party alignment over this issue.

CONFLICTS IN CIVIL SOCIETY: THE GERIN COMMISSION TESTIMONIES

Claims to consensus, both in my interviews with politicians and in the Gerin commission report itself, were not entirely borne out by the participants' testimonies. To the contrary, on the central question

Table 4.1
Position on face veil ban by type of participant

	Position on the face veil ban			
	Total	*For*	*Against*	*N/A*
Feminist individuals and associations	14	11	3	0
Secular associations	20	9	11	0
Members of the freemasonry	5	2	1	2
Individuals and associations representing the Muslim community	7	0	7	0
Academics, journalists and public intellectuals	13	2	7	4
Legal experts	7	2	4	1
Government actors	12	6	3	3
Total	78	32	36	10
Per cent in favour of ban	100	41	46	13

investigated by the commission – whether to legally ban the face veil in French public space – opinion varied widely, with the greatest support exhibited by feminists, pro-secular activists, members of the freemasonry, and government actors, and the lowest rates of support demonstrated by representatives of the Muslim community, academics, journalists, public intellectuals, and legal experts. In total, 41 per cent of the commission's invited participants openly advocated a legal ban, compared to 46 per cent who declared themselves opposed. The fact that a larger percentage opposed the ban was very much downplayed in the Gerin commission's report, which obscured these results beneath repeated claims to consensus.

In the following sections, I show that the conclusions of the Gerin report – including its declaration of consensus – required a strategic use and highly selective framing of the testimonies of three key groups of participants: individuals deemed to represent the Muslim community, feminists, and legal experts. Although small in number, the presentations by Muslim representatives were crucial in justifying the claim that the face veil is not a genuine prescription of Islam, but rather a tool for attacking the Republic. By utilizing the testimony of Muslim participants in this way, leading figures in the Gerin commission were able to deflect claims that a ban of facial coverings would violate Muslims' individual rights and freedoms. The testimonies of feminists, most of them supportive of a legal ban, were then mainly used to establish the contradictions between the face veil and the obligation to foster cohesion through acceptance of republican notions of liberté, égalité, fraternité, and laïcité. This portrayal of the feminist position heavily downplayed the objections of anti-ban feminists who, contrary to their pro-ban counterparts, saw the face veil proscription as a violation of their republican rights. Finally, and despite the fact that most of them objected to a ban, legal experts' testimonies were utilized to support the legal validity of prohibiting facial coverings on the basis of their reputed threat to a key collective dimension of French citizenship – protection of the public order.

Testimonies by Representatives of the Muslim Community

Four groups deemed to represent the interests of French Muslims made official statements before the Gerin commission. These include five representatives of the Conseil Français du Culte Musulman (French Council of the Muslim Faith, CFCM), a national Muslim association; Dalil Boubakeur, the rector of the Great Mosque of Paris; and Tariq Ramadan, a Swiss Muslim academic and controversial figure in Europe. Kenza Drider, a pro–face veil activist of Moroccan origin who wears the niqab, also testified. Because of the unique circumstances of her interview – its contents were not, like those of other participants, made public – I discuss it separately below. First, I provide contributing evidence to claims that these other testimonies were used by the Gerin commission members to create an "authoritative French version" of the Islamic tradition, one that strategically depicts the face veil as part of a political – rather than a religious – attack on French republicanism.[29]

Although they unanimously opposed a legal ban of facial coverings, all of the Gerin commission's Muslim participants (except, it appears, Drider) denied any characterization of this practice as a prescription of Islam.[30] That the CFCM and Boubakeur took this position is not wholly surprising given their previously expressed concerns about the face veil and their close ties to the French government. In 2002, when he was minister of the interior, Sarkozy handpicked Boubakeur to lead the CFCM. Links to the French government have continued to place pressure on both Boubakeur and the CFCM's leaders to abide by a promise of discouraging Muslim extremism in France.[31] This served the interests of the Gerin commissioners, who used the testimonies of these figures to frame the face veil as contrary to a "theologically proper Republican Islam."[32]

Ramadan's condemnation of the face veil was also to be expected given his writings and reputation. Grandson of Hasan Al-Banna, the founder of the Muslim Brotherhood in Egypt, Ramadan has openly repudiated his heritage and called on European Muslims both to embrace universal citizenship and to cease to demand recognition of Shariah law in Europe's legal systems. Although seen by many as providing a gateway through which "radical" Islam can be made acceptable in mainstream society, Ramadan is nevertheless a recognized and self-proclaimed non-extremist in French debates over religious integration.

While they themselves opposed the face veil, a key theme in the testimonies by representatives of the Muslim community was that, by the very fact of considering the advisability of a law to prohibit the practice, members of the Gerin commission were stigmatizing French Muslims. Speaking directly to the commission's leadership, for example, Mohammed Moussaoui, the president of the CFCM, warned that "there is a risk of manipulating the debate on the face veil. When you expressed your desire to set up a parliamentary commission of inquiry into the wearing of the burqa and niqab on the national territory, a debate opened up about this practice and it has taken on unexpected proportions. Muslims as a whole have found themselves increasingly confronted by an amalgam of attacks, resulting in the stigmatization of an entire religion."[33] In his testimony on 2 December 2009, Tariq Ramadan echoed these concerns, accusing the commissioners of intentionally popularizing a simplistic understanding of the face veil, which fails to consider the structural and socio-economic conditions that impel women to adopt the practice, causing them to "feel doubly stigmatized."[34]

Ramadan's testimony provoked a strong reaction from some commission members, who bluntly accused him of using the commission as a platform to broadcast a "double discourse," which, although it appears to condemn "radical" Islam, also fails to take a clear stand in defence of republicanism. The confrontational response of the Socialist commission member Jean Glavany demonstrates especially clearly how contrary views were shunned in an effort to assert the boundaries of the republican consensus. Following Ramadan's testimony, Glavany stated that:

> Your double discourse … half-truths, distortions, and manipulations have decreased your credibility in France and throughout Europe. There are fewer and fewer people willing to grant you any

> intellectual credit whatsoever. Your only talent, if indeed you have one, is coating discourse with unacceptable fundamentalist positions. The fact that you talked about secularism in terms far removed from the republican tradition and that you at no point referred to the equality between men and women confirms my opinion. I told the president and I said before the commission: this invitation will only serve to give you respectability and a forum that you do not deserve in my view.[35]

In this statement, Glavany very clearly depicts Ramadan as an outsider to the professed republican consensus around the need to restrict facial coverings. In failing to articulate republican principles in acceptable terms, and by omitting the question of gender equality altogether, Ramadan is portrayed as undeserving of the commissioners' respect. The stark boundaries thus drawn to exclude Ramadan from this debate are reminiscent of those erected to distinguish mainstream parties' "legitimate" positions on veiling from those of their shared enemy: the Front National.

In defending themselves against stigmatization charges by Muslim participants, members of the Gerin commission asserted that the face veil is not a religious prescription but rather a tool that religious extremists use to undermine the republican value system. To this end, the commission's report drew from passages of the Qur'an referring to the veil, to show that these "do not specifically mention the veils known in contemporary Muslim countries and, a fortiori, not the burqa or niqab."[36] In describing how a practice having no apparent basis in religious texts became (allegedly) commonplace in French Muslim communities, Gerin frequently referred to the face veil as "a political problem, to which there should be a political response."[37] He further proclaimed that the aim of this political project "is to destabilize our republic and its values of freedom, equality and brotherhood."[38]

An objective to dispel accusations of the stigmatization of Muslims appears to be a factor in the characterization of the face veil as political weapon rather than religious practice. When I inquired about certain commissioners' reasons for denying any genuine connection between the face veil and Islam, UMP member Georges Mothron candidly remarked that: "It was precisely so we would not be accused of stigmatizing. Because, if we admitted that it was a religious demand, we could be more easily attacked for being anti-Muslim or anti religion … So we strongly affirmed this because we did not want to fall into the trap of being considered anti-Muslim."[39] This quote suggests that deflecting charges of stigmatization was foremost in the commissioners' minds as they worked to validate a strong and pre-existing anti-veil stance.

By treating the face veil as a targeted, and ultimately non-religious, attack on republican values, the Gerin commission was able to downplay claims that restricting this practice amounted to a violation of Muslims' individual religious rights. This strategy also justified the very limited involvement of veiled women in the commission's proceedings. Indeed, as noted above, of the seventy-eight individuals invited to make formal presentations before the commission, only one was a woman wearing a full-face veil.[40] Taking place at the very end of the commission's deliberations, Kenza Drider's testimony was, for reasons that remain unclear, omitted from the public record. I gather from interviews with commission members that her remarks underscored the fact that the burqa is a choice for many women. Yet, this argument appeared to have very little impact. In fact, one commissioner whom I interviewed, Green Party MP François de Rugy, explained that his colleagues were highly unreceptive to Drider. In his words:

> I found that some deputies were not very respectful of her statement. That is to say, they had predetermined that she must have been manipulated, or that she necessarily held fundamentalist views on various topics. They were sort of mixing things together. They asked her questions like: "would you accept treatment from a male doctor in a hospital?" But that is another issue altogether. She was not there to express her view on that question. And so, I felt that there were many preconceptions. I think that the vast majority of commission members were there with the intention of saying: "radical Islam represents a great danger in France and we must prevent it by making a law that prohibits the face veil."[41]

This statement highlights, in strikingly straightforward terms, a commissioner's own belief that "preconceptions" played a role in encouraging a highly critical image of the face veil to take hold during the Gerin commission. Efforts to dispel those preconceptions were either met with disinterest or were read as confirming this practice's "radical" and threatening nature. For instance, when I asked Gerin whether Drider's testimony had influenced his point of view, he replied: "Not at all. In fact, it comforted me. It comforted me by reminding me not to let go, to continue, to go right to the end."[42] Almost in the same breath, Gerin reminded me how hard the commission had worked to be inclusive, explaining that he and his colleagues wanted the commission to consider all angles and "show the greatest possible openness."[43]

Despite commissioners' efforts to deflect charges of stigmatization – first, by downplaying the face veil's relation to Islam and, second, by limiting the participation of veiled women, the ostensible targets of the commission's work – these charges became widespread, permeating the testimonies of participants not affiliated with the Muslim community. For Jean-Michel Ducomte, president of the Ligue de l'enseignement (League of Education), a legal ban of face veils would "stigmatize the Muslim community and, within this community, those who most depend on the emancipatory virtues of republican secularism."[44] For other participants, the danger of stigmatization lay in the commission's potential to radicalize – by targeting – French Muslims. Journalist and sociologist Caroline Fourest insisted that "making the full veil a new flag for potential martyrs will only bolster recruitment [and] benefit fundamentalist propaganda."[45] A third group of critics maintained that, by focusing only on those practices related to Islam, the commission wilfully ignored the ostentatious symbols of other religious groups. In his testimony before the commission, Farhad Khosrokhavar, director of studies at the École des Hautes Études en Sciences Sociales (School for Advanced Studies in the Social Sciences, EHESS) and one of the first to study the issue of veiling in France, offered the following observation and warning: "Personally, it seems to me that a law banning the burqa would lead to other consequences: why not a law against bushy beards covering the entire face? Or against turbans? We risk entering into a dynamic of provocation and counter-provocation with a tiny minority of French and European Muslims, and creating "a desire to do battle" on the symbolic level."[46] These charges of stigmatization undermined the strategic efforts of leading commission members to assert the dangers of the face veil for republicanism, and to do so without offending the Muslim community or the French population at large.

Fearing the impact that charges of stigmatization might have on the commission's legitimacy, its leading members addressed these charges head on. André Gerin was especially defensive in denying the claim that he and his colleagues were predisposed to recommending a complete ban of facial coverings. At the opening of the commission's deliberative sessions, for example, Gerin often spoke to this issue, making statements like the following: "I'd like to emphasize with the greatest clarity that, contrary to what is being suggested by those who wish to discredit our work by deeming it unnecessary or by insinuating that our decision is already made, the eventual legal ban of the full veil is not an a priori objective of our commission, which, representative of all political currents in the Assembly, is taking a republican approach to this debate."[47] While seeking to deny a prejudgment of the issue, this statement may be seen as illustrating Gerin's desire to frame the face veil ban as stemming from a republican consensus. By underscoring the commission's "republican approach" and describing it as "representative of all political currents in the Assembly," he manages to portray that consensus as both highly inclusive *and* as having clear political boundaries. To remain outside those boundaries, this quote suggests, is to reject fundamental values shared by all France's (mainstream) political parties.

The Gerin commission thus drew heavily on a careful and strategic use of the contributions by participants deemed to represent the French Muslim community. Concerned that a law targeting a recognized religious practice would invite backlash, leading commissioners, including Gerin himself, redirected the conversation by presenting the face veil as an instrument of war against the Republic. By framing the commission's work in this way, commissioners were able to downplay concerns that restricting this practice amounted to a violation of veiled women's religious rights. In doing so, they also succeeded in redirecting the discourse of French citizenship away from an individual rights-based conception toward one that highlights citizens' collective obligation to foster reciprocity and social cohesion.

Testimonies by Feminists

Of the fourteen feminists who appeared before the Gerin commission, eleven supported the legal ban of facial coverings. The other three – two of them members of the same organization – opposed the law on the basis that it would threaten veiled women's right to religious expression. As we will see, the deep disagreements between these two camps over the implications of the face veil for women's rights belie the Gerin commission's claim that the proposed ban derives from a consensus among feminist activists.

Taking place early on in the commission's deliberations, testimonies by recognized pro-ban feminists and feminist associations set the moral case for condemning the face veil that would, from that point forward, mark the Gerin commission deliberations. Their arguments reinforced the perception of a deep and insurmountable contradiction between the practice of covering one's face and the republican values of liberté, égalité, fraternité, and laïcité.

Regarding liberté, pro-ban feminists argued that the face veil threatens women's capacity for individuality, a key aspect of freedom in the republican public sphere. In the words of Denise Oberlin, spokesperson for the Grande Loge Féminine de France (Grand Feminine Lodge of France), the face veil "dehumanizes women by erasing the features that render them unique." "Because the concealment of the face precludes meaningful communication or identification," she went on, "faceless women are deprived of their being."[48] Commentators claimed that, in addition to denying women's freedom by concealing their faces, the face veil makes women indistinguishable from one another.

When faced with the critique that a face veil prohibition would violate other aspects of liberté, such as freedom of conscience, pro-ban feminists called forth the notion of a hierarchy of rights. For instance, in her evidently influential presentation before the commission, the distinguished feminist Élisabeth Badinter dismissed the concern that a law would infringe upon women's freedom of dress. Such a claim, she insisted, reinforces "a hollow proclamation of freedom in rights." Other rights should take precedence, such as "the right to a free sexuality, the right not to be a virgin when one marries and to have to answer to no one."[49]

In addition to challenging the veil as violating the republican principle of liberté, pro-ban feminists also characterized it as contravening égalité. In this regard, their arguments reproduced the hybrid understanding of gender equality as sameness and as difference that I introduced in chapter 2. For instance, Élisabeth Badinter proclaimed that the veil threatens a conception of "equality as sameness," while simultaneously bemoaning the fact that "too many young girls in France are prohibited from wearing dresses and skirts."[50] This juggling act filtered into the testimonies of other pro-ban feminists. In her testimony before the commission, Olivia Cattan of the association Paroles de femmes (Women's Words) characterized the face veil as indicative of a pre-modern gendered ideology, which bars women from expressing their feminine traits and sexuality. Speaking to her encounters with Muslim high school students, Cattan then claimed that "only one girl in ten dares to wear a skirt" and that those "who do not cover themselves up risk being called easy."[51]

Believed by many feminists to reinforce gender equality, the concept of femininity also became central to claims that the veil undermines the third republican principle: fraternité. These carefully crafted arguments portrayed the free expression of femininity as essential to establishing meaningful contact and thus to securing social cohesion in the French public sphere. In this regard, Sabine Salmon, president of the association Femmes solidaires (Women in Solidarity), described the face veil as a "militant sign of belonging to a social project that seeks to create a private space within the public sphere and in which the laws of the Republic have no effect." "To conceal one's face," she continued, "is to deny one's own identity in favor of a collective physiognomy."[52] By obstructing fraternité, feminists also argued, the face veil undermines the rights of both veiled women themselves and those around them. Regarding the former, Nicole Crépeau, president of the Fédération nationale solidarité femmes (National Federation for Women's Solidarity), claimed that the face veil contradicts "the respect for fundamental rights – equality, freedom and integrity – and … women's right to a social life."[53] In terms of the latter, feminists argued that the face veil weakens the social order, thus constituting a violation of others' rights. According to Badinter: "To wear the face veil is to refuse absolutely to enter into contact with others or, more precisely, to refuse reciprocity: the veiled woman maintains her right to look at me but restricts my right to look at her."[54] By positioning veiled women as objects of society's collective gaze, statements such as this one led to a perception of the face veil as violating not only the values embodied by republicanism, but the fundamental rights allocated through it as well.

Claims by pro-ban feminists that the "voyeurism" involved in the practice of veiling weakens social cohesion and the republican sense of fraternité proved successful in shaping commission members' approaches to the face veil. Responding to a critique of a proposed ban by legal expert Cécile Petit, UMP commission member Jacques Myard replied: "I am the real victim; I am prevented from seeing the face of the one who watches me while escaping my gaze."[55] The notion that the face is the "mirror of the soul" bolstered this kind of argument, becoming a recurring theme in the Gerin commission deliberations and report. Citing French philosopher Emmanuel Lévinas, the report asserted that, "by preventing me from seeing his or her face, a person effectively makes his or herself inadmissible to the requirement of communication inherent in public space. I am thus entitled to interpret that behaviour as a symbolic violence against me."[56] By calling forth images of violence and victimhood in this way, the Gerin commission members and participants gradually crafted an image of the face veil as posing a threat, not only to the physical security of the French nation, but also to its social fabric.

In emphasizing the importance of communication to social cohesion, many pro-ban feminists also drew strategically on a fourth republican principle: laïcité. Speaking on behalf of the association Regards de femmes (Women's Outlooks), Michéle Vianès warned that, thanks to the veil, "we are no longer in our secular Republic, but in a world of pure communalism."[57] The notion that laïcité enriches fraternité – and discourages communalism – through its guarantee of individual rights and freedoms significantly shaped this argument. In her testimony before the commission, then president of Ni putes, ni soumises (Neither Whores, Nor Submissive, NPNS) Sihem Habchi cited laïcité as the solution to resolving the "breakdown in social order" allegedly brought about by the niqab and burqa. "Not only does it guarantee the separation of the political from the religious," she argued, "laïcité also permits a space of interaction between men and women, heterosexuals and homosexuals, rich and poor, allowing the creation of a social compact. Laïcité is the *sine qua non* condition for the exercise of democracy."[58]

Pro-ban feminists participating in the Gerin commission thus supported politicians' anti-veiling agenda by adopting a position that infuses the "universal" republican values of liberté, égalité, fraternité, and laïcité with a particularistic understanding of what it means to be "French" in order to place the face veil outside the legitimate boundaries of nationhood. This viewpoint easily overshadowed those of the three feminist participants who opposed a ban in the context of the commission.

Two such participants – Ismahane Chouder and Monique Crinon – appeared as representatives of the only anti-restriction feminist organization to testify: the Collectif des féministes pour l'égalité (Collective of Feminists for Equality, CFPE), a Paris-based organization that brings together Muslim and non-Muslim feminists who dispute measures to prohibit religious signs in France's public sphere. In her presentation before the commission, the group's headscarf-wearing president, Ismahane Chouder, echoed Muslim participants' concerns that the commission had become a platform for politicians to stigmatize French Muslims. Rather than punish women by forcing them to choose between the face veil and a life of isolation, Chouder argued, the commission should have sought to help these women. Instead, she maintained, by enforcing their unveiling through law, the French state was effectively turning these women into targets, and in the process continuing to ignore other, more perturbing expressions of gendered violence in France.[59]

Yet, in her remarks before the Gerin commission, Chouder also tried to rearticulate the meaning of French republicanism in a way that enables Muslim women to express their religion without sacrificing their belonging to the nation. Indeed, she demanded that lawmakers "treat the questions that concern women responsibly," by putting into action policies "that capture our belonging to the common project that is the Republic, founded on the principles of liberté, égalité, and fraternité."[60] In staking this claim, Chouder sought a treatment of Muslim women that conforms to republicanism's founding principles, noting that these principles form the basis of national cohesion in France.

Similar themes arose in my interviews with anti-ban feminists who were not invited to testify before the Gerin commission. In continuing to oppose the 2010 face veil ban, these groups have turned to the law to redefine the French republican values that upheld it. The key legal text they cite is the 1905 Law of Separation between Church and State, which protects the free exercise of religion (article 1) and prohibits the subsidization of religion by the French state (article 2). According to Ndella Paye, a member of the Collectif des féministes pour l'égalité: "We must correct the notion that Muslims and our organizations do not respect laïcité. We've been told that the 1905 law and the European and international conventions that France has signed protect our individual freedoms. But, in France, more and more, Muslims are being deprived of those freedoms. So, the legal argument is very important. The law is on our side."[61] This statement emphasizes that, by denying Muslims full and equal access to religious "freedoms," French politicians have disavowed the laws and "conventions" that fundamentally define republican laïcité. Studies based on interviews with Muslim women who wear the veil in France suggest that similar efforts to defend the veil by linking laïcité to religious freedom are underway at the broader community level.[62]

By calling forth the more universalistic conception of "freedom" implied in French legal definitions of laïcité, anti-ban feminists have also challenged their opponents' representations of women's agency, a key theme in the postcolonial feminist literature on veiling. That literature suggests that the "Western" liberal definition of "agency as domination"[63] mobilized in campaigns to unveil Muslim women obscures the multiple and nuanced ways that women negotiate between their wants and needs and the prescriptions of their cultures and religions. As a result, those who do not actively seek to dismantle hegemonic institutions and discourses, or whose day-to-day choices are circumscribed by custom or tradition, are not perceived by "Western" feminism as exercising their free will.[64]

In challenging this portrayal of women's agency, scholars and activists alike have worked to make visible the "agentic capacities of formerly non-agentic non-subjects, and underline their ability to resist/subvert Western hegemony."[65] For example, studies of activism regarding veiled women attempt to reposition the practice of veiling as being the result of women's own decision-making, rather than as a simple matter of submission.[66] This approach has led to proposals for an expanded and more inclusive view of agency as "embedded in intersecting social forces of domination and subordination."[67]

The anti-ban feminists I interviewed for this study were conscious of the need to challenge the "Western" liberal definition of agency that their opponents advocated. Consider the following exchange between Youssra H and Anissa Fathi, two headscarf-wearing members of Mamans toutes égales (Mothers for Equality, MTE), an organization created to oppose the 2012 *Circulaire Chatel*, a set of guidelines prohibiting veiled women from accompanying their children on school outings:

> Youssra: The government claims it wants to liberate us. But I say if you want to liberate us, liberate us from your Islamophobic ideologies. This is really the main freedom we're asking for.
>
> Anissa: They often describe us as women who are subservient to men, who do not have the right to speak, who do not go out, who remain cloistered in the kitchen.
>
> Youssra: But when it comes to a field trip, they won't let us go? It is really contradictory.[68]

By differentiating the quest to "liberate" them from the value attributed to "freedom" in French legal texts, this exchange serves to show

how the pro-ban feminist position effectively denies veiled women access to "universal" spaces – including the school – in which to enact their full and equal rights.

The rights-based discourse of laïcité that members of MTE employed has also served as a catalyst for critiquing the particularistic nationalism of pro-ban feminists in France. For example, Youssra stated in our interview: "I was born [in France]. I did all of my schooling here. I am affected by everything that's happening. I vote. I live, just like everyone else. Only the difference is ... well maybe it isn't really a difference, because we have the freedom to believe what we want. We can be secular, we can be Jewish, we can be Christian. I don't know why, when it comes to Islam, we create a whole polemic."[69] Youssra's statement juxtaposes the emphasis on "the freedom to believe" in French legal texts with the priority given to social solidarity and cohesion in pro-ban feminists' framing of the face veil, in order to constitute herself as fully and equally French. A graduate of the French school system – which in contemporary culture plays the role of "socialising individuals into Republican citizens"[70] – and having participated in the national polity through voting, Youssra believes she has earned recognition as a dutiful citizen.

Anti-ban feminists – including the very small number interviewed by the Gerin commission – were thus able to draw on French law to mobilize a republican opposition to the 2010 face veil ban. However, their position was severely downplayed by the commission board. Indeed, whether or not they ultimately endorsed a ban, Gerin commission members largely embraced the pro-ban feminists' position, granting particular praise to the arguments put forward by Élisabeth Badinter and Sihem Habchi. Commenting on the various submissions put forward in support of the law, for example, Socialist MP Sandrine Mazetier described Badinter's testimony as "very impressive and convincing" in establishing the principled and philosophical bases for seeing the face veil as a rejection of republicanism.[71] Likewise, though she also opposed a legal ban, preferring to tackle the veil through a parliamentary resolution, Socialist MP Danièle Hoffman-Rispal credited Badinter's testimony with shaping her own belief that the practice of veiling should be curtailed.[72]

Gerin himself claimed to be heavily impacted by pro-ban feminists' claims. In our interview, he described Badinter's testimony as "fundamental" to the commission proceedings, as it demonstrated that "facial coverings are not clothing; they represent the erasure of one's identity."[73] Taking place the same day, the presentation delivered by Sihem Habchi also influenced Gerin, who described it as crucial in illustrating the face veil's relationship to "problems associated with ghettos, communalism, fundamentalism, and especially women's submission."[74] Habchi's comments, Gerin concluded, were "very, very important to many people, including parliamentarians. They were floored."[75]

Testimonies by Legal Experts

While they managed to advance a convincing, principled basis for condemning the face veil – as a symbolic attack on republicanism's capacity to guarantee freedom and equality through a cohesive and secular public sphere – pro-ban feminists' testimonies could not speak to the legal implications of a general ban. For this, the commissioners would have to seek the advice of prominent legal scholars and practitioners. Testimonies by these participants served to channel the concern for reciprocity and cohesion that feminists introduced into a proposal to ban the face veil based on its threat to public order. This proposal further bolstered a discourse of national belonging that prioritizes collective obligations over individual rights.

Between the months of October and December 2009, eight legal experts appeared before the Gerin commission. Their testimonies echoed the feminists' arguments in that they also considered whether republican principles could serve as bases for a ban. However, the legal experts unanimously rejected a face veil ban based on laïcité, human dignity (which feminists cited as a component of liberté and égalité), and fraternité. The alternative justification that some did accept – that the face veil should be banned on the basis of its threat to public order – was rejected by many commissioners, who believed it did not sufficiently capture the affront to republicanism that the veil allegedly posed.

The legal experts testifying before the Gerin commission argued that laïcité does not justify a legal ban for two reasons. First, drawing on a strict interpretation embodied in the 1905 law, many pointed out that laïcité is a principle governing the state, but not individuals, in France. In the words of Marie Perret, national secretary of the Observatoire international de la laïcité contre les derives communautaires (International Observatory for Secularism against Communalist Threats), "the street is not under the authority of the state." "Individuals," she argued, "must have the freedom to express their belonging somewhere: we cannot prohibit it everywhere in the name of neutrality."[76] Adding to concerns over the legitimacy of using laïcité to regulate individual behaviour in the public space was a fear that a law based on this principle would likely be struck down by the courts.[77] (In this regard, although the European Court of Human Rights subsequently upheld the 2010 ban in a decision released in July 2014, it did not do so on the basis of laïcité. Instead, the Court accepted the claim that "a veil concealing the face in public could undermine the notion of 'living together.'"[78])

The human dignity argument, which anchored many feminists' claims that the face veil threatens liberté and égalité, also failed to pass legal muster, although only after a vibrant debate erupted over ways to define the concept. Basing their arguments on an objective measure of dignity, some feminist advocates of the ban claimed that, whether or not women describe themselves as choosing to wear the veil, the practice invokes a kind of "voluntary servitude."[79] However, the legal experts maintained that this argument relies on a "paternalistic," and therefore illegitimate, understanding of choice. Insisting that "it is the will of the person that counts and … merits protection," they reached the conclusion that to ban the face veil based on its threat to human dignity would be "imprudent."[80] Some even rejected the dignity argument on the additional basis that infringement of an individual's dignity can only be deemed to occur where a third party is involved.[81]

Although it garnered ample attention during feminists' testimonies – indeed, it became a primary foundation for pro-ban groups' condemnation of the face veil – the fraternité argument also failed to persuade legal experts. The first to testify before the commission, Remy Schwartz, reminded the commissioners that fraternité is not a legal principle.[82] Subsequent testimonies by legal experts confirmed this interpretation. Commenting on the possibility of invoking fraternité as a legal principle, law professor at the University of Pau, Denys Béchillon, stated that "the philosopher Emmanuel Lévinas would likely have been more susceptible to this argument than I. It seems to me this argument applies to a philosophical, but not a legal, order. I have difficulty imagining how we might craft a legally sound device using the notion of fraternité."[83] The doubt that such statements cast upon the legal applicability of fraternité quickly put to rest any discussion of a law based on this principle, despite its ample symbolic weight in pro-ban feminist discourses.

Legal experts' near unanimous rejection of a legal ban premised on republican principles enormously upset the Gerin commission's staunchest pro-law members. UMP member Georges Mothron complained that the legal experts had not proposed any real solutions to anticipate and prevent the challenge of the face veil.[84] Taking the most vigorous stance in denouncing the legal experts, Mothron's colleague Jacques Myard charged them with interfering in what he insisted should have been a democratic political process. In our interview, he asserted "We have to listen to the jurists until 10 o'clock, and at 10 o'clock, we throw them out the window … What is a jurist? What is a philosopher? It is someone who contradicts the opinions of others."[85] This charged statement captures the disdain for legal experts' opinions that seeped into the debate, as commissioners searched for other legal arguments on which to hang their cultural and moral discomfort with the face veil.

In his appearance before the commission, Guy Carcassone, a law professor at the University of Paris, provided such a solution, outlining a proposal to ban the face veil based on its threat to the public order. Although prior participants had explored this possibility to varying degrees, Carcassone's presentation provided the most developed and pragmatic outline of the public order argument. He claimed that a ban based on public order "would have the advantage of not being discriminatory for, rather than target the face veil in particular, it would apply to all face coverings – albeit with some exceptions."[86] Such a law, Carcassone argued, "would conform perfectly to our values," being based on the "irrefutable" notion that "the presence of persons refusing all communication constitutes a menace to be dealt with seriously."[87] Carcassone's proposal thus drew on an "immaterial" conception of the public order as dependent upon a commitment to a "social code derived from implicit shared values."[88]

This argument – that facial coverings threaten the public order and should thus be prohibited in public spaces – ultimately became the central justification for the 2010 face veil ban,[89] one that the European Court of Human Rights later upheld in its 2014 judgment.[90] However, in order to be considered legitimate, the 2010 law would also require strong campaigning by politicians. As we will see, this campaign was heavily influenced by the attempts of mainstream politicians to build consensus out of conflict as a way to deflect the electoral threat of the Front National. Those attempts, I will argue, have resulted in the proliferation of a closed national script, which positions those who wear the face veil outside the boundaries of French nationhood.

BUILDING CONSENSUS OUT OF CONFLICT: PARTY POLITICAL REPRESENTATIONS OF THE GERIN COMMISSION

As I indicated in chapter 2, when it came time to endorse a ban of face veils in public, contestation arose within the Gerin commission's membership over how best to proceed. In the final vote on the commission's recommendations, six members voted for and six against, with the rest of the commission board deciding to boycott.[91] The fact of these divisions speaks to the fragility and ultimate instability of the alleged republican consensus around Islamic veiling in France. Arising out of a contest for issue ownership among parties struggling to deflect the power of a common enemy – the Front National – that alleged consensus is not only wrought with its own internal tensions; it is also very much subject to the vicissitudes inherent in the fluid and ongoing social and political environment surrounding this very contentious issue.

Right-Wing Representations: The Face Veil as Economic Threat and Evidence of a "Clash" of Civilizations

In the parliamentary vote that took place in July 2010, all but one of the voting members of the UMP – which totalled 287 – voted in favour of a law to prohibit facial coverings in French public space. Although UMP members of the Gerin commission also overwhelmingly supported this law, they disagreed somewhat over which particular frame to use in justifying it to the public. Some drew on images of a "clash" between the French Catholic and Islamic religious cultures to condemn veiling as a highly dangerous practice. Others used the face veil debate as an opportunity to dredge up concerns that immigrants – particularly North Africans – are a drain on the welfare state system. Yet, as I will show, both sets of arguments ultimately bolstered the perception that the face veil symbolizes religious Muslims' incapacity to fully belong to the French nation.

In constructing an image of the face veil as a threat to France, UMP members of the Gerin commission relied on testimony by participants known for articulating the "clash" between "radical" Islam and the secular and Christian cultural norms that define certain representations of the French nation. Invited to participate in the commission by one of its UMP members, Pascal Hilout, a Moroccan-born blogger and activist of Muslim background, explained his objection to the face veil by asserting that Islam is "the most reactionary of all religions" and thus "a danger to national and social cohesion." "Democracy," Hilout argued further, "never manages to flourish where Islam is established."[92] Generalized claims of a "clash" of civilizations were echoed in statements made by certain UMP members of the commission. For example, speaking generally of Islam's impact on French society, UMP commission member Jacques Myard said: "we have allowed into our territory people who are inassimilable, because Islam is not a religion; it is a civil code." "If you assault the public sphere with religious elements," he continued, "it will be civil war."[93]

Both Hilout and Myard's statements underscore the belief that Islam poses a double threat. First, practices like the face veil are deemed to violate the *cultural* requirements of French national belonging, by fostering communal ties that weaken national social cohesion. Second, Islam is believed to threaten the *political* parameters of belonging by reducing citizens' engagement in, and thus commitment to, a civic model of participation.

In demonstrating the alleged "clash" between Islam and French republican conceptions of national belonging, some of the Gerin commission's UMP members also drew upon a common theme in the Front National's political platform: that immigrants – particularly those of North African origin – are a drain on the economy. In our interview, for instance, UMP commission member Georges Mothron raised the issue of social assistance fraud in this community, claiming that "The fraudsters are all of Arab origin. I see it every day and I fight against it. People who are 'Gaulois' like me, that is to say people of French origin who do not live off social assistance, know that these people are getting free health care."[94] Such complaints about social assistance fraud may be seen as deliberately linked to a desire to strengthen the boundary between native French citizens and domestic "others," at least in the case of Muslim immigrants and their descendants. As in the statements by Hilout and Myard, that boundary has both a cultural and a political meaning: insofar as they transgress the cultural norms of belonging in French society, Muslims also threaten the state system of redistribution.

In asserting the "otherness" that the face veil allegedly represents with regard to republican national belonging, right-wing politicians in the Gerin commission also frequently emphasized what they believed to be a stark cultural boundary between France and other immigrant nations. Speaking to the contrast with Britain in particular, UMP commission member Georges Mothron commented with regret that "Communalism has become a significant fact of life in Great Britain over the last twenty years. Here [in France] we have the impression that they abandoned the issue, making it difficult for people to live together. There really are, I won't say ghettos, but, neighbourhoods that are entirely Pakistani or African."[95] Equally convinced of basic differences between France and Britain on this issue, UMP commission member Jacque Myard used this comparison to underscore what he regards as France's historic commitment to gender equality. Adopting much more folkloric and hyperbolic language than his colleague, Myard claimed in our interview that "in France, women have always been equal to men. They accompanied men in combat in the Gaullist era and Joan of Arc drove the barbarous English out of France."[96]

The notion that gender equality constitutes a historic feature of French national identity, one that positions France above other immigration countries, was also cited by right-wing actors as evidencing the insurmountable boundary between France and the Islamic powers of the Middle East. In the words of UMP commission member, Nicole Ameline: "We are not in Saudi Arabia. We are in France. France protects you. It liberates you. Therefore, I fully support the law ... The [burqa] has no place in France, where women are free."[97] The link that Ameline draws here between women's "protection" and their "liberation" resonates with a common claim in the pro-ban feminist discourse on veiling: that women's capacity for freedom rests on the state's ability to protect them from the sexist cultural practices of foreign "others." Ameline's statement also strategically links the particularity of French culture to the protection of universal rights such as gender equality. By particularizing the universal in this way, she maintains an emphasis on France's cultural uniqueness while appealing to the human rights discourse of the international women's rights movement.[98]

Thus, although they overwhelmingly supported a legal ban of face veils, right-wing politicians in the Gerin commission diverged somewhat in the frames they adopted to justify this measure. A first approach was to suggest that the face veil symbolizes the broader "threat" of foreign elements to the French way of life, one that operates from within and from outside France's borders. Comments in this vein often underscored a need to protect France's unique cultural and religious heritage from the potential – and potentially violent – threat of "radical" Islam. A second justification advanced by UMP supporters of the face veil ban, and the one that most clearly suggests a co-optation of themes introduced by the Front National, was that laws such as this one contribute in a broad sense to discouraging North African immigrants from abusing the welfare state system. A third set of arguments treaded more closely on the territory of the left by highlighting France's commitment to protecting universal values, like gender equality. By emphasizing the particularity of the French perspective on this issue, however, even this line of argumentation served to draw a stark ethno-cultural boundary between native French citizens and foreign "others." Ultimately, all three sets of arguments bolstered a perception that Islamic practices like the face veil undermine the unique values that anchor the cultural and political terms of belonging to the French nation.

Left-Wing Representations: Deciding between "Rejection," "Rescue," and "Reclaiming"

With the UMP having claimed ownership of the face veil ban, Socialist representatives struggled to gain resonance in the debate. Deep schisms emerged as some members questioned the law's compatibility with the party's historic legacy of trying to foster immigrant inclusion. As they struggled to gain ownership of the face veil issue, Socialists and other left-wing actors deployed three main discursive strategies. I identify these below as: first, "rejecting" right-wing frames by condemning the law; second, seeking to "rescue" laïcité from its right-wing kidnappers; and, third, "reclaiming" the law prohibiting facial coverings by reframing its meaning in ways consistent with themes the left in France already "owns." The Socialist leadership ultimately chose the second and third strategies: asserting the party's ownership of the face veil issue without fundamentally disrupting the alleged consensus across parties, or rendering the boundaries of French nationhood more inclusive to Muslim minorities.

Rejection

A number of left-wing politicians – including some influential Socialist members of the Gerin commission – opposed the 2010 ban, claiming that it was rooted in racist colonial discourse. Building on a critique of similar restrictive laws by postcolonial academics and feminists, this approach targeted the cultural narrowness of the boundaries assigned to national belonging in both left- and right-wing articulations of the face veil issue. For example, according to Socialist member of the Gerin commission Sandrine Mazetier, "the motivations of those in favour of legislating seemed instrumental"; the law merely provided them "with an alibi for their racism and islamo-paranoia."[99] Others backed this interpretation, including the commission's sole Green Party member, François de Rugy, who considered boycotting the commission altogether because he knew "very well that, from the outset, Gerin and Raoult [the commission's rapporteur] were pushing a hostile, restrictive agenda."[100]

Similarly persuaded by critics' claims that laïcité is a guise for racism in French political discourse, other left-wing actors turned their gaze on the past, criticizing prior Socialist administrations for their complicity in allowing an anti-immigrant script to eclipse core progressive social values. Such was the view of Danièle Hoffman-Rispal, Gerin commission member and Socialist MP in the largely immigrant Parisian neighbourhood of Belleville. Although she supported a parliamentary resolution to condemn the face veil, Hoffman-Rispal expressed deep concern over her colleagues' neglect of this practice's relationship to underlying social inequalities. In her words, "I understand where [this reactive identity in the Muslim community] comes from. It comes from the Republic's failure to integrate and from the fact that politics no longer inspires people. In 1968, 1969, 1970, when I was 16–17 years old, we thought the world would be better. Today, this fundamental belief is rare. During the last electoral campaign, I spoke with young people in my neighbourhood. They told me: 'we're on welfare. We no longer know where we're from. We're not considered French. Even with degrees, we can't find work.'"[101] By capitulating to the right's obsession with religious signs, Hoffman-Rispal argued, the French left has lost its capacity to generate public concern around themes it previously "owned," like material suffering and inequality. A ban of facial coverings, she claimed, only exacerbates the marginalizing effects of prior governments' failure to meaningfully engage immigrants in the republican project. Others in the Socialist camp agree. According to Sandrine Mazetier: "The [face veil ban] does not in any way resolve the problem of affirming the republican pact and values of the republic … We could have legislated to outlaw actions that force particular garments on members of one sex but not the other. But this is not the choice that was made. Instead, the adopted approach merely causes tensions."[102] The statements by Hoffman-Rispal and Mazetier thus illustrate a deep concern among some Socialists that an anti-immigrant framing of secularism has displaced the values that once anchored the party's political brand and position within the French electoral system's axis of competition.

Given their strong opposition to the 2010 law, one might have expected Hoffman-Rispal and Mazetier to vote against the bill in parliament. However, the competition for issue ownership made this position untenable. Instead, hoping to maintain the appearance of party unity, the Socialist leadership called on its representatives to abstain from the parliamentary vote. This directive did not, however, prevent members of this or other left-wing parties from being compelled by the competition for issue ownership to attach their own meanings to the law and thus to participate in the production of French national belonging. Responding to what they claimed to be a "kidnapping" of laïcité by right-wing actors, leftists in France – many of them Socialists – have attempted to "rescue" laïcité and "reclaim" the left's ownership of the face veil issue in France. Yet, as we will see, these attempts largely perpetuate the status quo; they have little impact on whether and how laïcité is used to justify restrictions on religious dress. Nor have they fostered the creation of a significant alternative to the narrowness of right-wing articulations of belonging to the French nation.

Rescue

Ideological attempts to "rescue" laïcité and assert the left's ownership of the face veil issue involve an explicit denunciation, even ridicule, of right-wing conceptions of secularism in France. In particular, they seek to demonstrate that, in utilizing laïcité for political gain, the UMP and Front National have grossly misrepresented its meaning. Author and Gerin commission participant Patrick Kessel takes up this theme in his book *Ils ont volé la laïcité* (They stole secularism). Like others,[103]

Kessel maintains that right-wing articulations of laïcité contain remnants of a "counter-revolutionary" and "counter-republican" ideology.[104] This version of secularism – which some call *catho-laïcité* – ultimately undermines the secularity of public space by glorifying France's Catholic history and symbols.[105]

Left politicians' efforts to expose the fundamentally anti-republican character of right-wing laïcité similarly targeted the Front National. In this regard, the critique turned more explicitly on the racist undertones of this discourse. Commenting on Marine Le Pen's secularism, for example, the Socialist MP Christian Bataille described it as "a guise for anti-Islamism" and "a battle against Muslims." The arguments that she uses and the forces that she marshals, he further argued, demonstrate that Le Pen "is still mired in the spirit of the crusades."[106]

Thus, there was some attempt to assert a distinctly left-wing secular discourse that aligns more closely with the progressive goals of the Revolution. But these ideological attempts to "rescue" laïcité were largely overshadowed by a more strategic and procedural discourse, in which party political battles for ownership appear front and centre. "Rescuers" of this kind often target the left itself for abandoning, and thus ceding ownership of, laïcité. According to Alain Seksig, inspector general of national education and former member of the Haut Conseil à l'intégration (High Council of Integration, HCI),[107] had it not been for the left's own inability to take a clear stance on religious signs, including during the 1989 "headscarf affair," the right would not have managed to brand itself the defender of secular values and to pervert the definition of secularism in the process. In his words: "The left did not need the Front National to demonstrate its confusion around the issue of secularism. It did that all by itself, like a grown-up. Except that, by demonstrating that confusion over the years, it made a gift of secularism to the extreme right."[108] Seksig's remark demonstrates the frustration that pro-secular leftists feel toward prior Socialist administrations for allegedly failing to properly assert laïcité as a left-wing ideal.

For Gerin – a prominent Communist MP at the time of the face veil debate – the repercussions of the left's "abandonment" of laïcité, albeit quite different, are equally dire. In critiquing those Socialists who abstained from approving the face veil ban in the National Assembly, he pointed to the problem of *angélisme* ("otherworldliness"), a term he used to condemn those who lack the "courage" to take a clear stance on the face veil. Believing himself among the rare politicians to serve the real interests of voters, Gerin has bandied this term about to portray other leftists as elitists insufficiently committed to tackling issues of crime and delinquency that he perceives as aligned with "radical" religious behaviour. Without specifying exactly who falls into this category, Gerin commented in our interview "They beat around the bush. They don't have the courage to call a spade a spade. That is what I call *angélisme*. They don't have the courage to tackle the problems that are causing certain territories in our society to rot away, or to face the fact that religion is used for political means."[109] By referencing the "rotting" away of certain forgotten "territories" in this quote, Gerin is also embracing aspects of the Front National's script, particularly its attack on political elitism, to portray the Socialists as "lax" when it comes to defending laïcité. By asserting laïcité more firmly, he suggests, left-wing parties can begin to take back some of the electoral territory lost to the right.

Strategic and procedural attempts at "rescue" also laid blame directly on right-wing parties, claiming that politicians on that side of the fence have deliberately sought to shame the left by questioning its commitment to secularism. During the Gerin commission, these shaming attempts were mainly made by Jean-François Copé, then a prominent member of the UMP, who announced his party's intention to legally ban the face veil before the commission had finished deliberating.[110] Staunch proponents of the ban within the Socialist Party perceived Copé's announcement as disrespecting the process and as an attack on their own secular convictions. MP Jean Glavany reacted the most strongly, claiming in our interview that Copé's actions signalled "contempt for the commission." "It was shocking," he said, "so we refused to take part in the vote. We said: 'you take us for imbeciles. From the beginning, you have taken us for imbeciles.'"[111] Rather than take issue with the content of the right's pro-secular discourse, Glavany thus mainly disputed the perceived infringement on the left's territory that this discourse entailed.

Strategic and procedural attempts at "rescuing" laïcité resulted in overt efforts to redraw the partisan boundaries that have been obscured by the discourse of consensus around the face veil in France. In some cases, those boundaries demarcate competing parties on the left. In our interview, for instance, Socialist Jean Glavany complained that "[Gerin] is not a leftist when it comes to the emphasis on freedom that we generally find on the left." "From the minute he was appointed to chair the commission," Glavany asserted, "the French right manipulated and used him, turning him into an ally by granting him this position."[112] Here, Glavany is aiming to strengthen the boundaries around what can legitimately be considered "left-wing" in French politics. Although a major advocate of the strict regulation of religious signs in the public sphere, he opposes achieving that objective through total erasure of the ideological distinctions between Socialists and Communists.

In most cases, however, attempts to redraw partisan boundaries focused on disentangling the secular discourses of the Socialists from those of their main right-wing rival, the UMP. For example, although he referred to the consensus among members of the Gerin commission in other statements, Socialist member Christian Bataille also suggested in our interview that, in embracing laïcité, the UMP was effectively "rallying" around a principle that belongs to the progressive left.[113]

Left-wing attempts at "rescuing" laïcité during the Gerin commission ultimately served to reconstitute the partisan boundaries that have been obscured by parties' strategic claims to consensus over the face veil issue. By maintaining that ownership of particular issues belongs to certain political parties and not others, this defence of partisan boundaries can shape political manoeuvring in significant ways, as it did in July 2010 when the Socialists abstained from the National Assembly vote on the ban. Even Jean Glavany, an ardent advocate of a ban, declined to vote in favour of the law out of a refusal to be seen as supporting an initiative proposed by the rival UMP. Other Socialist members generally inclined toward a ban also abstained out of a concern for maintaining the appearance of party unity on the issue.

Socialists who opposed the law were similarly reluctant to take part in the vote, for fear of exposing fractures within their party. When I asked Socialist Danièle Hoffman-Rispal why she did not vote against the law, even though she preferred a parliamentary resolution, she replied: "I did not want to draw attention to myself, so I abstained. I told [the Socialist, Radical, Citizen, and Diverse Left] group I intended to vote against but they convinced me not to. It was really the only position we could all agree on."[114]

Driven by frustration and anger over the right's manipulation of laïcité for political gain, left-wing attempts at "rescuing" the term thus mainly turn on the question of who "owns" the religious signs issue in France. Although these attempts take an ideological form when targeting the so-called "counter-revolutionary" motivations behind right-wing secular claims, the need to "rescue" laïcité is articulated in largely strategic and procedural terms. What matters here is not so much *how* parties differ in their responses to the face veil question, but simply *whether* their positions can be clearly distinguished and which party best occupies the field. In this way, the discourse of "rescue" gives precedence to political boundaries rather than ones related to the building of nationhood. Its users are driven more by electoral objectives than discursive ones. As such, they do not directly engage with the question of where to situate the boundaries of belonging to the French nation.

Reclaiming

Since claims to a consensus that the face veil should be prohibited were so widespread during and around the Gerin commission, the margin in which left-wing politicians supportive of a legal ban could distinguish themselves was narrow. One of the strategies that pro-ban leftists deployed was to "reclaim" laïcité by tying it to issues that the left theoretically "owns." Unlike the discourse of "rescue," this approach went some distance toward identifying a distinctly left-wing approach to defining the political terms of belonging to the French nation.

Left-wing actors concerned with "reclaiming" laïcité as a legacy of the left used various methods to convey the intrinsic bond between left-wing ideology and the French project to preserve and promote the secularity of public space. Contrasting the face veil with the progressive goal of engaging citizens in public manifestations of their political belonging, Gerin himself bemoaned the fact that there are "some territories [in France] in which there is sharia in the public space." "For us," he went on, "the public space is the Republic."[115] By treating "the Republic" as synonymous with the "public space," Gerin made clear his belief that republican citizenship involves a particular kind of political engagement. To use Alba's terminology,[116] a "bright" political boundary is needed to exclude ways of organizing citizens' relationship to the state – such as "sharia" law – that contradict the republican political ethos.

Like his right-wing counterparts, Gerin thus regards the face veil as unsuited to French republican political culture. Unlike them, however, he attributes this unsuitability to the practice's alleged threat to the role of the state. Perpetuating the symbolic value attributed to the school in the debates preceding the 2004 law on religious signs in public education, Gerin cited in our interview "the fact that [Muslim] girls in some areas cannot go to Planned Parenthood because it is forbidden, cannot have relationships outside the Muslim community because it is forbidden, or young teenage girls in some high schools who have medical certificates to exempt them from participating in sports or going to the swimming pool. What does that have to do with the republic and secularism?"[117]

Socialist members of the commission have echoed Gerin's concern that Islamic religious practices impede participation in a progressive welfare state. Describing laïcité as "indistinguishable from the social struggle,"[118] for example, Socialist Jean Glavany imagines it as integral to the way France delivers services to its citizenry. Rather than simply defend laïcité when it is attacked, he further suggested in our interview that "we must promote it through training programs for teachers and in schools. It must be respected in hospitals."[119] Thus, for both Gerin and Glavany, "reclaiming" laïcité means re-establishing the state as the deliverer of services that enable citizens' full and active participation in the republican public sphere. This approach starkly contrasts with that of the UMP's Georges Mothron who, as I showed above, wishes to diminish North African immigrants' use of public services.

Efforts to "reclaim" laïcité as a discourse of the left also engendered symbolic images of statehood when they justified restricting the face veil on the basis of its alleged threat to republican universalism. Rather than imposing a particular way of life, left-wing defenders of laïcité claimed that, to the contrary, this concept promotes a respect for cultural and religious differences. By calling for citizens' emancipation from all doctrines of belief, they suggest, laïcité fosters a sense of the "common good" that transcends particularism. For this reason, left-wing secularists have tended to condemn right-wing discourses that have the effect of excluding newcomers by framing laïcité as part of the French cultural heritage.[120] In his testimony before the Gerin commission, for example, philosopher Henri Pena-Ruiz proclaimed that French national identity need not "mark itself through the valorisation of its particularities."[121] Rather, he argued, the Republic distinguishes itself by a commitment to universal rights and freedoms.

Yet, this emphasis on universalism has proven difficult to reconcile with efforts to compete with the right's defence of the particularity of republicanism in the face veil debate. Seeking to meld the universal and the particular, some left discourses of "reclaiming" echo UMP members' claims that protection of universal rights is precisely that which renders French republicanism unique. In her testimony before the Gerin commission, Sihem Habchi, former president of the feminist group Ni putes, ni soumises and former Socialist spokesperson, played on this notion of particular universalism. She claimed that if there is any country in which "it is possible to debate without killing each other, to manage conflicts in a secular and interactive social space, without tearing off veils or burning mosques, such as in the Netherlands, and to reach a solution that will advance the values of progress to which we are so attached, it is France."[122] This statement portrays progressive universal values, mainly secularism, as the route to unhindered engagement in a shared public sphere, the central criterion for political belonging to the French nation.

Statements intended to reinforce the particularity of republican universalism also drew on hyperbolic recollections of the French Revolution, an event that many leftists frame as anchoring modern notions of gender equality. In our interview, for instance, Danièle Hoffman-Rispal explained that all representations of Marianne – the iconic female figure symbolizing reason and liberty – feature her in a "low neckline," and with "practically no jewellery." Thus, Hoffman-Rispal went on, "the symbol of the Republic is a woman whose face we can see ... That is why we use this symbol to explain that [the face veil] is inconceivable."[123] Besides obscuring the many manifestations of gender inequality in France, statements like this one reinforce the image of an intrinsic bond between French political culture and universal values like gender equality.

Unlike the discourse of "rescue," which focuses on redressing the right's "kidnapping" of laïcité through a reassertion of partisan boundaries, efforts to "reclaim" laïcité as a legacy of the left thus reinforce the importance of universal republican themes as bases for articulating the political limits of inclusion in the French nation. These efforts underscore the need to re-establish the state as the key player in maintaining the secularity of public space and in reaffirming the importance of citizen engagement in the public sphere. When they bring about the search for ways to reconcile the particular and universal aspects of French political culture, attempts to "reclaim" laïcité fall short in providing a clear alternative to the right's restrictive response to veiling. This is because, ultimately, they justify narrowing the requirements for belonging in the French public sphere in ways that exclude religious Muslims.

CONCLUSION

In this chapter, I examined the debates that arose among civil society actors and politicians participating in the 2009 Gerin commission over ways to define secularism and national belonging in France. I showed that commissioners tasked with assessing the advisability of banning the face veil took a remarkably top-down approach, both in terms of selecting participants and in assessing and framing their testimonies. Nearly half of the seventy-eight invited speakers opposed a ban. Nevertheless, the authors of the Gerin commission report managed to frame the process as indicating a widespread consensus around the need to legally restrict the niqab and burqa in French public space.

This appeal to consensus, I argued, reflects mainstream French politicians' desire to "own" the religious signs issue in the context of a political system that, for decades, adhered to a class-based axis of competition. As I showed in chapter 2, the Front National has increasingly challenged that system by mobilizing popular concerns around issues of identity, particularly immigration. Although it was not itself invited to participate in the Gerin commission, the ultra-right party manifested its presence in that debate through the discursive and strategic dilemmas it created for the other parties.

However, the ostensible accord that emerged during the Gerin commission concealed underlying tensions within the major parties over how to reconcile opposition to veiling with both their individual historical legacies *and* extant republican ideas and institutions. The nature of those tensions differed significantly on the right and the left.

Within the right-wing UMP, there was vast support for a face veil ban. Whatever disagreement that did exist had to do with the frames individual politicians used to articulate their endorsement of this measure. Borrowing a theme popularized by the Front National, some emphasized the cultural "clash" embodied by veiling practices. Others called forth more universalistic themes, like gender equality, to propose that the face veil violates key republican ideals. However, even this approach remained heavily couched in a particularistic – and often exclusionary – image of French nationhood.

The conflicts that arose as a result of the struggle for issue ownership were much deeper on the left, where they spawned a real identity crisis. During and after the Gerin commission, members of the Socialist Party in particular struggled over how to reconcile a restrictive approach to religious signs with the party's legacy of trying to foster the integration of immigrant communities. This reconciliation proved impossible for some Socialists, who felt that denying individuals the right to religious expression contradicted historic left-wing values in France.

In resolving this dilemma, the left-wing participants in the Gerin commission offered three competing discourses. Those committed to "rejecting" the 2010 ban questioned the narrowness of the cultural boundaries that right- and left-wing politicians' articulations of laïcité draw around French nationhood. Motivated by a desire to reaffirm partisan boundaries, the second discourse – that of "rescue" – addressed the themes of nationhood and belonging only tangentially. Its users were far more concerned with whether the Socialist Party would be recognized as a dominant player in the face veil debate than with deciding how its positions on the issue should differ from those of the other parties. Finally, those concerned with "reclaiming" laïcité as a legacy of the left sought to strengthen the political dimensions of Muslims' national belonging by calling for greater state involvement in preserving the secularity of public space.

Ultimately, the Socialists chose a combination of "rescue" and "reclaiming," positioning the face veil as a threat to the Republic, but one that should be combatted through appeals to a left-wing, state-centred approach to laïcité. In so doing, the party as a whole failed to offer a clear and decisive alternative to the closed national scripts presented by the mainstream right in the face veil debate.

Focusing on republican ideas and institutions – and treating them as the driving forces behind restrictive laws like the face veil ban – misses crucial differences in the way politicians articulate the meanings of republicanism when addressing religious diversity. As we saw, staunch supporters of the 2010 law easily dismissed legal experts' objections to the 2010 ban on the grounds that these diverged from the interests of voters. Politicians advocating the ban were also remarkably creative in framing their positions as corresponding with the ideals and legal principles that constitute French republicanism. The resulting articulations of secularism bore the marks of inter- and intra-party conflict over the boundaries of political space.

5

"They Are Genetically Incapable" of Defending Québécois Values

Unresolved Struggles to "Own" the Nation in Quebec's Charter of Values Debate

From the time the press leaked its major orientations in August 2013 until the Parti Québécois' (PQ) electoral defeat in April 2014, the Charter of Values monopolized Quebec's airwaves, becoming the central focus of democratic debate, at the levels of both party politics and in much of civil society. Even before the government presented its bill to parliament, Quebec's newer, non-traditional opposition parties – the Coalition avenir Québec (CAQ) and Québec solidaire (QS) – issued alternative legislative proposals. Dated 9 October 2013, Québec Solidaire's Bill 398 proposed to adopt the Bouchard-Taylor report's recommended restriction of religious signs among public employees whose work embodies the authority and coercive powers of the state (namely the president and vice-president of the National Assembly, judges, Crown prosecutors, police officers, and prison guards). The Coalition avenir Québec quickly followed suit with Bill 492, in which it outlined a similarly narrowed restriction, although one that would also apply to schoolteachers and principals.[1] Only the Parti libéral du Québec – the main opposition to the Parti Québécois government – refrained from drafting its own bill, a move that exposed the party to damaging critiques.[2]

Unable – perhaps even unwilling – to forge a consensus based on its opponents' own proposals, the Parti Québécois forged ahead with its original project, presenting Bill 60 to Quebec's National Assembly on 7 November 2013. As anticipated, article 5 of the document outlined a proposal to restrict "ostentatious" religious signs in all public service employment.[3] When the opposition parties persevered in their objections to this measure, the government launched a series of public hearings to gauge the opinions of civil society actors and ordinary citizens on the Charter of Values. Taking place between January and March 2014, these hearings featured presentations by various groups, including feminists, legal experts, pro-sovereignty activists, unions, and social service providers.

This chapter unfolds in two parts. In the first part, I analyze the positions taken by concerned citizens and civil society actors in the public hearings on the Charter of Values. Drawing on a combination of textual and interview data, I show that, as in France's Gerin commission, there was significant disagreement among participants over the place of religion in the public sphere, the best ways to define gender (in)equality in the context of religious diversity, and the legal viability of outlawing religious signs in public sector employment. In debating all three issues, civil society actors mobilized highly disparate understandings of Quebec's national past, present, and future. Whereas proponents of the Charter believed the latter to be consistent with the development of a modern and secular national identity, in which women's equality is paramount, its opponents warned that Bill 60 would undermine secularism and gender equality, by obstructing women's participation in the workforce. Much more than a disagreement over policy, I argue, these divergent interpretations of the Charter amounted to conflicting ways of envisioning the meanings and boundaries of nationhood in Quebec.

The second part of this chapter turns from civil society debates to the contestations that took place among Quebec's main political parties over the Charter of Values. Drawing on parliamentary debates, party press releases and documents, and interviews with politicians, I show that, unlike in the French case, competition to "own" the religious signs issue by Quebec's political class did not involve a discourse of consensus. Rather, the major parties reaffirmed nationhood as the defining axis of electoral competition in Quebec by advancing conflicting understandings of what it means to be "Québécois." Those understandings formed the basis of three dominant discourses. Utilized by the Parti Québécois leadership, the discourse of "courage" portrayed the Charter of Values as a brave and audacious step in disentangling Quebec from the legal and political limitations imposed by Canadian federalism. A second discourse – that of "responsibility" – was used by the Parti libéral du Québec to emphasize discontinuities between the Charter and the universal rights and freedoms that designate belonging in a "modern" society. A third discourse, which I call nationalism's "third way," captures the dilemmas that the Charter posed for factions within the sovereignty movement that see immigrant inclusion as crucial to an independent Quebec.

PUBLIC HEARINGS ON THE CHARTER OF VALUES (JANUARY TO MARCH 2014): MANDATE, COMPOSITION, AND CANCELLATION

In January 2014, Quebec's governing Parti Québécois launched a series of public hearings aimed at assessing public and expert opinion on its proposed Charter of Values, or Bill 60. From the time they were announced in late fall 2013, the hearings themselves were widely scrutinized, with pundits claiming they were an empty gesture by a governing party that was intent on passing its proposed bill regardless of opposition. Comments by the minister in charge of the Charter, Bernard Drainville, were read as confirming these suspicions. During a televised interview that aired on *Radio-Canada* on 13 January 2014 – the eve of the start of the hearings – Drainville announced: "If there is a way to improve the bill, we will do that. However, we will certainly not empty the Charter of its contents. We will not dilute it. This is the Charter we will vote on."[4] Françoise David, who was then co-spokesperson of Québec solidaire, was quick to question the government's sincerity in seeking the public's opinion on the Charter of Values. In a statement published by *Radio-Canada on* 15 January 2014, she said: "The prohibiting of religious signs is the only proposal that profoundly divides the population, and yet, it is precisely this proposal on which Drainville refuses to negotiate. How can he claim to seek consensus?"[5] Thus, there was clear concern that the PQ government was unwilling to negotiate on the Charter's key proposals. Yet, unlike the highly selective and closely curated Gerin commission in France, the hearings held between early January and March 2014 were an open and public affair. In a statement printed by *Le Devoir*, Mathew Lagacé, deputy secretary of the Committee of Institutions – the provincial body tasked with organizing the hearings – told the press: "All those who wish to be heard will be heard. This is a general consultation that is truly open to all. Each and every brief submitted will be presented in public, one at a time, even if there is overlap."[6] Members of the public wishing to participate in the hearings on the Charter of Values were given until 20 December

2013 to submit a brief to the province's Committee of Institutions, with presentations scheduled to begin on 14 January 2014. On 28 December, *Le Devoir* reported that upwards of 200 briefs – with some estimates placing the actual number at 206 – had been received by the deadline.[7]

Recognizing that its Charter was popular among francophone voters – who make up the bulk of the electorate in Quebec – the PQ sought to strengthen its mandate by scheduling an election on 7 April 2014, thus prematurely concluding the public hearings. In the month-long campaign that ensued, the party called on the Québécois to get behind the Charter of Values, which it couched in a broader appeal to nationalist sentiment.[8] As the official opposition, the PLQ responded by promising to tackle "real issues," such as the economy, employment, health, and education.[9] It thus contrasted the PQ's nation-focused agenda by infusing economic questions into the election campaign.

Had the 2014 election occurred in late February, rather than early April, pollsters believe the PQ would have succeeded in obtaining a majority government, with approximately 40 per cent of the vote, compared to a projected 34 per cent for the PLQ.[10] Instead, on 7 April, by which time skirmishes over the sovereignty question unexpectedly took centre stage, the PQ obtained only 25 per cent of the vote, compared to 42 per cent for the PLQ. In the government that was subsequently formed, the PLQ held seventy of the 125 available seats, while only thirty seats were occupied by the PQ, and twenty-one and three seats for the CAQ and QS, respectively.

The 7 April election result laid the Charter of Values to rest, if only temporarily. In his speech, the incoming Liberal premier Philippe Couillard announced that, with his victory, "division is over" and "reconciliation has arrived."[11] However, it would not be long before the question of secularism in general, and of the public display of religious signs and practices in particular, resurfaced as a focus of party political contention in Quebec. In fact, the day following his election as premier, Couillard told the press he planned to move forward with legislation to counter religious fundamentalism, and promised to seek consensus on the question of religious accommodations and the secularity of the state.[12] "It is important for me," he said, "to address this issue early on in our administration."[13] As we will see in the epilogue, that consensus has, thus far, failed to materialize.

CONFLICTS IN CIVIL SOCIETY: BRIEFS SUBMITTED TO THE PUBLIC HEARINGS ON THE CHARTER OF VALUES

Between early January and March 2014, Quebec's parliament heard the testimonies of sixty-nine individuals and organizations on the subject of the proposed Charter of Values, or Bill 60. Ten additional presentations scheduled for March 2014 were cancelled when the PQ government called a provincial election on 5 March. The remainder of the briefs submitted – approximately 125 – were not made public. However, in order to capture the positions of civil society actors known to play a key role in the Charter debate, but whose briefs did not make it into the public record, I analyzed the briefs of an additional six organizations: the Quebec Bar Association; Indépendantistes pour une laïcité inclusive (Separatists for an Inclusive Secularism); the Commission des droits de la personne et des droits de la jeunesse (Human Rights and Youth Rights Commission, CDPDJ); the Association des juristes progressistes (Association of Progressive Jurists); the Fédération des femmes du Québec (Quebec Women's Federation, FFQ); and the Conseil du statut de la femme (Council for the Status of Women, CSF).

Individuals and organizations appearing before the public hearings on the Charter of Values can broadly be sorted into nine categories: "concerned citizens" (many of them former or current academics and retirees), representatives of "religious organizations," "pro-secular organizations," "feminist organizations," "atheist or humanist organizations," "university/school board or teachers' organizations," "organizations representing service providers," "labour market organizations," and "other interest group organizations."

Of the eighty-five briefs analyzed, most supported the PQ government's broad effort to give concrete meaning and recognition to secularism in Quebec law and to assert the importance of both the French language and gender equality (table 5.1). However, opinions differed widely with regard to article 5, the proposed ban of religious signs in public sector employment. Slightly less than half (45 per cent) of the briefs approved this ban, whereas 49 per cent opposed it and nearly 6 per cent did not state any clear opinion on the matter. Support for the ban was most prominent among concerned citizens, along with representatives of pro-secularism, feminist, and atheist/

Table 5.1
Position on prohibition of religious signs by type of participant, public hearings on the Charter of Values (January to March 2014)

	Prohibition of religious signs			
	Total	*For*	*Against*	*N/A*
Individuals	32	21	8	3
Organizations	53	17	34	2
Religious organization	2	0	2	0
Pro-secularism organization	5	5	0	0
Feminist organization	6	3	3	0
Atheist/humanist organization	2	2	0	0
University/school board/teachers' organization	9	0	9	0
Organization representing service providers	6	0	6	0
Labour market organization	4	1	3	0
Nationalist organization	4	2	1	1
Legal organization	4	1	3	0
Other interest group organization	11	3	7	1
N	85	38	42	5
Per cent	100	45	49	6

humanist organizations, whereas the lowest support rates were among representatives of religious groups, university/school board, teachers, and labour market organizations, as well as organizations representing service providers.

Three main themes were discussed in the briefs submitted to the public hearings: the role of religion and secularism in Quebec public life, the relationship between religious signs and gender (in)equality, and the legal viability of the Charter's main proposals (especially article 5). As in the Gerin commission, participants in the public hearings took a variety of positions on these themes. However, compared to their counterparts in France, civil society actors in Quebec tied those positions more explicitly to disparate understandings of what constitutes national membership and belonging in Quebec.

Briefs concerning the Role of Religion and Secularism

In debating the role of religion and secularism in Quebec public life, pro- and anti-Charter individuals and organizations took starkly different positions. Those in favour of the proposal to prohibit religious signs in public sector employment saw it as the next logical step in the historical process of forging a "modern" and secular national identity in Quebec, one that is dissociated from religious institutions. Those against the Charter of Values responded by characterizing its proposals as symbolizing a dangerous and "backward" reversal of Quebec's secularization project, which seeks a balance between the principles of state religious neutrality and individual religious freedom.

Pro-Charter participants in the public hearings were intent on framing article 5 of Bill 60 as consistent with Quebec's "modern" secular achievements. In constructing this narrative, they mobilized highly symbolic images of the Quiet Revolution – the period from the 1960s onward that many view as the birth of the "modern" Québécois nation. During this period, according to Yves Gauthier, the author of a brief, "The dictates of doctrinal thinking were booted out of our borders. A wave of freedom had swept through Québec … Today's Québec belongs to the modern world. Our fathers did not boot priests out of our civic space so that we could allow that space to be invaded once again by a new horde of 'religionists' and their symbols. It took nearly 400 years for us to get to where we are. Let's not go backwards."[14] In this statement, Gauthier draws a boundary between the "backwardness" of Québécois nationhood *prior* to the Quiet Revolution and the "modern" image of belonging that has prevailed *since* that defining period. That boundary, he argues, owes its existence to dedicated attempts to emancipate the Québécois from religious controls and to inscribe a sense of identity that is "free" from "doctrinal thinking." Thus, Gauthier concludes, maintaining a "modern" nationalist project requires ensuring that religion is never again allowed to penetrate into Quebec's public sphere.

Use of the Quiet Revolution to draw a discursive line in the sand between "backwardness" and "modernity" featured in numerous pro-Charter briefs. Indeed, according to members of the Société nationale des Québécoises et des Québécois de Chaudière-Appalaches (National Society of Quebeckers of Chaudière-Appalaches), the advances of the Quiet Revolution "are inscribed in a manifest desire for modernity as well as a constant concern for equality, equity and freedom."[15] Bill 60 "consolidates" these advances by allowing "us to construct a modern, inclusive Quebec that leaves no room for archaic retrograde values that penetrate our society and threaten to reverse the gains of the Quiet Revolution, which laid the groundwork for a modern state."[16] Like Gauthier's statement, this excerpt offers an image of religion as an "archaic" threat to the "values" that underpin the construction of a "modern state" in Quebec.

In the discourse constructed by advocates of the Charter, immigrant religious signs were even portrayed as intentional efforts to betray the historical legacy that underpins "modernity" in Quebec society. According to the brief submitted by the Mouvement des Janette (The Janette Movement), a pro-Charter feminist group named after the actress Janette Bertrand, "certain other religious groups have sought to make us revert to the past and once again make women subservient to men by veiling their bodies, which they treat as objects of concupiscence. We are back to a discourse in which Eve causes Adam's fall … For the sake of our daughters and granddaughters, we must not allow such a retreat."[17] This statement positions "other religious" groups as threatening to dissolve the boundary between "backwardness" and "modernity" that the Quiet Revolution instilled. The authors of this particular brief emphasized the importance of that boundary for ensuring that women's rights are never again allowed to be governed by religious doctrine and authorities.

The notion of a linear historical trajectory – from "backward" to "modern" – was thus essential to claims that there is a contradiction between the religious practices of "other" groups and contemporary social life in Quebec. Citing that trajectory, Mathieu Gauthier encouraged the government to "take this courageous and necessary step of adopting a Charter that preserves a strict separation of religions and the state," adding that "respect for our history commands it!"[18] Similarly, the authors of the brief submitted by the Rassemblement pour la laïcité (Rally for Secularism) described the Charter as "the last phase in [Quebec's] democratic evolution." Criticisms of the Charter were framed by this discourse as anathema to this "evolution." Phrases such as "let us not take a step backward"[19] and "we do not want regression but evolution"[20] served to denigrate both the challenged religious practices themselves and the view that such practices should be tolerated in public sector employment. Not surprisingly, given the politicized responses it generated, the Bouchard-Taylor report became the ultimate lightning rod for those seeking to present the Charter as the culmination of a historic modernizing project. According to the Rassemblement pour la laïcité, that commission's report constituted "a rupture in modern Québec's path to secularization."[21]

When addressing the themes of religion and secularism in public life, opponents of the Charter of Values appealed to a very different understanding of what defines "modernity" in the context of Quebec's religious signs debate, which they then couched in an alternative recollection of the legacies of the Quiet Revolution. For these actors, being "modern" presupposes an ability to incorporate all religious creeds into a conception of the nation that values state religious neutrality, but without denying individuals their right to religious expression. To forbid religious signs in various public spaces and institutions, anti-Charter participants argued, is to reproduce the historically repressive actions of the Catholic Church in Quebec.

In conveying this competing understanding of "modernity," anti-Charter actors also condemned what they saw as politicians' instrumentalization of Quebec's Catholic past to vilify (mainly Muslim) religious symbols. Such was the position of Jean Dorion, a long-time nationalist and supporter of the Parti Québécois. In our interview, Dorion suggested that feminist members of the pro-Charter camp in particular have projected their anger with the Catholic Church onto Muslim women. In his words: "the hunt for nuns is active but there aren't any more nuns. So [pro-Charter feminists] are looking for game that resembles their actual target and firing at it. These women have accounts to settle with the Church, but they have decided to settle them with Muslim women instead."[22] According to Dorion, attempts to anchor the Charter of Values in a "modern" understanding of Québécois nationhood obscure a strongly resonant discomfort with religion tied to recent memories of Catholic Church dominance. Thus, far from embodying a "modern" vision of Quebec's future, this argument suggests that the Charter's proposals derive their salience from a past that continues to generate anti-religious sentiment in the province.

Those who concur with this proposal believe that the referencing of Quebec's Catholic past to advance the PQ's agenda proves that the secular regime contained in the Charter of Values is far from culturally neutral. According to a brief submitted to the parliamentary hearings by Daniel Laguitton, "we cannot define as neutral a discourse so impregnated with a desire to avenge centuries of cohabitation by religious and political powers."[23] By using memories of the Catholic Church to justify restrictions on religious dress, Laguitton also argues, those in the pro-Charter camp are merely mimicking the tactics of their historical oppressors. Indeed, he suggests, "the proposed clothing restrictions have much in common with the measures historically imposed by a patriarchal and infantilizing clergy whose traces we hope to erase."[24] Not only is the Charter of Values not "modern" or "neutral" according to this line of argument; its proposals are reminiscent of measures regarded as embodying the "backwardness" in Quebec's religious past.

Thus, the anti-Charter camp had recourse to a different conception of Quebec's history – rooted in a distinct understanding of the secular legacies of the Quiet Revolution – than that advanced by its opponents. One of the briefs presented stated that "Québec has a tradition of pluralism (evident, for example, in the recognition granted to its minority anglophone and native populations) and has never intervened to prohibit the wearing of religious signs. Bill 60 goes against this tradition."[25] For others taking this view, the Quiet Revolution represents an opening up to the world and a recognition that, in order to form an enduring national project, Quebec must learn to incorporate the minorities within its territory. "In that sense," one brief argued, "the perspective adopted in Bill 60 constitutes a surprising reversal of public policies and law that have formed the basis for social cohesion and willful integration since the 1960s."[26]

Far from wrenching Quebec out of the past and into the future, as many pro-Charter activists claimed, those opposed to its recommendations maintained that the bill constituted a dangerous "regression." In one such instance, the Ligue des droits et libertés (League of Rights and Freedoms) described the Charter of Values as "reminiscent of the period preceding the Quiet Revolution when a superior moral authority, the Catholic Church, could dictate which modes of thinking and acting were acceptable and unacceptable on a society-wide basis."[27] Critics of the Charter expressed concern that, besides representing a reversal of Quebec's pluralist commitments, it would draw damaging criticism on the world stage. According to a brief submitted by researchers at various Quebec universities, "Quebec has been a pioneering figure [of secularism], adopting its own Charter of Human Rights and Freedoms in 1975 and declaring its adherence to the International Pact on Civil and Political Rights under the auspice of the United Nations."[28] By reneging on these commitments, many argued, the PQ government was behaving in a way that threatened Quebec's reputation as a "modern state of law": "From the perspective of a global normative legacy, the about-face in which Québec is currently engaging neither opposes 'multiculturalism' to 'laïcité' nor a 'Canadian model' to a 'Québécois model.' Rather, it compromises Québec's contribution to the modern state of law ... The fundamental issue at stake is therefore the following: does Québec want to continue to contribute to the development of the modern state of law or will it begin to contribute to its stagnation, even retreat?"[29] The threat to Quebec's "modern" reputation would have drastic consequences for the economy, many in the anti-Charter camp argued. As has been the case for French secular laws, the restrictive measures contained in Bill 60 would convey an image to the world of being closed off, with multiple negative consequences. Among these was the concern that, by restricting access to employment, the Charter might diminish foreign companies' willingness to invest in the Quebec economy. According to the Conseil du patronat (Council of Employers), an organization representing employers' interests, it is essential in the context of global competition that Quebec "project, as a society, an image of openness and stability."[30]

Therefore, when it came to defining the parameters of religion and secularism, those for and against the Charter of Values took diverging positions, each of which embodied a different understanding of what constitutes "modernity" versus "backwardness" in relation to Quebec's national project. Indeed, those on both sides of the debate mobilized what Bouchard has described as the "myths" attending the 1960s Quiet Revolution,[31] but to significantly different ends. They did not agree on the *meaning* of secularism, nor did they converge around a shared understanding of its role in forging a "modern" society in Quebec. In this way, civil society actors participated in the making, remaking, and unmaking of Quebec's national identity that Zubrzycki has chronicled and analyzed.[32] As in the Quiet Revolution, the understandings of religion, secularism, and nationhood that became inscribed through this debate were wrought with paradoxes and contradictions.

Briefs concerning Gender (In)equality

Disagreements over the meanings of secularism and nationhood similarly marked the contestation among feminists in the Charter of Values debate. The terms of that contestation crystallized during the November 2013 meetings of the États généraux de l'action et l'analyse féministes (General Assembly for Feminist Action and Analysis), an umbrella organization that holds periodic symposia to reflect on the current status of, and set future goals for, feminism in Quebec. Scheduled to take place just as the debate over the Charter of Values was ramping up, the event gathered 800 participants to discuss various topics, including secularism and religious diversity.

As they unfolded, the meetings became the site of heated exchanges between feminists who opposed the Charter of Values – whose viewpoints were broadly represented by the Fédération des femmes du Québec (Quebec Women's Federation, FFQ) – and those who believed the FFQ had failed to project a "universal" feminism, by catering to minority interests and culturally relativist arguments. For instance, Diane Guilbault, a former FFQ member, accused the organization of attempting to silence the pro-Charter position, by inviting a larger-than-usual number of Muslim women to attend the November 2013 meetings. In her words: "A bus filled with veiled women pulled up. They all exited the bus together, but once inside, they separated themselves from one another. And so everyone was seated next to, in front of, or behind a veiled woman. It was extremely well done, extremely well done."[33] In the votes held to determine the movement's future agenda, meeting participants overwhelmingly opposed proposals to restrict religious signs in public spaces. As a result, they later explained to me, Guilbault and other pro-Charter feminists found themselves unable to remain with the FFQ. Citing the organization's "manipulation of feminism," as well as "contradictions and half-truths" in its directives, they subsequently formed an alternative pro-Charter association, Pour les droits des femmes du Québec (For the Rights of Women in Quebec, PDFQ).

When I met with Guilbault and her colleague, Leila Lesbet, in late February 2014 – at a time when most political pundits expected the Parti Québécois to prevail in the upcoming election in large part due to its popular Charter of Values – they were remarkably pessimistic about the prospects of the pro-Charter cause. They described being "ignored" and "verbally assaulted" by established associations like the FFQ.[34] They also felt marginalized and silenced by what they regarded as prevailing norms of political correctness in Quebec. For instance, Guilbault lamented her impression that, "as soon as you say you're for the Charter, you're seen as 'racist.'" "Many of those who supported the Charter from the start," she continued, "were reluctant to say so, because the opposition was so strong."[35]

Guilbault and Lesbet maintain that these charges of racism derive from a hegemonic feminist discourse in Quebec that prioritizes "intersectional" and "black" feminist themes, as well as a multicultural approach to diversity and women's rights.[36] Although not formalized as policy in Quebec, where in fact it is heavily criticized, multiculturalism is seen by many pro-restriction feminists as constituting a barrier to "universal" feminism. For example, having immigrated to Canada from Algeria in the early 2000s, Leila Lesbet believes that multiculturalism fosters religious fundamentalism by allowing Islamists in Quebec to behave "the same way" as in her home country.[37] Other PDFQ members echoed these sentiments, regretting the ways in which multiculturalism "recognizes, empathizes with, and legitimizes cultural particularities."[38] In these ways, one argued, this ideology "reinforces sexist patriarchal practices in Québec and Canada."[39]

In order to challenge the cultural relativism that they believe to be fostered by multiculturalism, members of PDFQ took to claiming that they represent the interests of "all" women in Quebec. Echoing the universalist claims of their pro-restriction counterparts in France, they insisted that "feminism has no colour."[40] "Being a woman," Lesbet stated, for instance, "is not related to being of a certain colour. We have a sex, yes, but we do not have a colour."[41] To ignore the "universal" aspects of womanhood by recognizing plural definitions of gender equality is to "pit women against other women," according to Diane Guilbault. In her words: "Our goal is to defend women's rights. And when we defend access to daycare, it is all women who benefit, regardless of their skin colour or whether they have a disability. And when we defend the right to work, or pay equity, it is all women who benefit. So, you see, these struggles have been fruitful for all women."[42] These representations of "all women" are consistent with a history of downplaying the significance of race in certain factions of Quebec's feminist movement.[43] In the context of the religious signs debate, this universalizing narrative has pinpointed multiculturalism – seen as a by-product of Canada's British colonial heritage – as reinforcing divisions and inequalities among women, preventing a real emancipatory feminism from taking root.

Although they oppose the intersectional representations of women's rights that they see embodied in Canadian multiculturalism, pro-Charter feminists did draw on a certain kind of anti-colonialism – one that underscores Quebec's own historical subjugation to colonial rule – in staking their claims.[44] For example, in highlighting the importance of laïcité, many recalled dark memories of Quebec's Catholic past, during which the Church, with the support of the British colonial administration, treated women as second-class citizens. Marylise Hamelin, a member of the Association féminine d'éducation et d'action sociale (Women's Association for Education and Social Action, AFEAS), remembers the era of Catholic dominance as a period of rampant sexism and inequality. In her words: "We used to be very Catholic compared to the rest of Canada, but we have rejected that oppression ... What my grandmother lived through ... she was not allowed to do anything. When she was pregnant, she could not walk on the street because of shame. That was Catholic Québec. It was a hell that still sickens people to think about."[45] Hamelin and her colleagues view this oppression as part of a deliberate strategy by the Catholic Church to obstruct women's access to political power and influence in Quebec.

Unlike their French counterparts, whose defeat by pro-ban feminists left them marginalized in the 2010 burqa debate, anti-restriction voices dominated the feminist response to Quebec's Charter of Values. Krista Riley of the Collective des féministes musulmanes du Québec (Collective of Muslim Feminists of Quebec, CFMQ), a group created in 2013 to impart a Muslim perspective on the Charter, recalls the November 2013 meetings as demonstrating feminists' "overwhelming" opposition to restricting religious signs. "I'm not talking about a 60/40 split," Riley explained. "It was like a 90/10 split."[46] For fellow CFMQ member Bochra Manai, these results clearly showed that "intersectional or postcolonial approaches were beginning to take up much more space" in Quebec's feminist politics.[47] The exchanges that took place as part of the 2013 meetings also served as a visible sign that the issue of religious diversity "was becoming less of a Muslim issue and more of a women's issue" and that "racialized women or Muslim women had inscribed ourselves in a renewal of the feminist perspective."[48]

Like their French counterparts, anti-restriction feminists were also concerned about the exclusionary effects of attempts to project a "universal" feminism in Quebec. According to Manai, pro-Charter feminists claim "there is one way to be feminist, that if what you bring to the table is uncomfortable to us, it is not feminist."[49] In challenging this perspective, Manai has advocated the embrace of plural definitions of gender equality and emancipation. This is necessary, she told me, because "we all carry wounds. We are all searching for equality, among ourselves and in relation to men."[50] In order to address the multiple wounds that women face, Manai has proposed a feminist outlook based on solidarity across difference, rather than sameness. In her words: "[Feminism] is taking another woman's hand to claim equality in society and craft a vision out of our recognition of injustice. That is what being a feminist means to me. Yes, there is patriarchy. But what can we do to ensure that women who suffer from patriarchy join with us? It is not to point the finger at certain women because they are racialized."[51] Thus, rather than obscure the multiple sources of injustice by prioritizing causes common to "all" women, Manai has argued that feminism should encompass diverse perceptions and experiences of patriarchy. The parallels to the pluralist feminist discourse in France are striking. In making the case there for pluralism, Ismahane Chouder of the Collectif des féministes pour l'égalité (Collective of Feminists for Equality, CFPE) has similarly rejected the claim that a "superior emancipatory model" exists, and called for the "respect for all women's voices and pathways to emancipation."[52]

However, the greater visibility of anti-restriction voices in Quebec's – compared to France's – feminist movement has not led to closer alignment with the state. Indeed, just as the FFQ and CSF asserted their political independence by publicly opposing the Charter, the CFMQ challenged the PQ government by boycotting its consultation hearings. The main motivation for this, both Manai and Riley explained, was to prevent the Parti Québécois from further "instrumentalizing" feminists and feminism to justify its proposals. In Manai's words: "We knew the process was not being conducted in good faith, that it was not actually a process of genuinely wanting to consult anybody about this Charter. It was really more about the government being able to say, 'Hey, look, we had a consultation process and we talked to people.' It was a way of giving them legitimacy in what they were trying to do. We didn't want to be part of that."[53] The mention of "legitimacy" in this quote underscores pro-Charter feminists' awareness of the symbolic power of feminism to uphold and validate state projects involving the control of women's bodies. Having no intention of providing such legitimacy, Manai and her colleagues took steps to prevent any attempt at co-optation by the governing party. By refusing to engage, they maintained, they could ensure their participation would not be used to validate policies that infringe on women's rights.

Relations among feminists in the deliberations surrounding Quebec's Charter of Values were thus highly fluid and indeterminate. As the above quotes demonstrate, at least some of that indeterminacy stemmed from the fact that, thanks to a complex colonial history, both pro- and anti-Charter feminists were able to anchor their claims in differing anti-colonial discourses. In the case of pro-Charter feminists, the adopted discourse underscored the need to assert Quebec's independence vis-à-vis a Catholic history and contemporary federal multiculturalism that some perceive as emanating from Britain's historic colonial role in Canada. By contrast, anti-Charter feminists viewed colonialism in much the same way as anti-ban feminists in France: as a foundation for "Western" feminists' subjugation of alternative conceptions of women's equality, agency, and emancipation. The disparate uses of these discourses by pro- and anti-Charter feminists fed into, and reinforced, the larger debate around what constitutes Québécois nationhood in the context of religious diversity.

Briefs concerning the Legal Viability of the Charter of Values

Just as feminists mobilized competing interpretations of gender equality and women's emancipation to validate their positions on the Charter of Values, legal experts participating in the public hearings interpreted the same stock of legal and policy material in different ways. Their arguments also similarly illustrated the fundamental conflicts that exist in Quebec over ways to define and articulate the meanings of secularism and nationhood.

As in France, experts speaking to the role of law in the Charter of Values debate battled over whether the matter at issue – religious dress in public sector employment – should be addressed through political, as opposed to legal, means. The main question for those on the pro-Charter side was whether the Supreme Court of Canada would cite violation of religious freedom to strike down the proposed prohibition of religious signs in public sector employment.

Some argued that the matter should be determined by Quebec's democratically elected officials. Describing the court system and religious dogma under the joint rubric of "divine law,"[54] these individuals worked just as hard to convince the public that the legislature – as opposed to the court system – is the appropriate venue in which to define the parameters of secularism as they did discussing what those parameters should be. In this regard, many pro-Charter legal experts advocated that the Marois government invoke the notwithstanding clause in the event that Bill 60 were to be struck down by the courts. When hailed in the public debate around the Charter of Values, this clause became a symbolic tool in affirming the superior legitimacy of democratically elected officials over legal experts. In its brief submitted to the public hearings, for instance, the group Mouvement national des québécoises et québécois (National Movement of Quebeckers) "invite[d] the Québec government to consider, if circumstances call for it, using the notwithstanding clause to assert the political character of the secularism debate and prevent it from being swallowed up by a judicial logic that dangerously undermines contemporary democracy. It is crucial, in the current period, that we bring the larger questions that divide us back into public debate, that we remind ourselves of the value of representative democracy and that we do not let ourselves be mystified by judges' attempts at governing."[55] This call to protect "representative democracy" against "judges' attempts at governing" closely mirrored the discourse used by French politicians (see chapter 4) to insist upon the legitimacy of the face veil ban regardless of the court's approval.[56] Thus, in both Quebec and France, we see dedicated attempts by advocates of restriction to couch their demands in a distinctly political – as opposed to judicial – understanding of ways to circumscribe religion, secularism, and belonging in the context of diversity.

Recognizing the challenges associated with invoking the notwithstanding clause – including the danger that it would provoke a public backlash – pro-Charter figures in Quebec's legal community set about identifying legal precedents for Bill 60's article 5 in Canadian jurisprudence. Their analyses demonstrate just how deeply rooted are the disagreements surrounding the meaning(s) of state neutrality and religious freedom in Quebec.

As I mentioned in chapter 1, the Quebec Bar Association rejected the proposal to prohibit religious signs among public sector employees (including judges), claiming that such a move would contravene Canadian and international human rights law. In its brief, the association argued that the proposed ban violated the protection of freedom of religion based on the principle of "subjective belief."[57] This principle was established by the Supreme Court of Canada in *Syndicat Northwest v. Amselem* (2004), in which the Court held that religious freedom is based on the "subjective aspect of the believer's personal sincerity rather than the objective aspect of the conformity of the beliefs in question with established doctrine."[58]

Legal experts who supported the Charter of Values constructed elaborate responses to the Quebec Bar Association's objections. Diverging from the notion of laïcité ouverte (open secularism) proposed in the Bouchard-Taylor report, they invoked a secular discourse mirroring that advanced by pro-restriction forces in the French face veil debate. The basic argument is that, by allowing religious expression by civil servants, the government risks threatening – rather than *protecting* – individuals' religious freedoms in Quebec. For those freedoms to flourish, they claimed, the state must rid itself of all religious symbols and practices.

This argument was deployed by Julie Latour, former member of the Quebec Bar Association and representative of Juristes pour la laïcité et la neutralité religieuse de l'état (Jurists for Secularism and the Religious Neutrality of the State, JPLNE) at the time of the Charter of Values debate. In our interview, Latour suggested that "One of the greatest flaws of *laïcité ouverte* is that it eradicates freedom of conscience. If people working for the state wear religious signs, it is as if the state were saying that to have a religious posture is predominant. The state must treat all citizens equally. Freedom of religion and conscience requires that the state equally protect believers and non-believers. At the moment, the non-believers are being ignored."[59] To bolster this interpretation, Latour undertook an elaborate examination of prior Supreme Court of Canada rulings regarding religious freedom, which she claimed provide precedent for restricting religious signs in public sector employment. Since 2006, when it overturned the 2004 decision by Quebec's Court of Appeal prohibiting a Sikh boy from wearing a kirpan to school,[60] decisions by the Court, according to Latour, have introduced possible avenues for circumventing the right to religious freedom in certain cases. For example, she cited *Bruker v. Marcovitz* (2007), a case involving the validity of the *get* (the Jewish divorce procedure in which a woman cannot obtain a divorce from her husband unless he agrees), in which the Supreme Court ruled that freedom of religion should be balanced and reconciled with countervailing rights and principles, such as equality and protection of public interest.[61] Latour also referred to *Alberta v. Hutterian Brethren Church of Wilson* (2009), in which the Court denied Alberta's Hutterite community's request for exemption from having their photos taken to receive driver's licences, claiming that such an allowance would increase the risk of identity theft.[62]

For those who support restrictions of religious signs in public service, these recent rulings open a doorway for reinterpreting the principle of religious freedom in Canadian jurisprudence.[63] In particular, they point to the Supreme Court's willingness to limit said freedom if and when it contravenes rights and/or the general interest.[64] In lieu of that outcome, however, many supporters of the Charter advocated the use of the notwithstanding clause, a measure that they framed as upholding the legitimacy of politics and politicians in deciding questions of rights in Quebec.

AT AN IMPASSE: PARTY POLITICAL REPRESENTATIONS OF RELIGION, SECULARISM, AND BELONGING

The fact that the Quebec Bar Association, and other legal organizations, considered the Charter of Values unconstitutional did not deter the Parti Québécois from advancing its agenda. Indeed, the party framed the legal objections as another example of the unacceptable limitations imposed on the province by Canadian legal bodies. In making this case, the PQ developed a discourse of "courage" that portrayed the Charter as part of Quebec's historical and incomplete struggle for national self-determination. As I will show, this discourse became a prime vehicle by which the government tried to claim sole ownership of Québécois nationhood.

Legal experts' objections to the Charter of Values also served as a backdrop to the PLQ's competing discourse of "responsibility." Indeed, in trying to snatch ownership of the religious signs issue from the PQ, members of this party asserted their opponents' dangerous neglect of fundamental rights and freedoms. The PLQ then used that discourse of "responsibility" to craft an alternative definition of Québécois nationhood, one that underscores its universal – rather than its particular – dimensions.

The notions of "courage" advanced by the PQ, and of "responsibility" by the PLQ, were challenged by a third discourse, which I call nationalism's "third way." I use this label to describe the claims of long-time and prominent sovereigntists – including former Quebec premiers – who regarded the Charter of Values as undermining Quebec's project to gain independence from Canada by alienating minority communities.

Because they derive from parties' positioning along an axis of competition that is highly nation-centred, these three discourses ultimately proved irreconcilable. Rather than claiming a general consensus, like their mainstream counterparts in France, the Parti Québécois and Parti libéral du Québec continued to compete for ownership of the religious signs issue, while the smaller opposition parties, the Coalition avenir Québec and Québec solidaire, advanced alternative ways of conceiving the link between class concerns and the national project.

The Parti Québécois and the Discourse of "Courage"

In presenting its Charter of Values as part of a "courageous" battle to confront historical and contemporary barriers to Quebec's self-determination, the PQ leadership and prominent members developed a vocabulary for articulating the relationship between religious minorities and the state in terms of "values," rather than "rights." This emphasis on "values" was evidenced in the very title of Bill 60: *Charter affirming the values of State secularism and religious neutrality and of equality between women and men, and providing a framework for accommodation requests*.

PQ press releases and flyers also sought to link the measures proposed by Bill 60 to the core "values" of secularism, gender equality, and protection of the French language. Consider the following excerpt from a PQ document entitled *Charter of Québec Values: Affirming who we are and who we wish to be*: "In Québec, the equality of all citizens, equality between women and men, and the separation of Church and State are core values ... This Charter is an important milestone in our history. It affirms who we are and defines the Québec in which we want to live together, regardless of our origin or religion. Forty years ago, we entrenched the primacy of French as a shared value among the Québécois. Today, we affirm the shared values of secularism, religious neutrality of the state and equality between women and men."[65] By connecting gender equality, secularism, and commitment to the French language, and placing them in the realm of "values" rather than "rights," this quote signalled that the Parti Québécois intended to frame the parameters of national belonging in political (and therefore value-laden) – rather than legal (and thus rights-centred) – terms. Indeed, in its official advertisement of the Charter, the PQ went so far as to raise the status of those values to a "sacred" level, comparable to that of a "church, synagogue or mosque" (see Figure 5.1).[66]

Because they upheld a political – as opposed to legal – conception of nationhood, the "values" identified by the Charter of Values would require an act of "courage" to assert. Speaking before parliament on 23 October 2013, Premier Pauline Marois described her party's bill as

Figure 5.1 PQ poster promoting the Charter of Values, 2013. It reads: "Equality of men and women. Religious neutrality of the the state. These are also sacred." *Source*: Parti Québécois: http://www.nosvaleurs.gouv.qc.ca.

addressing "a major societal debate, one that requires *courage* since it involves particularly important cultural, political, and sociological changes."[67] Those "changes," it became clear, would entail a shift in the definition of secularism from a principle of state religious neutrality to one that restrains the actions of individuals. From this point forward, Marois herself was portrayed as personifying the "courage" entailed in asserting this alternative secularism. In December 2013, the minister in charge of the Charter of Values, Bernard Drainville, announced that "it is thanks to the courage of the Premier that we have a Charter of Values."[68]

In explicitly characterizing the Charter of Values as a "courageous" move in the project to secure the "values" of state religious neutrality and gender equality in Quebec, PQ members juxtaposed their proposals against actors and institutions whom they charged with lacking the "courage" to defend Québécois nationhood, chief among which was the Parti libéral du Québec. Addressing this theme head-on in parliament, Bernard Drainville claimed that demonstrations of "courage" have always been absent in the PLQ. Just as they lacked the "courage" to defend Quebec's linguistic heritage, he suggested, the Liberals have been ineffective in enforcing secularism. In the minister's words:

> This [debate over the Charter of Values] strongly resembles the debate we had over Bill 101. It's actually quite fascinating, Mr President, to go back and review the headlines and commentaries that were made in the period that Bill 101 was adopted, or in the months preceding its adoption. Because Bill 101, Mr President, precisely sought to strike a balance between individual and collective rights; it was a foundational piece of legislation that marked and continues to mark our history ... And I will remind you, Mr President, that in 1977 the Liberals were opposed to Bill 101.[69]

In this statement, Drainville is citing the debate over Bill 101 to make a larger point: that the PQ is the only one of the two traditional parties to recognize, and seek to protect, the collective parameters of nationhood in Quebec. The Liberals, he maintains, have ignored the collective by anchoring their approach to language and religion solely in legal terms, citing individual rights.

Attempts to showcase the PLQ's lack of "courage" in matters of identity were reinforced by allegations that the party is incompetent when it comes to upholding the secular principles that define membership in the contemporary Québécois nation. Indeed, Marois herself took aim at the PLQ's track record on secularism in Quebec, citing the party's failure to implement the recommendations of the Bouchard-Taylor commission in 2008: "when they were in power for nine years – indeed Mr. President, the Liberal Party formed the government for nine years – they put in place a commission, which became the Bouchard-Taylor commission, from which they retained nothing on the question of reasonable accommodation. They made some attempts. They had a majority of seats at the time; they could have shown some leadership."[70] Unwilling to take concrete action on the issue of secularism, Marois concluded, the Liberals have chosen a discourse of ambiguity that suffers in comparison with the PQ's "clarity and respect for rights."[71] Elaborating on this claim, Minister Drainville complained in parliament that the Liberals "would like a policy of religious neutrality that is invisible and abstract."[72]

According to PQ representatives, the Liberals' cowardice and incompetence are illustrated by the party's mishandling of the debate – fueled by the deliberations around the Charter of Values – over whether the province should remove all Catholic iconography from public buildings. Indeed, some argued that by supporting the removal of the crucifix from the wall of the National Assembly, while advocating that individuals in the public service be able to maintain their religious appearance, Couillard and the rest of the PLQ were confusing the Québécois as to the meaning of secularism. In Drainville's words: "it is a strange kind of neutrality that the Liberal Party proposes. They want neutral brick and plaster, but they certainly don't care that the face of the state be neutral ... Our state must speak to us, welcome us, and give us services that embody this religious neutrality. If the state itself is neutral, those who represent it should be also, not only in their actions and decisions, but also in the images they convey to us."[73] Although they had insufficient "courage" to propose it, Drainville argued, the Liberals would eventually see the necessity of the Charter, as they did with Bill 101.[74]

Allegations that the Liberals did not have the "courage" to enforce the religious neutrality of the state through legislation aimed at its employees fed into a discourse that positions the PQ as the sole legitimate "owner" of nationhood in Quebec. This discourse came to the fore when key figures in the PQ transitioned from arguments about the specifics of the proposed policies to claims that Liberal politicians are intrinsically unable to mobilize on behalf of Quebec's interests. Launching the most direct assault of this kind, PQ minister Bernard Drainville charged Liberal members with being "genetically incapable of defending and affirming Québec's values."[75] The reference to genetics in this statement implies a conception of politicians as either inherently capable or incapable – depending on their partisan associations – of recognizing and defending the terms of Quebec's national identity. Premier Marois herself waded into this territory when she stated that, "according to the Liberals, it's as if we should apologize for defending Québec's interests. It's as if we should apologize for wanting to live in French in our own home. It's as if we should apologize for defending our common values."[76] These comments reinforce an image, integral to Quebec's nation-centred axis of political competition, of the PLQ as the vehicle for interests and values that threaten the shared identity of the Québécois.

The notion that, by virtue of its stance on the Charter of Values, the PLQ lacks the nationalist credentials necessary to govern in Quebec also filtered into claims made by members of the CAQ party, which supported some but not all aspects of Bill 60. In the parliamentary debates, party leader François Legault denounced Philippe Couillard and his Liberal caucus for being "not much interested in defending Québécois identity and values."[77] Nathalie Roy, the party's key spokesperson on issues of secularism, echoed this claim in our interview, suggesting that Couillard lacks a nationalist "sensibility." Roy explained, "That is to say that, for him, the [Canadian] Charter of Rights [and Freedoms] is a sacred text. He does not even believe in the rights afforded to the provinces allowing them to bypass it when it is justified, which is very rare."[78]

Representations of the Charter of Values as legally "impossible" thus served as an impetus for efforts to construct a "courageous" nationalism on the part of the Parti Québécois and its allies in this debate.[79] Rather than undermine its legitimacy, the fact that Bill 60 was expected to fail the tests of Québécois and Canadian jurisprudence instead bolstered its validity as a tool in the battle to confront the political obstacles to Quebec's national self-determination. The national script thus generated also took on an essentialist dimension when it was used to suggest that the Liberals are "genetically" predisposed to placing individual rights above the interests of the collective. Ultimately, the discourse of "courage" – combined with the attacks on the PLQ – amounted to a conception of national belonging that excludes those who are unprepared to adopt the "values" that are bound up in the PQ's conceptualization of secularism.

The Parti Libéral du Québec and the Discourse of "Responsibility"

In lieu of proposing a bill in parliament to rival that of the PQ, Liberal politicians and their civil society allies embraced a competing discourse of "responsible" nationhood and governance, one that builds on legal experts' representations of the Charter as "impossible" to elicit public skepticism over the PQ's program. Like the discourse of "courage," this approach draws resonance from parties' positioning along Quebec's nation-centred axis of competition. While the government emphasized "values" over legal tradition in order to justify the Charter, recourse to the law and "rights" was the primary tool used by the PLQ to advance a "responsible" opposition to Bill 60.

The discourse of "responsibility" that the Liberals deployed in the Charter of Values debate was predicated in large part on a portrayal of the document as an affront to the rule of law in Quebec. In its press releases and submissions before the National Assembly, the PLQ repeatedly warned that prohibiting religious signs would dangerously infringe on citizens' rights to religious expression and to employment, thus contradicting Quebec's legal framework. Linking these two issues together in a broad condemnation of Bill 60, Liberal representative Marc Tanguay explained to his colleagues in parliament that: "[The bill] would lead to discrimination, of women and minorities, but also of all those who believe – and they are right to believe they have freedom of religion – in the neutrality of the state, who do not seek to proselytize, but who wish, for example, to be able to wear jewelry that resembles a cross. These individuals have the right, Mr. President, to access jobs offered in the public and semi-private sectors."[80] This statement asserts a distinctive and "responsible" brand of nationalism, by linking the illegitimacy of the Charter on legal grounds to two prominent themes in the Liberal party brand: the economy (employment) and defence of individual "rights."

In elucidating their concerns about the rights-based implications of Bill 60, prominent Liberals openly questioned the government's respect for the rule of law. On 23 October 2013 – before the government had officially presented its bill to parliament – the party proposed a motion demanding that the Parti Québécois hear the opinion of Quebec's Commission des droits de la personne et des droits de la jeunesse (Human Rights and Youth Rights Commission, CDPDJ) and formally promise to respect the province's Charter of Human Rights and Freedoms in drafting its bill. In his comments following the motion's introduction, Liberal MNA[81] Marc Tanguay outlined his party's concerns, effectively daring the PQ to vote against a proposal that merely articulated the importance of the rule of law.[82] Although it was forced to support the motion – to do otherwise would be politically unviable – the PQ responded by accusing the Liberals of "using the Human Rights Commission to political ends."[83]

Liberal members' efforts to prove their superior commitment to the rule of law were woven into a broader discourse of nationhood centred on the promise of "responsible" government. Characterizing the PQ as "irresponsible," Marc Tanguay stated in parliament: "We will always represent this responsible opposition, Mr President, and we will always do our part to ensure that, in all the measures taken by this government, whether they be measures of the government or the legislature, we maintain that respect for the rights and freedoms of all Quebeckers."[84] This liberal discourse of "responsibility" was picked up by the other opposition parties, particularly the Coalition avenir Québec, whose program, entitled *Religious Accommodations: A Responsible Approach*, called on the National Assembly to "take its responsibilities" and adopt a proposal that "balances" respect for the neutrality of the state, gender equality, and Quebec's heritage.[85] In affirming the legitimacy of its proposals, the CAQ further suggested that its "balanced" and "responsible" approach embodies principles established during the Quiet Revolution, the period during which "education was notably entrusted to secular authorities rather than religious ones."[86]

The discourse of "responsibility" that the Liberals and CAQ adopted transferred seamlessly onto warnings that, if elected, the PQ would likely try its luck at a third referendum. Keen to capitalize on the public's ambivalence over sovereignty, Liberal leader Philippe Couillard claimed in a television interview: "It's irresponsible to deliberately introduce division between the communities of Québec [through mentions of a referendum]. I cannot accept that. We will correct that. We will work hard to make it so that all Quebeckers feel united under the umbrella which is our Québec identity."[87] By linking the referendum issue to the question of national belonging, Couillard was able to frame the PQ as "irresponsible" in its approach to both major themes addressed by the Charter of Values: individual "rights" and the "values" that constitute Quebec's national identity.

Underlying these charges that the PQ had been "irresponsible" in its management of the religious signs issue was a palpable frustration among PLQ members that ownership of Québécois nationhood was slipping from their hands. This theme of ownership came visibly to the fore in the party's campaign posters, which asserted that: "Our identity is not exclusive to a political party. It belongs to all of us Québécois."[88]

Other opposition parties picked up on this theme of ownership. Recognizing the threat it posed to their capacity to "own" Quebec's national identity, they accused the PQ of using the term "values" for strategic purposes. Although it "might appear semantic," the CAQ's Nathalie Roy claimed in parliament, this choice "reflects the government's desire to profit from Québécois identity through electioneering."[89] Roy's colleague Gérard Deltell further sought to expose the PQ's hidden strategy, stating in parliament: "I think it sad that the government has once again attached the adjective 'Québécois' to one of its bills, because it makes it such that, if we disagree with the content of the Charter … we can be accused of being less Québécois than others? Are we not sufficiently Québécois if we disagree with what's inside [the Charter]? That adjective belongs to all Québécois, and certainly not only to a bill defined by the current government. Québec deserves much better."[90] Such skirmishes over who owns the term "Québécois" speak to the symbolic importance of this label in Quebec politics. While French politicians battled over the precise meanings of secularism, they stopped short of claiming to be more or less "French" than their opponents. In Quebec, by contrast, the political contestation over the Charter became a site for reaffirming a zero-sum understanding of nationhood and its capacity to be "owned" by a particular party.

Having proclaimed itself an equal "owner" of Québécois national identity, the PLQ went about elaborating the parameters that this identity would take on in the event of a Liberal victory in the 2014 provincial election. The party committed itself to protecting Québécois culture by supporting calls to allow the crucifix to remain in the National Assembly.[91] However, the Liberals also remained adamant that focusing on the particularistic elements of Québécois identity did not serve the national project in the long run. If they did not support the Charter of Values, party members argued, it was precisely because they value Quebec's distinctiveness and hope to protect it from being governed by nationalist "extremists" who allow a discourse of "fear, humiliation and retreat" to guide their secularism policy.[92] Indeed, offering this protection was central to the PLQ's "responsible" and "rights"-based articulation of nationhood.

A "Third Way" for Nationalism? The Charter of Values as a Wedge Issue in the Sovereignty Movement

While nationhood remained the primary axis of competition throughout the debate over the Charter of Values, the proposed legislation deepened the cleavage between two factions within the Quebec sovereignty movement: those who believe openness to diversity strengthens the independence project and those who, by contrast, seek to restrict the requirements for participation in Quebec's public sphere along cultural, religious, and linguistic lines. This conflict came to the forefront early on in the Charter debate, when prominent sovereigntist politicians – including former Parti Québécois premiers Bernard Landry, Lucien Bouchard, and Jacques Parizeau, and former leader of the Bloc Québécois Gilles Duceppe – openly repudiated the project. The confrontations that ensued illustrate the dilemmas that arise as politicians who agree on the "national question" begin to frame it in different ways.

A major criticism of the Charter of Values by pro-sovereignty actors was that Bill 60 betrays the sovereignty movement's historic pluralist inclinations. In the words of Gérard Bouchard, the Charter "perverts" the legacy of civic nationalism that the Quiet Revolution established.[93] Long-time nationalist Jean Dorion concurred, arguing that "people like René Levesque and Jacques Parizeau would never have taken things in this direction."[94] According to Gérard Bouchard, however, the objections of known sovereigntists "passed like butter in a pan," failing to influence the governing party's agenda.[95] This, he argued, was because the Charter was a ploy by the PQ to attract votes and gain an electoral majority.

In addition to denouncing the Charter on ideological grounds, sovereigntist critics of the proposed bill warned of the strategic threat it posed for the sovereignty movement. Specifically, they argued, Bill 60 would derail Quebec's independence project by reviving discourses of division and isolation.[96] This was the central argument put forward by former PQ member Jean Dorion in his 2012 opinion piece in *Le Devoir* entitled "The Charter of Secularism: When a Separatist Separates Himself." Dorion argued that restricting the religious freedom of Quebec's minorities would weaken the potential for sovereignty by drawing a wedge between francophones and immigrants and by undermining the province's capacity to one day be recognized as a liberal nation state. In his words: "For the first time since the PQ was created, I did not vote for the party. The project it is pursuing will divide a society already too divided. It will make independence more difficult to achieve, as it alienates us from liberal sectors in the rest of the continent, the only ones likely to respect our choice."[97] Pursuing a restrictive secular agenda, Dorion further argued, will encourage outsiders to view Quebec as a "fortress of intolerance" in North America, with possible negative impacts on support for sovereignty.

Dorion's colleagues in the group Indépendantistes pour une laïcité inclusive (Sovereigntists for an Inclusive Secularism) took up this argument in the context of the Charter of Values debate. They claimed in their brief that, if implemented, the Charter would only serve to convince the province's immigrant minorities that a united Canada would be more committed to protecting their rights than would an independent Quebec. In their words: "It is not enough to win the next election. In order for the independence project to succeed, sovereigntist governments must bring people together; they must have the widest possible embrace. They should start by pursuing an agenda that unites sovereigntists themselves."[98] This quote speaks directly to the close association between the strategic concerns brought about by the quest for Quebec sovereignty and activists' articulations of religion, secularism, and belonging. Although actors share a commitment to sovereignty, differences in the way they view the road to independence shape how they frame issues of diversity and national membership. Those who opposed the Charter believed that by conceiving the sovereignty struggle in terms of short-term electoral goals, the PQ has failed to project an inclusive image of the nation, thus alienating potential sovereignty supporters in the long run.

Concern over the party's present and future direction has resulted in great tensions among prominent PQ supporters. Jean Dorion stated in our interview: "[The Charter] has made discussion very difficult. I've had some very amicable and long-term friendships that were completely destroyed when I published my book. And those relationships are over. We don't talk anymore. Many relationships have ended the same way. It won't be easy to put the pieces back together."[99] Disaffection with the PQ's strategy alienated other key members of the sovereignty movement, including Maria Mourani, a Bloc Québécois member of federal parliament evicted from her party for opposing the Charter. In December 2013, Mourani publicly dissociated herself from the sovereignty movement, citing irreconcilable differences with the movement's new leadership. In a statement published by *La Presse*, Mourani stated that the "flagship of sovereignty is nothing like the one I have known. Some sovereigntist leaders remain who defend an inclusive vision of Québécois identity, but it is clear that they are marginal."[100] Further on in her statement, Mourani justified her decision as being based on a concern for universal rights, which she claims are better protected under Canadian federalism: "The ease with which Québec's Charter of Individual Rights and Freedoms can be modified, even abolished, has convinced me of the value of the Canadian federal system. I have concluded that belonging in Canada, with its Charter of Rights and Freedoms, better protects citizens' Québécois identity. I am no longer sovereigntist."[101] This quote points to the perception of an inherent connection between the promotion of universal "rights" and the preservation of a distinct Québécois national identity among sovereigntists opposing the Charter of Values. A threat to the one entails a threat to the other, and it is for this reason that Mourani abandoned the sovereignty movement.

Above all, these quotes demonstrate how issues having to do with the incorporation and accommodation of immigrant religious minorities are intersecting in new ways with the prevailing focus of party political competition in Quebec: nationalism. Indeed, the Charter of Values brought to the fore a deepening divide within the province's sovereignty movement, between those who view independence as contributing to and propelled by an inclusive national project based on universal rights, and those who utilize sovereignty as a vehicle to mobilize linguistic and cultural cleavages. As I discuss in the epilogue, the vacuum produced by this divide has enabled the non-traditional Coalition avenir Québec and Québec solidaire to occupy a much more prominent place in Quebec electoral politics, particularly since 2018.

CONCLUSION

Rather than instigating a battle between left and right, Quebec's Charter of Values debate reinvigorated latent struggles over the province's national identity and potential to achieve sovereignty. As in prior nation-building periods in Quebec, two parties – the pro-federalism Parti libéral du Québec and the pro-sovereignty Parti Québécois – dominated the airwaves, using the issue of religious signs to distinguish themselves in this ongoing struggle. Evidence from party press releases, parliamentary debates, and interviews with politicians demonstrates the important ways in which these parties' strategic concerns prompted them to attach opposing meanings to existing ideological structures and legal frameworks. In promoting the Charter, for instance, PQ members emphasized ways in which it solidified prior policies that pushed forward a similarly "courageous" defence of national identity. In seeking to demonstrate its own credentials in the nationalist debate, the PLQ rebutted by claiming to be the party of "responsible" nationhood and governance.

Competing articulations of nationhood were equally relevant to civil society debates over the Charter of Values, in which the three key themes were religion and secularism in Quebec public life, gender (in)equality, and the legal viability of outlawing religious signs in public sector employment. Those who supported the Charter maintained that its proposals reflected a "modern" commitment to secularism and women's equality, consistent with Quebec's national trajectory since the Quiet Revolution. Fueled by the perception that opposing views constitute a "rupture" with Québécois law and history, and by a deep dissatisfaction with the partial solutions proposed by the Bouchard-Taylor report, this discourse framed the particularistic dimensions of national identity in terms consistent with the universal requirements of modern liberal state building.

In stark contrast, opponents of the Charter perceived its recommendations as betraying a longstanding commitment to pluralism in Quebec, one that earlier leaders of the sovereignty movement willingly embraced. Bolstered by a strong feminist critique of article 5, as well as by the disenchantment of sovereigntists who viewed the Charter as threatening the prospect of independence, this argument conveyed a different image of nationhood in Quebec, one that sees recognition of diversity as both a faithful reflection of existing policy frameworks and as the surest way to guarantee Quebec's long-term cultural and political survival.

Existing ideas and institutions informed these party-political articulations of secularism, but in limited ways. Recognizing that many prominent legal experts opposed their proposals – including the highly respected Quebec Bar Association – PQ supporters strategically framed the Charter of Values as part of a "courageous" battle to assert the Quebec government's political authority over the terms of citizenship and belonging within its territory. This discourse of "courage" in turn compelled party leaders to redefine the "rights" associated with secularism in terms of "values" that they could then present as widely shared. Recognized legal frameworks played a different role in the anti-Charter discourse. Claims that the Charter's article 5 was legally "impossible" were used by leading PLQ representatives to situate their opposition to the bill within a program of "responsible" government. This discourse of "responsibility" meant that the party hewed more closely to "rights"-based – as opposed to "values"-centred – articulations of secularism.

Thus, while extant ideas and institutions did not dictate the broad stances that parties adopted in Quebec's Charter of Values debate – indeed, these were far more influenced by overarching structures of competition and the articulation strategies they generated – they did place some constraints on the precise frames that party representatives adopted in articulating those positions for the public. Ultimately, however, because they represent a highly fractious debate around how to define and defend Quebec's national identity, the PQ and PLQ were unable to achieve consensus in the Charter of Values debate. Whereas politicians in France agreed on the need for restrictive legislation to protect French secularism – a fact that limited that debate to detailed aspects of the 2010 law – the nation-centred character of Quebec's political system was such that competing actors remained intent on proving themselves to be "more Québécois" than their opponents. As a result, politicians and civil society participants in the Charter of Values debate were able to represent Quebec's past, present, and future in remarkably different ways.

Conclusion

Why Politics?

Scholars are continually searching for ways to understand the link – if there is one – between countries' unique personalities, reputations, or "creeds,"[1] and the methods they adopt for selecting newcomers and incorporating minorities. Underscoring the historical production and institutionalization of nationhood, many have concluded that nation-specific identity discourses or "models" provide the essential clue in explaining why states respond differently to immigration-related diversity. I have argued in this book that the resulting focus on ideas and institutions fails to account for the important role that politics plays in driving states' responses to religious signs. I showed that as they compete for the power to dictate the terms of religious minorities' incorporation, political parties continually define and redefine the meaning(s) of nationhood.

This conclusion elucidates the theoretical advantages of placing the study of nationhood – its construction and boundaries – in dialogue with the literature on party politics, in order to better understand states' disparate reactions to immigrant religious diversity. Drawing examples from the foregoing chapters, I emphasize that the struggles to demarcate boundaries between and among political parties both *mirror* and *shape* the process of demarcating the boundaries of nationhood. Moreover, I suggest that the context of partisan conflict – specifically whether axes of competition are rooted primarily in issues of class or national identity – shape the religious signs debate by impacting the likelihood that parties will compete over, rather than attempting to share, ownership of this issue.

LINKING BOUNDARY DRAWING IN POLITICS TO THE DEMARCATION OF NATIONAL BOUNDARIES

In chapter 1, I surveyed the scholarly work that depicts republicanism as the driving force behind immigration and integration policy in France. I showed that, whether they use the term "cultural idiom," "synthesis," or "philosophy of integration" to characterize the role that it plays, this body of work generally reifies republicanism, treating it as the main independent variable in understanding policy outcomes. I critiqued this research on the basis that it obscures the numerous and often contradictory incarnations of republicanism that exist, particularly in debates over immigrants' religious diversity. This multiplicity of meanings applies equally to Quebec's burgeoning intercultural discourse of citizenship and integration. While it prescribes a level of tolerance for diversity, interculturalism also embodies a desire to preserve the culture and language of the province's francophone majority.

The fact that the meaning(s) of French republicanism and Québécois interculturalism are heavily contested should come as little surprise, given scholars' growing appreciation of the tensions that mark the production of national identities. Those tensions can shape even the most fundamental aspects of nationhood, including whether membership is determined by ethnic ancestry or birthplace. Studies suggest that both logics can coexist in shaping national "models" of identity. For instance, in her study of Polish nationalism, Zubrzycki found that, in order resolve the tension between liberal intellectuals and the Catholic Church, the preamble to Poland's 1991 constitution juxtaposes the civic and ethnic dimensions of nationhood by referring to the "citizens" of the "Polish nation."[2] My collaborative work with Carson and Korteweg has shown that a similar interplay exists between civic and ethnic articulations of nationhood in Quebec's religious accommodation debates.[3]

The fact that political actors interpret the parameters of religion, secularism, and belonging differently is thus consistent with what we now know about nationalism as a "category of practice," whose meaning is situational and contingent.[4] Why, then, have some scholars held on to the notion that republicanism, especially, is an analytic category? Part of the answer lies in the interests that social scientists, historians, political theorists, and philosophers have in maintaining this state of affairs. According to Bowen, for example, scholars' penchant for looking to the genealogy of institutions to explain their current functions bolsters a desire to find continuities in history, and to impose those continuities on contemporary debates.[5]

However, there are real dangers to remaining committed to the notion that fixed ideas or institutions drive policy responses to immigration-related diversity. In the French case, for example, it can lead scholars to reproduce certain assumptions about the nature of diversity, with real effects on research and policy. As Amiraux and Simon have argued, French academics' hesitation to break with the illusion of a universal and colour-blind republicanism places a taboo on studies that take seriously racial and ethnic differences. The power of this "republican myth" is such that discrimination based on race has tended to be under-recognized in politics and academic research in France.[6] Recognizing the contestations that underlie the production of national "models" such as republicanism is one step toward reversing this tendency. It has been my argument in this book that comprehending the roots of those contestations is critical to knowing why states like France adopt laws that restrict the boundaries of minorities' belonging to the nation.

There are two main ways in which boundary drawing in politics "matters" to the production of nationhood. First, efforts to demarcate the boundaries of the nation *mirror* boundary-drawing processes in politics. Indeed, in the same way that political struggle engenders a complex interplay between agreement and disagreement among political actors, the project of constituting the nation involves a juxtaposition of images of sameness and difference. Second, struggles over boundaries in the electoral field can *shape* the production of nationhood.

Beginning with the first point, I have demonstrated that the boundaries that delimit the French electoral sphere – in terms of both the divisions among parties and the separation of electoral politics from civil society – are subject to intense and ongoing negotiation. Because the articulation of these boundaries is a shared and contested endeavour, political parties look to one another for clues in deciding how to respond to the issues of the day. Eager to defend and expand its electoral territory, each party struggles to "own" the political themes deemed important to voters. When they encounter competition from opponents who intentionally disrupt the traditional axis of competition for political gain, parties face additional dilemmas. If they are to "own" the issues introduced by their new competitors, they must construct solutions that both coincide with their historical legacies *and* further their electoral interests.

Depending on how parties respond to them, these dilemmas can result in a rearticulation of the boundaries of the electoral sphere. As in the boundary drawing that takes place in the context of ethnic group relations, that rearticulation process calls forth an interaction between internal and external forces of self-ascription and ascription by others. In addressing the electoral threat posed by the ultra-right Front National, for example, the UMP and Socialist parties in France have sought to bolster the division between "us" and "them." They have done so by framing the FN as the "outsider" to "legitimate" politics, and identifying themselves as "insiders" who share the responsibility of defining the limits of political space. The Front National has in turn appropriated its reputation as an "outsider" and mobilized it for political gain. Indeed, one of the key claims made by the party in the 2017 presidential election was that it, unlike the rest, does not belong to the "elite" political class.

This process of identifying the "insiders" and "outsiders" of politics closely maps onto the project of constructing nationhood and its boundaries. Indeed, according to Korteweg and Yurdakul, belonging to the nation is "always constituted vis-à-vis what or who we are not."[7] In producing a bounded sense of national identity, national actors must construct a kind of "imagined homogeneity" that downplays "the realities of difference in the populations constituting the nation."[8] The illusion of internal sameness thus created is necessary to delineate the external boundaries that render national projects different from one another. Changes to the balance between sameness and difference can result in a reconstituting of the boundaries of nationhood. Thus, boundary formation processes in the realms of politics and nationhood mirror each other.

The struggle to demarcate the boundaries of the electoral sphere can also *shape* articulations of secularism and national belonging. For instance, in seeking to deflect the threat posed by the Front National in the context of the face veil debate, France's traditional political parties converged around a narrow definition of political membership, one that excluded both the ultra-right political movement *and* religious Muslims. Moreover, by making full participation in the public sphere dependent on the concealment of personal religious beliefs, that definition has effectively denied women wearing the face veil full access to belonging in the French nation. Conversely, in the Quebec case, parties' interest in maintaining strict partisan boundaries around issues of identity has rendered nationhood and its boundaries a much more contested terrain. Viewing the ownership of the religious signs issue as a zero-sum game, politicians there have summoned distinct understandings of national membership based on "rights" versus "values." The resulting tensions are replicated in the feminist field, where competing conceptions of women's emancipation and equality resonate.

DEMARCATING THE BOUNDARIES OF THE NATION IN CLASS- VERSUS NATION-CENTRED POLITICAL SYSTEMS

A second proposition of this book is that, in thinking about how boundary drawing in the realm of politics mirrors and even shapes the demarcation of nationhood, scholars should pay closer attention to the *contextual* and *processual* factors at play in shaping political articulations in different political systems. A rich literature now exists showing that the degree to which ideological dimensions – class, culture, religion, regionalism, language, et cetera – constitute the axis of electoral competition differs across countries. As a result, scholars are becoming increasingly dissatisfied with the notion that a single measure – that of left versus right – determines electoral divides.

The left-right dichotomy has its origins in the French Revolution, when the supporters of the king sat on the right side of the National Assembly and the supporters of the Revolution sat on the left.[9] Although the "liberals" of this period consisted of "bourgeois intellectuals who objected to the involvement of the state in economic affairs," by the nineteenth century, "leftist" politics had become the territory of socialist and communist ideologies.[10]

However, the notion of left versus right is incapable of capturing the multiple dimensions that impact both the demand for, and supply of, ideological forces in contemporary electoral systems. Politicians are continuously introducing new issues into public debate. Parties that find the current structure of voter loyalties unfavourable may find it beneficial to introduce, and then claim ownership of, new controversies.[11] The restructuring of politics around a "new politics" or "new social movements" has thus had a clear impact on the range of party political options that exist in contemporary electoral systems.

There is a growing number of ideological dimensions over and above the right-left dichotomy. The extent to which these have displaced the traditional left-right axis varies cross-nationally. Studying the effects of globalization on the structure of political space in Europe, for instance, scholars have found that while parties are repositioning themselves in light of this new cleavage, the extent of the realignment is less in some countries, with France being a prime example.[12] Indeed, compared to its counterparts elsewhere in Europe, the French electoral system has – until the 2017 presidential election – remained relatively centred on the left-right axis.[13]

In Quebec, by contrast, where the national question has long constituted a "great divide,"[14] political processes adhere much less to a traditional left-right axis. While economic and social issues crosscut the debate over sovereignty, parties stake their claims primarily in disparate understandings of what it means to be Québécois and in divergent visions of the province's future as a real or quasi nation-state. The ways that economic values intersect with articulations of nationhood vary across the different parties. The economy is most relevant to support for the Parti libéral du Québec and to the now governing Coalition avenir Québec party. By contrast, support for the Parti Québécois and Québec solidaire is driven mainly by the nationalist question, although competition between the two is marked by voters' differing attitudes to social class.

France and Quebec's political systems thus follow different conventions for deciding who wins elections and on what basis. Those differences are key to determining whether or not, when it comes to navigating immigration-related religious diversity, parties will seek consensus or conflict. In particular, it has been my contention that the success of campaigns to restrict religious covering in France derives in part from the fact that, while intent on maintaining at least the semblance of a left-right partisan structure, mainstream political parties are willing to claim consensus – whether real or imagined – around questions of national identity if it enables them to deflect the ultra-right political threat. Meanwhile, in Quebec, where distinct nationalist visions dictate much of the battle between parties, consensus around matters of identity is less desirable. Therefore, at least for the time being, religious accommodation is the object of intense political debate and division.

CONCLUSION

In describing the challenges to French national identity at the turn of the new millennium, French philosopher Alain Finkielkraut famously wrote: "The contradictory metaphysics of modernity are today nothing but two variants of the same discourse: all is equal because all men are equal. Faced with this triumphant nihilism, there is nothing left but small nations and fragile heritages. We are all Québécois."[15] Finkielkraut intended these words as a call to intellectual action, a plea for the protection of French national heritage in the face of what he saw as a false and faceless modernity. In using the phrase "we are all Québécois," he further proposed that, like minority nations whose fate depends on a constant and vigilant promotion of their language and culture, France must be diligent in protecting and preserving its heritage if it is to survive.

Yet, at the same time that Finkielkraut was expressing a shared fate with Quebec, that province was itself shifting toward a much more majority-like conception of its national identity, manifested in the development of a unique, though unofficial, intercultural approach to integrating minorities. Over the last several years, Quebec has seen an upsurge in controversies surrounding religious accommodation and the meaning(s) of secularism. However, its major political parties have not – as yet – established anything resembling a "consensus" around these issues. Instead, measures to restrict religious signs in public spaces and institutions remain the subjects of heated political contestations, in which the question of who "owns" the Québécois nation looms large.

In this work, I have used the French and Québécois religious signs debates as empirical entry points from which to demonstrate the underappreciated role of politics – and particularly the *context* and *processes* of competition between parties – in the production of nationhood in religiously diverse societies. I have shown that the strategies political parties use to make gains vis-à-vis established axes of competition impact articulations of minorities' belonging to the nation. Highly gendered and racialized, those articulations have real material and symbolic implications for the lived experiences of religious communities, particularly Muslims.

By bringing party politics to the forefront in analyzing campaigns to restrict religious signs in France and Quebec, we can gain new insights into how nationhood is produced in contexts of religious diversity. By taking a politics-centred approach, and by thinking more methodically about how nations' discursive and institutional structures map onto party political interests, we can better appreciate the ways that ideas about who belongs to the nation are defined, redefined, and ultimately contested.

Epilogue

As I stated in the introduction, proposals to restrict certain religious signs in the public sphere ostensibly aim to set the present and future parameters of religious accommodation in diverse societies. Yet, such proposals *also* serve as key sites in which to negotiate the boundaries of national identity, membership, and belonging. As such, we can think of France's 2010 face veil ban and Quebec's 2013 Charter of Values as "events" that prompted political actors to rethink the question of who belongs to the nation and how. The significance of these "events" is likely to be longstanding.

In this epilogue, I consider how parties' articulations of the religious signs issue have evolved since the 2010 face veil ban in France and since the (proposed but never implemented) 2013 Charter of Values in Quebec. As we will see, the consensus alleged by France's mainstream political parties over the public prohibition of face veils remains intact, albeit in a fractured and unstable form. The establishment of that consensus during the 2009–10 debate continues to inform the discursive terrain of French secularism, bolstering campaigns to extend restrictive legislation to private – as well as public – spaces and institutions. Meanwhile, in Quebec, the political debate over Islamic religious signs remains as divisive as ever. In 2017, the PLQ government acquiesced to pressures to intensify its secular agenda, passing a bill prohibiting the wearing of facial coverings in public services. Yet, its proposals did not meet the demands of the opposing parties, whose members wished the government to go much further. In the larger political debate that ensued, opposition members of the National Assembly excoriated the Liberals as feeble defenders of Quebec's national interest, reaffirming a nation-centred axis of electoral competition in the process. This zero-sum battle among parties for ownership of the religious signs issue arguably helped to propel the Coalition avenir Québec to a majority government in the transformative provincial election of October 2018.

France

In effect since 2011, France's ban of facial coverings in public space has had significant consequences for the country's Muslim population. Even before the law was implemented, veiled women were the targets of harassment, notably, studies suggest, from middle-aged women in the majority population.[1] When women who wore the burqa or the niqab were asked what they would do after the law came into effect, many said they would consider leaving France for countries, such as the United Kingdom, that are reputed to be more tolerant toward Muslims.[2] Others said that they would refuse to remove their face veils, preferring to stay home. Still others proposed to conceal their faces through other non-restricted means, such as surgical masks, when out in public.[3]

By 2015 – four years after the face veil ban took effect – approximately 1,000 fines had been issued to women for refusing to remove their facial coverings in France's public spaces.[4] Some of those women purposely infringed the law out of protest, incurring multiple fines as a result. Many were simply reluctant to leave their homes in the aftermath of the ban.[5]

With the face veil banned in all public spaces, tensions around Islamic religious symbols have shifted back to the headscarf, and focused on women's right to wear this garment in three contexts: as mothers accompanying their children on school outings, as employees in daycare centres receiving public funding, and as students attending university courses.

The 2004 law prohibits students from wearing the headscarf in schools, but it says nothing about parents' rights. Over the last few years, some schools have taken the matter into their own hands, adopting regulations that require mothers to remove their headscarves before joining their children on school outings. A 2011 ruling by a court in Montreuil – a Parisian suburb – upheld such regulations, holding that schools have the right to exclude headscarf-wearing mothers. A subsequent memo released in 2012 by Sarkozy's minister of education backed this decision, leaving school principals free to decide whether or not to accept the headscarf in this context.

However, in 2013, the Conseil d'État issued an advisory ruling the other way, recommending that women be allowed to wear the veil when accompanying their children on school trips on the basis that they are "users," rather than "agents," of the public service.[6] This ruling has put the issue of parents' religious dress in the school setting to rest for the time being. In the meantime, groups advocating on behalf of veiled mothers – such as Mamans toutes égales (Mothers for Equality) – have expanded their mandates, becoming part of the larger network of associations opposing Islamophobia in France. This network includes the Collectif des féministes pour l'égalité (Collective of Feminists for Equality, CFPE), for whom the right of mothers to wear the headscarf on school property is fundamental. This right is also supported by Les mots sont importants (Words Are Important, LMSI), a group that came into being in order to oppose the prohibition of religious signs in schools in 2003–04.

Debates about the headscarf have continued to emerge, even in quasi-educational settings that are not clearly part of the public system. In March 2013, France's Cour de Cassation[7] – the highest court in the French judiciary – held that the Babyloup daycare centre located in the town of Chanteloup-les-Vignes discriminated against a female Muslim employee when it fired her for refusing to remove her headscarf while on the job. The incident became a national media sensation, with supporters of the daycare – including prominent feminists, philosophers, writers, and politicians – drafting petitions demanding that the National Assembly take action to affirm the principle of laïcité in early childhood education.[8] Opposition to the court's decision gained further attention when Manuel Valls, then Socialist minister of the interior, issued a statement claiming it undermined the principle of laïcité.[9]

In justifying its decision to sanction the Babyloup daycare centre for firing its headscarf-wearing employee, the Cour de Cassation relied on what it deemed a key distinction between private enterprises (like the Babyloup daycare) – which cannot use laïcité to deprive employees of the protections granted to them by the labour code – and public service enterprises, or private enterprises that provide a public service – which can apply laïcité to sanction employees' dress.[10]

Since the decision's release in March 2013, there have been mounting pressures to deepen the commitment to laïcité in France by extending the requirement of religious neutrality in public schools to early childhood education and, in some cases, to other private companies. Socialist Party president Hollande responded to these calls, proposing in 2013 that the rules applied to the public service also be applied to enterprises that have regular contact with the public or that provide services that are of general interest to the public. In March of that year, the UMP went even further, proposing a bill that would allow all companies to include the requirement of religious neutrality in their internal regulations.[11] In the June 2013 National Assembly debate over this bill, the leftist group, including the Socialists, rejected this proposal, condemning it as an opportunistic vote-grabbing strategy on the part of the UMP.[12]

The united front against the UMP's proposal, however, conceals deep discord among leftists, particularly Socialists, over how to address religious coverings in daycare centres and other establishments that are not directly under state control. A number of left-wing politicians, including Prime Minister Manuel Valls, openly supported the daycare manager's position. As a result, they received heavy criticism, drawing condemnations from progressive pluralist associations, including the Ligue des droits de l'homme (Human Rights League) and the Fédération nationale de la libre pensée (National Federation for the Freedom of Thought).

In order to diffuse conflict over the Babyloup Affair, President Hollande turned the question over to the Observatoire de la laïcité (Observatory of Secularism), the consultative body appointed in 2013 to advise his government on questions of laïcité in public services.[13] Made up of twenty-three individuals, mostly representatives in the National Assembly and Senate, civil servants, and scholars, the group is divided in its perspective on laïcité. Both the president and the rapporteur, Jean-Louis Bianco and Nicolas Cadène, are clear advocates of a moderate position, aimed at appeasing conflict over religious dress by reminding the public of the laws that already exist to address these issues. A second contingent within the Observatoire – comprising four of its members – disagreed with this position in the context of the Babyloup daycare debate. While they are no longer members, the Socialist MP (and Gerin commission member) Jean Glavany, Socialist Senator Françoise Laborde, journalist and essayist Patrick Kessel, and philosophy scholar Abdenour Bidar led a campaign to further restrict religious symbols in this and other settings.

Contrary to the wishes of these former members, the Observatoire de la laïcité has so far been a force for moderation in the debate over religious signs. In its advice pertaining to the Babyloup case, which it submitted to the government in October 2013, the group rejected any laws allowing daycare providers to restrict the religious symbols worn by their employees.[14] However, a subsequent reversal by the Cour de Cassation of its original 2013 judgment takes a contrary position. In June 2014, the Court ruled that a private enterprise or association can restrict an employee's freedom to exhibit his or her religion so long as such a restriction is warranted by the "nature of the task," "fulfills an essential professional requirement," and is "proportional to the goals" of the workplace.[15]

In addition to backing proposed legislation applying to daycare employees, dissident members of the Observatoire de la laïcité advocated restricting the headscarf on university campuses. This issue became the subject of a heated debate in February 2015, when, in a situation that had already occurred elsewhere, a professor at the Paris XIII University threatened not to lecture in front of headscarf-wearing students. Days later, the UMP responded with a statement calling for a prohibition of ostentatious religious signs in institutions of higher education. Drafted by the party's Secrétaire nationale aux valeurs de la République et laïcité (National Secretary to the Values of the Republic and Secularism), the statement claimed that: "For several months, incidents in universities that undermine the serenity of teaching have multiplied." The document further maintained that: "As in schools, the public university must be sanctified and neutrality must prevail."[16] Shortly thereafter, and only days before the first round of regional elections of March 2015, the UMP leader Nicolas Sarkozy came out publicly in support of a proposed ban,[17] sparking a media controversy that once again brought parties' competition to "own" the religious signs issue to the forefront of French electoral politics.

Both the UMP and Socialist parties showed signs of disunity when articulating their positions on a potential headscarf ban in universities. In a media interview following Sarkozy's announcement, former UMP prime minister Jean-Pierre Raffarin expressed strong reservations about a ban, arguing that a more effective strategy would be to "appease, rather than stigmatize."[18] The Socialists were similarly divided on the issue. Although the government's official position was a largely neutral one, various members' off-the-cuff remarks suggest that a cleavage existed within the Socialist Party caucus. In March 2015, the secretary of state in charge of women's rights, Pascale Boistard, wavered in her response to journalists' inquiries about a headscarf ban in this context. Admitting that she is "against" the wearing of headscarves in universities, Boistard stopped short of advocating a ban, proposing instead that "It is up to university presidents to dialogue with the students."[19] Similarly, although he previously described a proposed ban of the headscarf in universities as "worthy of interest," the former prime minister Manuel Valls avoided taking a strong position, dodging questions from journalists during a public appearance in Strasbourg.[20]

Criticisms of the UMP and Socialists by their opponents testify to the continued salience of concerns over issue ownership to the way that parties and their critics frame the religious signs issue in France. In a bid to protect its own political territory, the Front National accused Sarkozy of borrowing from the party's script to gain votes in the departmental elections. In a press release, the party stated: "Following his usual habit, Nicolas Sarkozy is chasing after the Front National, pulling out his machine of un-kept promises days before the elections. Not one French citizen remains duped by this electoralist masquerade."[21] The Socialists' more neutral position drew similarly harsh criticism. In an interview with the magazine *Marianne*, feminist writer Élisabeth Badinter stated that she cannot forgive the Socialists for having "abandoned laïcité" during the "headscarf affair" of 1989. It was at that crucial moment, Badinter maintained, that the left, "contrary to its long tradition, allowed religion to enter the public school."[22]

Subsequent instances in the debate over religious signs testify to the continued desire for consensus among politicians in this matter. In the summer of 2016, the mayors of approximately thirty southern communities announced their intention to prohibit the "burkini" – a swimsuit for women that covers the whole body except the face – on public beaches, in the name of laïcité. Despite an August 2016 ordinance by the Conseil d'État – which ruled that any such prohibition would constitute "a grave and manifestly illegal violation of fundamental rights"[23] – the burkini affair became the stage for parties to once again showcase their concern with upholding the boundaries of laïcité. Across the spectrum, the responses were remarkably similar.

Adopting his usual hard stance on the issue, Manuel Valls criticized the burkini, calling it a "provocation" and a demonstration that "radical Islamism" is attempting to "impose itself in the public space."[24] This statement echoed one made days earlier by Sarkozy, who was then campaigning to become the presidential candidate for the Républicains (formerly the UMP) in the 2017 election. In trying to lead the charge against the burkini, Sarkozy described wearing one as a "political, militant act," committed with the goal of "testing the resistance of the Republic." Using the burkini issue as an opportunity to claim ownership of the religious signs issue more broadly, Sarkozy further proposed a law that would "prohibit all ostentatious religious signs, not only in the school, but also in the university, in the public service, and in businesses."[25]

The positions taken by Valls and Sarkozy not only mirrored one another, but also coincided with that of the Front National. Echoing the intensity of her opponents' rejection of the burkini, Marine Le Pen announced in a press release that it is now "up to the French legislator to as soon as possible pass a law that extends the 2004 law in schools by banning ostentatious religious signs in public space." Demonstrating a strong proprietary impulse over the religious signs issue, which trumped that of her opponents, Le Pen added that her party "alone has made this proposal, since 2012."[26]

The tug-of-war among parties for ownership of the religious signs issue in France took on very different dimensions in the context of the 2017 presidential election. That election – which saw the dramatic decline of traditional mainstream parties in favour of non-traditional "outsider" candidates – carved new ideological divisions into the French political landscape. The material and class-centred discourses associated with the left-right axis of competition were diminished in favour of a debate over identity-related themes, such as the nature of patriotism and the place of immigrants in the nation.

In some ways, upheavals in the Socialist Party prior to the 2017 presidential election foreshadowed this outcome. For the first time in French history, the sitting president – François Hollande – did not seek his party's nomination for re-election due to his abysmal approval ratings.[27] His decision to step down in December 2016 cleared the path for Hollande's second-in-command, Manuel Valls, to stand for the Socialists. However, thanks to the unprecedented unpopularity of his administration, Valls was easily knocked out in the second round of the party primaries by Benoit Hamon, the "rebel" candidate, whose radical left program included a proposal to introduce a basic universal income.[28] Hamon also distinguished himself from the pro-business party establishment by supporting a more tolerant and pluralist approach to laïcité, in which Islam is no longer framed as a "problem for the Republic."[29]

While the Socialists chose a candidate for change – one whose secular vision challenged that of the Hollande administration by being less restrictive – the UMP (now Républicains) opted for continued emphasis on the "dangers" of Islam in selecting François Fillon, who was prime minister under Nicolas Sarkozy, to lead them in the 2017 presidential election. A committed Catholic with a socially conservative agenda, Fillon repeatedly claimed that Muslims must "catch-up" to France's other religious communities during his campaign. In a speech, he announced his intention to "impose upon the Muslims of France the communal rules that Christians and Jews – often only after drawn-out struggles – have accepted."[30]

The main challenge to Fillon's candidacy came from Alain Juppé, long-time mayor of Bordeaux and prime minister under Jacques Chirac from 1995 to 1997. Like Hamon for the Socialists, Juppé challenged his party's discourse of fear of the "other," in his case by invoking the notion of *identité heureuse* ("happy identity"),[31] which places hopefulness and optimism at the centre of France's integration discourse. This vision was resoundingly rejected in the second round of the right-wing primaries, in which Fillon received a comfortable 66.5 per cent of votes cast.[32]

Yet, neither of the traditional parties' candidates – Hamon for the Socialists and Fillon for the Républicains – received sufficient votes to advance to the second round in the 2017 presidential election. Once seen as a favourite to win the presidency, Fillon was badly damaged by a judicial investigation into a string of corruption allegations, including one that he had used state funds to pay his wife and children to perform "fake jobs."[33] While he still managed to secure 20.01 per cent of the first round votes – a figure that exceeded Jacques Chirac's first-place finish in 2002 with 19.88 per cent – it landed Mr Fillon in third place. The first-round results were much more dire for the Socialists. Thanks in part to the late-campaign surge of the far-left candidate, Jean-Luc Mélenchon,[34] the party saw its score plummet to 6.4 per cent.

With both of the traditional parties having been knocked out in the first round, the battle for the French presidency was left to two non-traditional candidates: the Front National's Marine Le Pen – who received 21.3 per cent of first-round support – and the young, independent centrist, Emmanuel Macron – who came in first with 24 per cent.[35] Macron's popular En marche! ("Onward!")[36] movement promised to reinvent French politics by challenging the Socialists' and Républicains' monopoly over the instruments of government. Eschewing the labels "left" and "right" in his campaign, Macron also sidestepped any fixed ideology, instead conveying an image of personal and charismatic leadership. His approach combined a liberal and pro-business attitude to the economy with a leftist slant on social issues.[37]

The second-round run-off between Macron and Le Pen was very much a battle between "two Frances": one that saw hope and prosperity in the prospect of a revived economy with close ties to the EU, and one that built on anti-immigrant fears and economic despondency to call for much tightened borders and limited trade. Along with this polarization came new ideological divisions, which no longer reflected the traditional left-right axis of political contention.

A first such division – which Marine Le Pen herself injected into the debate – was that of the Front National's appeal to so-called "patriots" versus the "globalists" allegedly represented by Macron.[38] As has been the case elsewhere in Europe, the 2017 French election was very much dominated by the question of France's position in the EU. For years now, Le Pen has capitalized on the economic dejection of her base to suggest that globalization will, if left unfettered, destroy the French economy and the cultural integrity of the Republic along with it. Describing herself as a "patriot" in the battle to "protect" France, she has frequently deployed apocalyptic imagery, claiming that Macron represents "a morbid continuity, littered with the corpses of jobs transferred offshore, the ruins of bust businesses, and the gaping holes of deficit and debt."[39]

In challenging these claims during the campaign, Macron appropriated the term "patriot" for himself. For example, in his first-round victory speech, he pledged to be "the president of all the people of France, for the patriots facing the threat of nationalism."[40] In this way, Macron sought to reframe the division alleged by Le Pen of "patriots" versus "globalists" to one of "patriots" versus "extreme nationalists."

A second ideological division that gained resonance in the second-round showdown between Macron and Le Pen was that of the so-called "people" versus the "Republic."[41] Particularly in the final weeks of the campaign, Le Pen honed an image of herself as *la candidate du peuple* ("the people's candidate"), which she then juxtaposed against her characterization of Macron as a calculating banker, unconcerned with the plight of French workers. This tactic was illustrated in the highly mediatized stand-off between the two candidates at a Whirlpool dryer factory in the northern town of Amiens, where the workers were striking. Arriving unexpectedly, just as Macron was touring the site, Le Pen stood before a crowd of workers at the factory gate and said: "Everyone knows what side Emmanuel Macron is on – he is on the side of the corporations. I am on the workers' side, here in the car park, not in restaurants in Amiens." She then added: "He's showing disdain for workers, so I've come to see them."[42]

Le Pen tried – although less successfully according to the subsequent polls – to reinforce her image as "the people's candidate" in the *entre deux tours* ("between rounds") debate on 3 May 2017. In her opening remarks, the Front National leader called her opponent "the candidate of unfettered globalization, uberization, precarity, social brutality, and the war of all against all."[43] Macron responded to these remarks by asserting that, while Le Pen speaks for *la France de la colère* ("the France of anger"), he embodies *la France de la conquète* ("the France of the conquest"). His vision of the future, he further claimed, best captures the power and influence of the French language and culture on the world stage.[44]

A third ideological divide, which intersected somewhat with the other two, was that between Macron and Le Pen's competing approaches to the questions of Muslim integration and laïcité. From the outset of the campaign, the En Marche! candidate called for "reconciliation" and "cohesion" with respect to the religious signs issue. While he remained firm in his commitment to "making French citizens of the Muslim culture prouder to be French than to be Muslim,"[45] Macron was also clear in stating that, when it comes to religious signs, "freedom is the rule, and prohibition, the exception."[46] For that reason, he opposed prohibiting the headscarf in universities and the burkini on public beaches. This contrasted with Le Pen's presidential election platform, which included proposals to shut down mosques deemed to have fundamentalist links.[47] Moreover, during the election campaign, Le Pen reiterated her proposal to extend the 2004 ban of "ostentatious" religious signs in schools to all public spaces.[48]

Macron's vision ultimately captured the imaginations of French voters. On 7 May 2017, the thirty-nine-year-old was elected president, with 66.1 per cent of the vote, compared to Le Pen's 33.9.[49] In his victory speech, President Macron sought to unify a divided France, saying: "tonight, there are but French women and men, the people of France reunited."[50] However, the atmosphere of division remained palpable in the wake of Macron's comfortable victory. In delivering her concession speech, a visibly disappointed Le Pen reminded the French public of the divide that supposedly exists between her "patriots" and Macron's "globalists." Foreshadowing the struggles that will likely surround future elections, the Front National leader called on all "patriots" to join her in a "decisive political battle that begins tonight."[51] In setting the stage for such a battle, and recognizing in many ways the transformation effected by the 2017 election result, the party renamed itself Rassemblement national (National Rally, RN) in June 2018.

The 2017 presidential election and its result thus marked a dramatic redrawing of the French political landscape. As the traditional parties faded into the background, so did the former left versus right divide that has long dictated the terms of party political contention. Compared to that left-right axis, the newly formed ideological divisions – those of so-called "patriots" versus "globalists," and "the people" versus "the Republic" – map more directly on to the identity-related themes of nationhood and belonging. Yet, this rearticulation of the electoral terrain has not displaced the party-political consensus formed in 2010 around the curtailment of facial coverings in the French public sphere. If anything, that ostensible consensus has set a precedent for current and future calls to further exclude Islamic symbols from the boundaries of nationhood.

Quebec

Since it took place more recently, the impacts of the 2013 Charter of Values on the dynamics of party competition and on the lived experiences of Quebec Muslims have yet to be fully seen. What *is* clear, however, is that, despite having been sidelined by the Parti Québécois's electoral defeat on 7 April 2014, Bill 60 has shaped the conversation around religious signs debate in Quebec – as well as Muslims' lived experiences – in significant ways.

The upsurge in reports of verbal and physical violence against visibly religious groups in 2013–14 has led many commentators to conclude that the Charter of Values fuelled linguistic, ethnic, and religious tensions in Quebec. As early as September 2013 – before the PQ presented Bill 60 to the National Assembly – national and provincial media outlets began reporting incidents of intimidation, particularly of hijab-wearing women.[52] In one widely reported instance, a man was caught on tape telling a woman on a Montreal city bus to "go back to her country."[53] That same week, a Muslim mother and son shopping in Sainte Foy – a suburb of Quebec City – were approached by a woman yelling "change your religion."[54]

These and numerous other incidents led some Muslim association leaders to conclude that the Charter of Values was contributing to an atmosphere of fear and anxiety in Quebec, with Muslims as the collateral damage. Following the first Montreal bus incident, for example, Samer Majzoub, then president of the Canadian Muslim Forum, rejected suggestions that this was an isolated event by announcing that his organization had received "a lot of reports, people complaining about racist comments, about aggression, about stereotyping."[55]

In response to these allegations, PQ representatives called "on all Quebeckers to have a respectful debate [about the Charter] and to be particularly concerned and sensitive to our citizens who are wearing religious symbols, as is their right."[56] However, reports of intimidation continued to surface throughout the public hearings on Bill 60, and even appeared *after* the election of 7 April 2014, which removed the Charter from the province's policy agenda.[57]

In addition to affecting the lived experiences of Quebec Muslims by inflaming linguistic, ethnic, and religious tensions, the Charter of Values has also impacted the dynamics of political contention in the province. Specifically, it has reinforced the importance of nationhood and identity as the main objects of electoral struggle. Increasingly, however, that struggle has been articulated by Quebec's newer, non-traditional parties – the Coalition avenir Québec and Québec solidaire.

After it won the 2014 provincial election on an anti-Charter platform, the Parti libéral du Québec immediately took measures to demonstrate that it too is committed to upholding the secularity of the state in Quebec. In keeping with some of the recommendations of the Bouchard-Taylor report, the government presented a bill to the National Assembly in 2015, which proposed to prohibit the wearing of facial coverings by providers and users of public services. Bill 62, which would turn this proposal into law, contained additional measures to clarify the meaning of "religious neutrality" in public sector employment and to make such neutrality a legitimate requirement for services provided by companies that are contractually linked to public agencies. But the government also limited the restrictive nature of the bill by specifying, albeit in vague terms, what would constitute a "reasonable" request for exemption of the facial coverings ban.[58]

The consensus among journalists was that Bill 62 represented an attempt by the Couillard government to show that, despite having condemned the Charter of Values, it too is committed to secularism.[59] Yet, other motivating factors may also have played a role. For instance, commentators speculated that the government's proposals were prompted by security concerns in response to international terrorist events.[60] This was corroborated by the fact that Bill 62 was announced shortly after the January 2015 attacks on the headquarters of the French magazine *Charlie Hebdo*, and that the PLQ framed it as part of its agenda to ensure "communication, security, and identification" in the public service.[61]

From the time it was proposed, Bill 62 was the object of intense party political debates. Proponents of the law cited its consistency with the Bouchard-Taylor report – which proposed what many view as a moderate set of secular guidelines – as a condition for their support.[62] However, this justification came into question when Charles Taylor – who co-chaired the commission along with Gérard Bouchard – published an op-ed in *La Presse* in February 2017, in which he retracted his previous support for any religious restrictions. Reproducing the title of the commission's report – *A Time for Reconciliation* – he argued that the definition of public servants in positions of authority has, since 2008, been extended "almost indefinitely, to the point of including teaching and daycare workers, which is something we had not at all envisioned." Taylor also cited the Charter of Values as having created an atmosphere of "stigmatization" in Quebec, which came to a head with the terrorist attack on a Quebec City mosque in February 2017, which killed six people.[63] Published only days after this attack, the article concludes with a warning that the Québécois "cannot afford the luxury of new measures that would renew that effect of stigmatization, however good the intentions of those who would defend them." By way of conclusion, Taylor asked that politicians not "open the wounds again," and instead "make full room for reconciliation."[64]

Taylor's article reinforced Couillard's own uncertainty over Bill 62. Despite having committed – both during and after his 2014 election campaign – to affirming Quebec secularism through legislation, the premier expressed concerns about the potentially divisive and discriminatory effects of laws that target (certain) religious signs in the public sphere. According to journalists, Taylor's "about face" was a "blessing" for Couillard, as it gave him justification to reject any sort of compromise with the opposition.[65] That opposition responded in kind. Asked to comment on Taylor's declaration, for instance, the PQ leader, Jean-François Lisée, said: "I have great respect for Charles Taylor the sociologist, but the argument he presents essentially holds that: if we act [on facial coverings in the public service], it will antagonize extremists, which we don't want to do. It is as though our democratic debate were taken hostage by the least reasonable citizens."[66] CAQ leader François Legault followed suit, suggesting that, while Charles Taylor "can change his mind, Quebeckers have not changed theirs."[67]

There thus remains significant polarization around the question of religious signs in Quebec's political landscape. That polarization is especially visible within the sovereigntist camp. By tying the recommendations of Bill 60 to its nationalist program, Marois's PQ government added fuel to what has been described as a "civil war"[68] among sovereigntists. The two sides of that "war" crystallized in the races to succeed Pauline Marois as leader of the Parti Québécois, one in 2015 and the other in 2016.

The election of media mogul and businessman Pierre Karl Péladeau to succeed Marois as leader of the PQ in 2015 was largely a foregone conclusion. Leading in the polls throughout the campaign, Péladeau prevailed over his opponents in the first round of voting, held in May 2015, earning the support of 58 per cent of the party delegates.[69] Although he had begun the race for leadership advocating a relatively restrictive approach to religious signs – one that coincided with the proposals of the Charter of Values – Péladeau changed tack partway through the campaign, when he proposed a more conciliatory stance that was modelled after the Bouchard-Taylor report. This revised platform, Péladeau told the press, derived from his desire to form "the largest possible consensus" in the matter of religious signs.[70]

While he appeared to desire reconciliation on the question of secularism, Péladeau left no one in doubt as to the strength of his sovereigntist ambitions. Using his business success to position himself as the most equipped of the leadership candidates to manage the economic transition to a sovereign Quebec, Péladeau invited party delegates to imagine a future in which Quebec City could be a nation-state capital "in the same way as Washington, London, and Paris."[71]

Péladeau's victory in May 2015 marked a crucial change in the PQ's positioning within Quebec's electoral politics. It suggested that the party's sovereigntist project would no longer be linked to social democratic goals. Instead, it would be framed as a path to business and economic success. However, less than a year after becoming leader of the PQ, Péladeau resigned from politics on 2 May 2016, citing "family reasons."[72] His departure cleared the path for candidates who subscribed to different visions of Quebec's national and secular future.

Two of the three frontrunners in the 2016 race for the PQ leadership – Alexandre Cloutier and Martine Ouellett – advocated a moderate secular agenda, which aligned with the recommendations of the Bouchard-Taylor report. Their main rival, Jean-François Lisée – who had served in Pauline Marois's cabinet from 2012 to 2014 – opted for a restrictive approach to laïcité, which some of his critics labelled "Charter 3.0." This approach would involve reintroducing measures to forbid the wearing of religious signs by public sector employees.[73]

As the campaign wore on, however, Lisée softened his position, arguing that efforts to forbid "ostentatious" religious signs are discriminatory, since they typically target minorities. Based on these concerns, he maintained, it would be more prudent for Quebec to pursue a "gradual" and "pedagogical" strategy for upholding laïcité in the public sector.[74] Then, once he became leader of the PQ – obtaining just over 50 per cent of votes in the second round held on 6 October 2016[75] – Lisée hardened his position on laïcité once again. In November, the PQ leader proposed to extend the Bouchard-Taylor report's recommended ban of religious signs by public employees in positions of authority to include teachers and daycare workers. Additionally, Lisée proposed to ban the chador – the veil which covers the whole body, but *not* the face – for all state employees.[76]

Like all of the other opposition party members, the PQ voted against the Liberals' proposed Bill 62, when it came to a vote on 18 October 2017, claiming that it did not go nearly far enough. As in the debate over the Charter of Values, moreover, PQ representatives even contended that the PLQ leadership lacks the capacity to identify and appropriately defend Quebec's national interest. According to PQ MNA Agnès Maltais, for instance: "The only consensus that exists on the subject [of secularism] is the opposition parties' unanimous opposition to this law that goes nowhere. Many of us do not share the DNA of the Liberal Party of Québec … After ten years of consultation – it's been ten years since Bouchard-Taylor – no one is rallying to the Liberal position."[77] Not only does it deny outright the potential of a "consensus" around religious signs in Quebec; this statement by Maltais further deems such a "consensus" to be impossible, given the Liberals' allegedly inherent incapacity to reach appropriate conclusions concerning this issue.

Though it faced unanimous rejection by the opposition parties, Bill 62 passed by a comfortable margin of sixty-six to fifty-one in the vote held on 18 October 2017, thanks to the PLQ's majority position in the National Assembly.[78] Yet, the legislation quickly faced significant political and legal challenges. Hours after legislators approved the bill, media and opposition party members began questioning whether its prohibition of facial coverings could feasibly be applied, given the prevalence of other garments – including winter scarves and sunglasses – that similarly conceal the face. Capturing the satirical tone of the ensuing debate, *Toronto Star* columnist Chantal Hébert remarked on the uniqueness of the Quebec government's decision to "declare war on sunglasses."[79]

Bill 62 was further challenged on legal grounds, with some Muslim organizations and civil liberties groups maintaining that the law – as it stood – violates the right to freedom of religion, which is guaranteed by both the Canadian and Québécois Charters. These concerns were echoed in a subsequent court challenge, in which two face veil-wearing women issued sworn statements to Quebec's Superior Court asserting that they fear having to remove their veils to receive government services, and claiming that aggressive responses from the public have increased since the law came into effect.[80] These challenges resulted in a decision by Quebec Superior Court justice Babak Barin to suspend the law until appropriate guidelines for determining which precise garments are to be prohibited, and clear criteria for accommodations, are established.[81]

The PLQ government acquiesced by providing the requested guidelines on 9 May 2018. In a much-anticipated press conference, Minister of Justice Stéphanie Vallée announced that, to be granted, requests for exemption from Bill 62's face-covering ban would need to be "serious and based in sincere belief," as well as demonstrate that the ban impaired the rights of the applicant. The minister further stated that only accommodations that are "reasonable,"[82] and in line with the principles of "equality of all people" and of "the state's religious neutrality," would be granted. The sixth and final criterion announced by Vallée suggests that accommodations will only be granted in cases in which the "person making the request is co-operating in seeking a solution, including making concessions."[83] Individual requests for accommodation, it was further specified, are to be assessed by a designated representative of the public agency in question. These specifications did not prevent Bill 62 from facing further legal push-back, however. In June 2018, another Quebec judge suspended the bill for a second time, concluding in his ruling that it would cause "irreparable harm" to Muslim women.[84]

Vallée's pronouncements sparked renewed criticism from members of the opposition and among some public commentators. Resuming her critique of the Liberals' secularist program, the PQ's Agnès Maltais accused the government of offloading the responsibility to adjudicate accommodation requests onto public employees, thus failing once again to take a firm and definitive stand on legally upholding the religious neutrality of the province. In her words: "The hot potato again lands on the shoulders of the person sitting in front of the person asking for an accommodation. The law is not sufficiently strict."[85]

The other opposition parties echoed the PQ's characterization of Bill 62 as further proof of the Liberals' ineffectiveness in the matter of state religious neutrality. The CAQ's Nathalie Roy responded to the government's proposed guidelines by asserting that "It was a hodgepodge, now it's a catch-all."[86] Roy's colleague, justice critic Simon Jolin-Barrette, followed suit when he pronounced that, with Bill 62 to take effect on 1 July 2018, "absolutely nothing is resolved. We are still at the same place we were: [state employees] in positions of authority can still don religious symbols."[87]

Conflicting visions of Quebec's national future continue to loom large in these debates. While vacillating somewhat on the question of secularism, recent PQ leaders have been firm in advocating a cautious approach to sovereignty. Convinced that talk of holding a third referendum has threatened the PQ's chances at the ballot box in the past, Lisée promised that, as premier, he would implement a moratorium on referenda until 2022.[88] The PQ leader's supporters were optimistic that this move would limit the PLQ's ability to "stir up passions by brandishing the effigy of a referendum."[89] Lisée also moved to broaden the PQ base by toning down the party's approach to the hot-button issue of language. While promising that, if elected, he would move ahead with extending the provisions of Bill 101 (the legislative cornerstone of Quebec's official language policy) to medium-sized businesses, Lisée also pledged to allow municipalities to keep their bilingual status and to entrench anglophone rights in the party's manifesto.[90]

At the same time as he reoriented the PQ's platform around principles for governing Quebec as a province, rather than transforming it into an independent nation-state, Lisée worked to reconsolidate, and take the helm of, the sovereignty movement. As I discussed in chapters 3 and 5, the PQ's shift toward an anti-immigrant agenda under Marois led some voters to shift their allegiance to Québec solidaire, thus splitting the sovereigntist vote. It was among Lisée's main objectives, therefore, to foster a merger of the two parties, thus re-establishing the PQ as the central voice for sovereignty in Quebec politics.

The leaders of Québec solidaire have so far turned down these invitations. However, the party *did* agree to a strategy of convergence, in which the two parties – along with Option nationale (National Option, ON), a third pro-independence party, which merged with QS to form a single party in late 2017 – refrain from contesting each other's candidates in certain ridings, so as to avoid splitting the sovereigntist vote.[91]

Whether QS should maintain this strategy of convergence was a key object of debate among the candidates vying to replace Amir Khadir as the party's male spokesperson in May 2017. Labelling himself the "candidate for political convergence," Jean-François Lessard launched a website entitled Alliance populaire du Québec (Quebec Popular Alliance), which outlines the reasons why the Parti Québécois and Québec solidaire should cooperate to defeat the Liberals in the 2018 provincial election. According to the site, such cooperation would not override these parties' differing positions in other matters, such as the economy.[92] Gabriel Nadeau-Dubois, the candidate who succeeded in replacing Khadir as co-spokesperson of QS in May 2017, claims to advocate a more "moderate" and "prudent" approach to inter-party convergence. While willing to cooperate with the PQ to prevent Liberal victories in select ridings, he has drawn a strict boundary between QS and its sovereigntist ally on economic policy, warning in an interview that the Québécois "must not replace the red neo-liberals [the PLQ] with blue neo-liberals [the PQ]."[93]

Jean-François Lisée tried to deflect these criticisms, and save the PQ from possible extinction, by resuscitating his party's economically progressive legacy. Tying his cautious two-term sovereigntist approach to a program to rebuild the welfare state, the PQ leader espoused the slogan "A strong state to achieve independence" during his party's convention in 2018. Using this strategy to carve out a distinctive territory within Quebec electoral politics, Lisée further denounced his opponents in the PLQ and CAQ as intent on keeping Quebec "in a permanent state of austerity."[94] Despite efforts to appease its progressive flank, and renew Quebeckers' "taste for sovereignty" by reinvesting in a state-centred economic program,[95] the PQ continued to occupy a tenuous – and some would say untenable – position within Quebec politics. Poll after poll suggests that the public is at best ambivalent about sovereignty, and emerging academic research indicates that the growing vote share of millennials could threaten the resonance of independence and the PQ long-term.[96] As such, promising to delay a referendum was perceived as the only path to gaining office in 2018.

This promise proved vastly insufficient in securing support for the PQ, however. To the contrary, as the October election approached, the party plummeted in the polls, while the non-traditional CAQ and QS parties grew in voters' esteem. Taking advantage of the PQ's internal strife and indecision over sovereignty, and building on Quebec residents' growing distrust for the Liberals, the CAQ sky-rocketed to power, earning 37.41 per cent of the popular vote and establishing a comfortable majority in the National Assembly. This victory proved devastating for both the Liberals – who obtained less than a quarter of the vote – and the Parti Québécois – whose inability to surpass the 20 per cent threshold cost the party its official status and prompted Lisée to step down as leader.[97]

As in the 2014 election, questions of national identity were at the top of the 2018 election agenda. Among the CAQ's main promises was to slash immigration levels from 50,000 a year to 40,000.[98] The party also resuscitated Quebec's language debate when it proposed to impose a values test and French-language assessment on immigrants wishing to become Canadian citizens. Those who failed such a test would risk losing their selection certificate and could even be subject to deportation.[99] The newly elected government also wasted no time in reigniting the religious signs debate, by indicating its willingness to invoke the notwithstanding clause in order to prohibit the wearing of "ostentatious" religious signs among public elementary and secondary school teachers.[100]

While the exact implications of the CAQ's victory for religious rights in Quebec remain to be seen, one thing is certain: the "national question" remains a – if not *the* – primary object of party political contention in the province's electoral system. It has, as I have shown, impacted the ways parties respond to successive challenges around religious diversity, with important implications for ways of articulating Muslims' and other minorities' material and symbolic belonging to the nation. The recent fracturing of Quebec's political system also suggests that the religious signs debate is generating new cleavages, which intersect in complex ways with the nation-centred axis of competition. Thus, not only do the dynamics of party political contestation shape outcomes with respect to the religious signs debates; those outcomes in turn can redefine the boundaries and content of political struggle.

Appendix

Data and Methods

In order to analyze how electoral contexts and processes shaped the demarcation of the boundaries of nationhood in France's face veil debate, I conducted a detailed qualitative analysis of the 2009 Gerin commission and its surrounding debates. Primary data sources for this portion of the study include the Gerin commission's 200-page report and the full 400-page transcripts of its deliberations, including presentations by all seventy-eight of its invited participants. I also spent the months of October 2012 and March, April, and October 2013 conducting interviews in Paris and Lyon, France. Of a total of twenty-nine interviews, nine were conducted with politicians who were members of the commission board (see table A.1), ten with individuals belonging to various organizations who appeared before the commission as participants (see table A.2), and ten with other individual actors who did not appear before the commission but played a key role in the surrounding public debate (see table A.3).

My methods for recruiting participants differed according to the type of interviewee in question. For Gerin commission members, I used email contact information provided on the French National Assembly's official website. I then drew from the list of commission participants to identify relevant organizations, finding contact information for most of these online. These initial interviews then led me to discover other key actors, whom I contacted via referrals from prior interviewees. Because all participants are public figures – either public officials, political party members, interest group representatives, or well-known academics – and given the relatively small number of individuals prominently involved in the Gerin commission and surrounding debates, I did not guarantee anonymity to my interviewees.

Table A.1
Interviews with members of the Gerin commission (France)

Name	*Party affiliation*
André Gerin	Parti communiste français (PCF)
Jacques Myard	Union pour un mouvement populaire (UMP)
Georges Mothron	Union pour un mouvement populaire (UMP)
Nicole Améline	Union pour un mouvement populaire (UMP)
Jean Glavany	Parti socialiste (PS)
Christian Bataille	Parti socialiste (PS)
Danièle Hoffman-Rispal	Parti socialiste (PS)
Sandrine Mazetier	Parti socialiste (PS)
François de Rugy	Parti Vert

The Office of Research Ethics at the University of Toronto provided ethics approval for the project in May 2012.

Lasting 40–120 minutes, interviews were open-ended and touched on a wide range of questions. I began each conversation by asking the respondent to describe his or her personal role in the French face veil debate. Having established the basic facts of each participant's involvement, I then asked them to describe the key actors, ideas, and institutions underpinning the 2010 law. In the case of politicians directly implicated in the process of passing this law, I inquired about the dynamics of contention in the National Assembly, about the sources of agreement and disagreement with their political foes, and about internal party dynamics during this period. When interviewing civil society actors, I asked about goals and strategies for gaining traction in the face veil debate, about their allies and opponents in the electoral field, and about the discourses that they deployed when engaging publicly with this issue.

Interview data for the French case was supplemented with evidence obtained through participant observation in lectures, conferences, and organizational meetings pertaining to the face veil ban and its surrounding debates. Lectures and conferences include: (1) a lecture by sociology professor Jean Baubérot entitled "La laïcité falsifiée" (Falsified Secularism) organized by Plateforme de Paris (Paris Platform) and delivered on 24 September 2012; (2) a one-day conference entitled "Laïcité et collectivités locales" (Secularism and local collectivities) attended by academics, legal experts, and public servants in Paris on 9 October 2012; (3) an academic seminar on Islamophobia hosted

Table A.2
Interviews with participants in the Gerin commission (France)

Organization name	*Organization type*	*Interviewee name*
Ligue du droit international des femmes (International League for Women's Rights)	Feminist	Annie Sugier
Regards de femmes (Women's Outlooks)	Feminist	Michèle Vianès
Collectif des féministes pour l'égalité (Collective of Feminists for Equality)	Feminist	Ismahane Chouder
Égalité Laïcité Europe (Equality Secularism Europe)	Feminist	Martine Cerf
Riposte Laique (Secular Answers)	Secular	Pascal Hilout
Ligue des droits de l'homme (Human Rights League)	Secular	Jean-Pierre Dubois
Fédération nationale de la libre pensée (National Federation for the Freedom of Thought)	Secular	Marc Blondel and Christian Eyschen
Conseil d'État (Council of State)	State/legal	Remy Schwartz
École Pratique des Hautes Études (Practical Institute for Higher Learning)	Academic	Jean Baubérot

Table A.3
Other interviews (France)

Name	*Role/Occupation*
Alain Seksig	Inspector general of national education
Nicolas Cadène	Socialist MP and secretary of the Observatoire de la laïcité (Observatory of Secularism)
Patrick Weil	Political Scientist, director of research at the Centre national de la recherche scientifique (National Centre for Scientific Research)
Christine Delphy	Feminist scholar
Naima Bouteldja	Author of 2011 Open Society report on veiled women in France
Eric Thiers	Advisor and division chief, Division du secrétariat de la Commission des lois constitutionnelles, de la legislation et de l'administration générale de la République (Division of the Secretariat of the Commission of Constitutional Laws, of Legislation, and of the General Administration of the Republic)
Pierre Tévanian	Member of feminist organization Une école pour tous et toutes (A School for All)
Ndella Paye, Anissa Fathi, and Youssra H	Members of feminist organization Mamans toutes égales (Mothers for Equality)

by Sciences Po in Paris on 3 April 2013; (4) a two-day academic conference on laïcité organized by the Centre national de la recherche scientifique (National Centre for Scientific Research, CNRS) in Paris on 11–12 April 2013; (5) a two-day academic conference entitled Enseignement laique de la morale et enseignement des faits religieux (Teaching Secular Morality and Religious History) organized by the Institut européen en sciences des religions (European Institute for the Scientific Study of Religions) in Paris on 18–19 October, 2013; and (6) a symposium entitled "La laïcité en actes" (Laïcité in action) organized by the Association de culture berbère (Berber Cultural Association, ACB) in Paris on 26 October 2013. In addition, I attended an event organized by the pro-laïcité feminist organization Regards de femmes (Women's Outlooks) at a Paris café on 23 April 2013. It was attended by numerous feminist organization representatives and the author Jeanette Bougrab, a lawyer of Algerian background who supports the restriction of Islamic religious signs.

In order to study the relationship between electoral contexts and processes and the production of Québécois nationhood in the context of the Charter of Values, I draw on primary evidence pertaining to party politicians' and civil society actors' involvement in the surrounding debate. To capture the role of politicians, I draw primarily from parliamentary debates, and the documents and press releases issued by the major opposition parties. I cover the eighteen parliamentary sessions in which the Charter of Values was debated between 25 September 2013 – when the first discussion of the Charter took place in parliament – and 20 February 2014 – the date of the last parliamentary session prior to the calling of an election on 5 March 2014. Press releases by the major opposition parties cover the period from 15 August 2013 to 7 April 2014, and include nine statements by the Parti libéral du Québec (PLQ), eleven by the Coalition avenir Québec (CAQ), and thirteen by Québec solidaire (QS). I supplement this data with interviews I conducted with Nathalie Roy, the Coalition avenir Québec (CAQ) spokesperson in matters of immigration, secularism, integrity, and the status of women, and with Amir Khadir, co-president of Québec solidaire at the time (see table A.4).

To capture the influence of civil society actors in deliberations surrounding the Charter of Values, I turn to the parliamentary hearings organized by the Parti Québécois government to tap public responses to Bill 60, which would make the Charter into law. Between January and late February 2014, representatives of Quebec's National Assembly heard the testimonies of sixty-nine individuals and organizations. Ten additional presentations scheduled for March 2014 were cancelled when the PQ government called a provincial election on 5 March 2014. In addition to the total seventy-nine briefs made public on the government website, I analyzed those of another six organizations known to play a key role in the Charter debate but whose briefs did not make it into the public record. These include briefs by the Quebec Bar Association; Indépendantistes pour une laïcité inclusive (Separatists for an Inclusive Secularism); the Commission des droits de la personne et des droits de la jeunesse (Human Rights and Youth Rights Commission); the Association des juristes progressistes (Association of Progressive Jurists); the Fédération des femmes du Québec (Quebec Women's Federation); and the Conseil du statut de la femme

Table A.4
Interviews with politicians (Quebec)

Name	*Party affiliation*
Nathalie Roy	Coalition avenir Québec (CAQ)
Amir Khadir	Québec solidaire (QS)

(Council for the Status of Women). I supplement this evidence with interviews I conducted with civil society actors participating in the public hearings and surrounding debates (see table A.5) and with four prominent members of the Bouchard-Taylor commission (see table A.6).

As in the French case, interviews consisted of open-ended questions and lasted 40–120 minutes. When interviewing politicians, I posed questions aimed at probing the dynamics of competition between and within political parties in the National Assembly, at identifying key sources of agreement and disagreement with competitors, and at gaining insight into the internal party mechanisms for deciding which positions to put forward with respect to the religious signs issue in general and the Charter of Values in particular. Exchanges with civil society actors were geared primarily to gaining a sense of the field of organizations involved in the Charter of Values debate, to probing the mandates and internal decision-making procedures of the specific organizations in question, and to identifying the main sources of agreement and discord between differently positioned actors. A final set of interviews, those conducted with members of the Bouchard-Taylor commission, was undertaken with the aim of understanding the mechanisms for reaching conclusions and generating recommendations with regard to religious accommodation in Quebec.

In my study of both the French and Québécois cases, I coded and analyzed field notes from events attended, as well as textual and interview data pertaining to the Gerin commission and the Charter of Values debate, through a multi-step iterative process. After noting which themes were most prevalent in a first open round of coding in Nvivo, I then grouped codes together into broader themes and conducted focused coding to understand (1) how the electoral context and estab-

Table A.5
Interviews with organization members (Quebec)

Organization name	*Organization type*	*Interviewee name*
Conseil du Statut de la Femme (Council for the Status of Women)	Feminist	Leila Lesbet, Julie Latour
Fédération des Femmes du Québec (Quebec Women's Federation)	Feminist	Bochra Manai, Krista Riley
Association féminine d'éducation et d'action sociale (Women's Association for Education and Social Action)	Feminist	Marylise Hamelin
Pour les droits des femmes du Québec (For the Rights of Women in Quebec)	Feminist	Diane Guilbault, Leila Lesbet, "Céline"
Collective des féministes musulmanes du Québec (Collective of Muslim Feminists of Quebec)	Feminist	Bochra Manai, Krista Riley
Mouvement laïque québécois (Secular movement of Quebec)	Secular	Michel Lincourt
Indépendantistes pour une laïcité inclusive (Sovereigntists for an Inclusive Secularism)	Sovereigntist	Jean Dorion
Juristes pour la laïcité et la neutralité religieuse de l'état (Jurists for Secularism and the Religious Neutrality of the State)	Legal	Julie Latour
Barreau du Québec (Quebec Bar Association)	Legal	Pierre Bosset
Association des musulmans et des arabes pour la laïcité au Québec (Muslims and Arabs for Secularism in Quebec).	Cultural/religious	Haroun Bouazzi

Table A.6
Interviews with actors in Bouchard-Taylor commission (Quebec)

Name	*Role/Occupation*
Gérard Bouchard	Professor of sociology, Université du Québec à Chicoutimi; co-chair of Bouchard-Taylor commission
Charles Taylor	Professor emeritus, philosophy, McGill University; co-chair of Bouchard-Taylor commission
Jacques Beauchemin	Professor of sociology, Université du Québec à Montréal; advisor to the Bouchard-Taylor commission
Daniel Weinstock	Professor, Faculty of Law, McGill University; advisor to the Bouchard-Taylor commission

lished processes of party political contention shaped parties' competition for issue ownership during the period surrounding France's 2010 ban of face coverings and Quebec's 2013 Charter of Values and (2) how the resulting discourses define nationhood, religion, secularism, and belonging in the two societies.

Notes

INTRODUCTION

1 Jean Raspail, "Serons-nous encore français dans trente ans?," *Figaro Magazine*, 26 October 1985, author's translation.

2 Valéry Giscard d'Estaing, "Immigration ou invasion?," *Figaro Magazine*, 21 September 1991, author's translation.

3 Jim Jarassé, "Nicolas Sarkozy défend le projet de loi sur la burqa," *Le Figaro*, 19 May 2010, author's translation.

4 Manuel Valls, "Déclaration de Manuel Valls, ministre de l'intérieur, en réponse à une question sur l'application de la loi du 11 octobre 2010 concernant le port du voile intégral, à l'Assemblée Nationale le 23 juillet 2013 (2013). Ministère de l'intérieur."

5 Gagnon and Iacovino, *Federalism, Citizenship, and Québec*.

6 Baubérot and Milot, *Laïcités sans frontières*; Koussens, "Comment les partis politiques québécois se représentent-ils la laïcité?"; Koussens, "Neutrality of the State"; Koussens, "Religious Diversity"; Milot, *Laïcité dans le nouveau monde*.

7 Koussens, "Religious Diversity," 4.

8 "Public sector employees" includes those working in the ministries, in government institutions, in public elementary and secondary schools, in *centres de petite enfance* and private subsidized daycares, as well as judges, police officers, and employees of correctional institutions. Health care institutions, CEGEPs, universities, municipalities, and constituency offices would be exempt for five years on a renewable basis. Elected officials would also be exempt from the Charter's requirement regarding ostentatious religious signs (Drainville, *Charter*).

9 Many authors use the term “Quebecker” when writing about the population of Quebec in English. However, I follow others (Zubrzycki 2016) in adopting the French adjective “Québécois” because, first, it is a cornerstone of the territorial definition of Quebec nationhood that has framed discussions of the province’s identity since the Quiet Revolution of the 1960s (Juteau, “‘Pures laines’”) and, second, this territorial identity is so heavily anchored in the French language.

10 Bill 62 contains additional measures to clarify the meaning of “religious neutrality” in public sector employment; to make such neutrality a legitimate requirement for services provided by companies that are contractually linked to public agencies; and to specify what constitutes a “reasonable” request for accommodation of religious signs and practices.

11 Boundary formation has become a key analytic device in theorizing processes of symbolic and social differentiation in various social groupings (Lamont and Molnar, “Study of Boundaries”). In its early usage, the notion of boundaries was employed primarily to conceptualize the production of ethnic group similarities and differences (Barth 1969). In a more recent and ambitious effort to draw conceptual links between theories of boundary formation, ethnic identity, and ethnic conflict, Wimmer (2008) introduces a multi-level process framework to explain how group characteristics are generated and transformed over time. According to the model he develops, four factors account for variation in the characteristics of ethnicity across cases: institutions, power, and networks; conflict and consensus; boundary closure and differentiation; and boundary stability and path dependency. Institutions, power, and networks determine the boundary strategies that actors pursue and where boundaries are drawn. Depending on whether there are overlapping interests across boundaries, group interaction may result in conflict or consensus. Moreover, the higher the degree of ethnic inequality between groups and the more encompassing the consensus between actors belonging to the same group, the more closed and differentiated the boundary. Socially closed ethnic groups, Wimmer (“Making and Unmaking”) concludes, will tend to produce higher levels of identification and stable boundaries through path dependency.

12 Gellner, *Nations and Nationalism*.

13 Smith, *The Ethnic Origins of Nations*.

14 Anderson, *Imagined Communities*.

15 Calhoun, *Nationalism*; De Cilia, Reisigl, and Wodak, “The Discursive Construction of National Identities”; Zimmer, “Boundary Mechanisms and Symbolic Resources.”

16 Brubaker, *Citizenship and Nationhood*.

17 Yuval-Davis, *The Politics of Belonging*, 20.
18 Korteweg and Yurdakul, *The Headscarf Debates*, 3.
19 Al-Saji, "The Racialization of Muslim Veils"; Amiraux, "De l'empire à la république"; Bilge, "Beyond Subordination vs. Resistance."
20 Hajjat and Mohammed, *Islamophobie.*
21 Meer, "Islamophobia and Postcolonialism."
22 Sheehi, *Islamophobia*.
23 Bilge, "Beyond Subordination vs. Resistance"; Korteweg, "The Sharia Debate in Ontario"; Korteweg and Yurdakul, *The Headscarf Debates*; Salzbrunn, "Performing Gender and Religion"; Scott, "Symptomatic Politics"; Scott, *The Politics of the Veil.*
24 See also: Ahmed-Gosh, "Dilemmas of Islamic"; Bilge, "Beyond Subordination vs. Resistance"; Dot-Pouillard, "Les recompositions politiques"; Killian, "The Other Side of the Veil"; O'Neill, Gidengil, Côté, and Young, "Freedom of Religion."
25 Farris, *In the Name of Women's Rights*.
26 Ahmed, *Strange Encounters*; Mohanty, "Under Western Eyes"; Yegenoglu, *Colonial Fantasies*.
27 Amiraux, "De l'Empire à la République."
28 de Leon, Desai, and Tugal, "Political Articulation," *Building Blocs*.
29 A preliminary version of this argument with respect to the French case can be found in my sole-authored article 'We are all Republicans': Political Articulation and the Production of Nationhood in France's Face Veil Debate," published by *Comparative Studies in Society and History* in 2018. In terms of the France-Quebec comparison, readers may also be interested in a co-authored study, with Anna C. Korteweg, entitled "Party Competition and the Production of Nationhood in the Immigration Context: Particularizing the Universal for Political Gain in France and Québec," also published in 2018.
30 Somers, "Narrativity, Narrative Identity, and Social Action"; Somers and Gibson, "Reclaiming the Epistemological 'Other'"; Tilly, "To Explain Political Processes"; Tilly, *Stories, Identities, and Political Change*.
31 Somers, "Narrativity, Narrative Identity, and Social Action," 594.
32 Ibid., 598.
33 Tilly, "To Explain Political Processes," 1595.
34 Ibid.
35 Somers, "Narrativity, Narrative Identity, and Social Action," 593.
36 Berezin, *Illiberal Politics in Neoliberal Times*; Brubaker, *Nationalism Reframed*; Sewell, "Historical Events as Transformations."
37 Sewell, "Historical Events as Transformations," 843.

38 Berezin, *Illiberal Politics in Neoliberal Times*, 56.
39 "MP" – for "member of parliament" – is the term used by the English-language version of the French National Assembly website: http://www2.assemblee-nationale.fr/langues/welcome-to-the-english-website-of-the-french-national-assembly#node_9511.
40 Gerin, "Rapport d'information."
41 Assemblée Nationale de France. *Proposition de loi interdisant le port de tenues ou d'accessoires ayant pour effet de dissimuler le visage dans les lieux ouverts au public et sur la voie publique*, Pub. L. No. 2283. 5 February 2010, http://www.assemblee-nationale.fr/13/propositions/pion2283.asp, author's translation.
42 Drainville, "Charte affirmant les valeurs."
43 Frosh and Wolfsfeld, "ImagiNation," 106.
44 Helbling and Tresch, "Measuring party positions," 176.
45 Ibid., 177.

CHAPTER ONE

1 Jon Henley, "Europe's Governments Signal Relief after Dutch Election Defeats Far Right," *The Guardian*, 16 March 2017.
2 Philip Oltermann, "Angela Merkel Endorses Party's Call for Partial Ban on Burqa and Niqab," *The Guardian*, 6 December 2016.
3 Brubaker, *Citizenship and Nationhood*.
4 Alba and Foner, "Comparing Immigrant Integration."
5 Favell, *Philosophies of Integration*.
6 Zubrzycki, "'We, the Polish Nation.'"
7 Brubaker, *Citizenship and Nationhood*.
8 Esping-Andersen, *Three Worlds of Welfare Capitalism*; Lewis, "Gender and the Development"; Orloff, "Gender and the Social Rights."
9 Ahmed, *Strange Encounters*; Benhabib, "The Return of Political Theology."
10 Milot, *Laïcité dans le nouveau monde*.
11 Korteweg and Yurdakul, *The Headscarf Debates*.
12 Laborde, "The Culture(s) of the Republic," 720.
13 Laborde, *Critical Republicanism*, 4.
14 Ibid.
15 Brubaker, *Citizenship and Nationhood*.
16 See Simon, "Contested Citizenship in France," for an update on the republican "consensus" post-1990s.
17 Kawar, "Juridical Framings of Immigrants."
18 Favell, *Philosophies of Integration*.

19 Giry, "France and Its Muslims."
20 Gokariksel and Mitchell, "Veiling, Secularism."
21 Lefebvre, "Republicanism and Universalism."
22 Thomas, "Keeping Identity at a Distance."
23 Silverman, "The French Republic Unveiled."
24 Scott, "Symptomatic Politics."
25 Lépinard, "Migrating Concepts"; Wiles, "Headscarves, Human Rights."
26 Soper and Fetzer, "Explaining the Accommodation"; Soper and Fetzer, "Religious Institutions, Church-State History."
27 Baubérot, *Les Sept Laïcités Françaises*; Bowen, "A View from France"; Joppke, "State Neutrality"; Laborde, "On Republican Toleration."
28 Laborde, "On Republican Toleration." Other scholars similarly identify the diverging interpretations of *laïcité* in France. For instance, Weill discusses the divide between "eradicators" and "moderates" in the secular movement. See Weill, "What's in a Scarf?" Similarly, Kuru addresses the dichotomy between "assertive secularism" and "passive secularism." See Kuru, "Passive and Assertive Secularism." Jennings emphasizes the distinction between "traditional," "modernizing," and "multicultural" republicanism. See Jennings, "Citizenship, Republicanism and Multiculturalism."
29 Gouvernement du Québec, "Au Québec pour bâtir ensemble," author's translation.
30 Bouchard, "What Is Interculturalism?," 451, 463–4. For an extensive analysis of interculturalism, see also Bouchard, *L'interculturalisme*.
31 Bouchard and Taylor, "Building the Future."
32 David, "Charte de la laïcité de l'état québécois"; Parti libéral du Québec, "Déclaration identité québécoise."
33 Bouchard, "What Is Interculturalism?"
34 Blad and Couton, "The Rise of an Intercultural Nation"; Gagnon and Iacovino, "Interculturalism"; Juteau, "The Citizen Makes an Entrée."
35 Zubrzycki, "Negotiating Pluralism in Québec."
36 Laxer, Carson, and Korteweg, "Articulating Minority Nationhood."
37 Pierson, *Politics in Time*.
38 Bleich, "Integrating Ideas into Policy-Making Analysis"; Campbell, "Ideas, Politics, and Public Policy"; Surel, "The Role of Cognitive and Normative Frames."
39 Hall, "Policy Paradigms, Social Learning," 289.
40 Ferree, "Resonance and Radicalism"; Tilly and Tarrow, *Contentious Politics*.
41 Pierson, "Increasing Returns."

42 Bleich, "Integrating Ideas into Policy-Making Analysis," 1056–7.
43 Bowen, "A View from France."
44 Conseil d'État, "Étude Relative Aux Possibilités Juridiques D'interdiction Du Port Du Voile Intégral," 30–5. Also charged with assessing the proposed law's compatibility with the French Constitution, the Conseil Constitutionnel (France's highest constitutional authority) gave its approval in a decision released on 7 October 2010 (Conseil Constitutionnel, 2010).
45 Joppke and Torpey, *Legal Integration of Islam*.
46 *O'Malley and Ontario Human Rights Commission v. Simpsons-Sears Limited*, 1985 SCC, [1985] 2 SCR 536.
47 Beaman, "Conclusion."
48 *Alberta v. Hutterian Brethren of Wilson Colony and Hutterian Brethren Church of Wilson*, 2009 SCC 37, [2009] 2 SCR 567.
49 Barreau du Québec, "Mémoire du Barreau du Québec"; Commission des droits de la personne et des droits de la jeunesse, "Mémoire à la commission des institutions."
50 Morel, "La coexistence des Chartes"; *Chaoulli v. Quebec (Attorney General)*, 2005 SCC 35, [2005] 1 SCR 791.
51 *Chaoulli v. Quebec (Attorney General)*, 2005 SCC 35, [2005] 1 SCR 791.
52 This option was suggested by numerous organizations in the Charter of Values debate. See, for example: Coalition Laïcité Québec, "Mémoire présenté à la commission"; Mouvement laïque Québécois, "Charte de La Laïcité"; Rassemblement pour la laïcité, "Mémoire Sur Le Projet de Loi."
53 Initially, the notwithstanding clause was used extensively by the Quebec government. Following the establishment of the federal Charter in 1982, the PQ Government of René Lévesque protested its enactment by invoking the notwithstanding clause in every single piece of Quebec legislation. This practice came to an end when the PLQ won the election of 1987 under Robert Bourassa. The Liberal government itself invoked the notwithstanding clause in 1988 after the Supreme Court of Canada struck down the province's law restricting the posting of certain commercial signs in languages other than French. However, Mr Bourassa amended that legislation in 1993 in order to bring it in line with the federal constitution to obviate the need to renew the clause for another five years.
54 Marco Fortier, "L'effet PKP profite aux libéraux de Couillard," *Le Devoir*, 15 March 2014.
55 Statham and Geddes, "Elites and the 'Organised Public.'"

56 For an exception, see: Joppke and Torpey, *Legal Integration of Islam.*

57 Bale, "Turning Round the Telescope," 316.

58 Triadafilopoulos and Zaslove, "Influencing Migration Policy."

59 Schain, "Commentary: Why Political Parties Matter," 465.

60 Lipset and Rokkan, "Cleavage Structure."

61 Evans, Rueschemeyer, and Skocpol, eds., *Bringing the State Back In*; Skocpol, *States and Social Revolutions.*

62 Brooks and Manza, "Do Changing Values Explain"; Clark and Lipset, "Are Social Classes Dying?"; Clark, Lipset, and Rempel, "The Declining Political Significance of Social Class"; Inglehart, *Culture Shift in Advanced Industrial Societies*; Inglehart and Rabier, "Political Realignment"; Lipset, "The Decline of Class Ideologies"; Lipset and Rokkan, "Cleavage Structure"; Pakulski, "The Dying of Class"; Putnam, "Bowling Alone."

63 Inglehart and Rabier, "Political Realignment."

64 Lipset, "The Decline of Class Ideologies."

65 Inglehart and Rabier, "Political Realignment."

66 Fraser, "From Redistribution to Recognition"; Fraser and Honneth. *Redistribution or Recognition?*

67 Bale, "Politics Matters," 453 (emphasis added).

68 de Leon, Desai, and Tugal, eds., *Building Blocs*; Mair, "Political Parties, Popular Legitimacy"; Pakulski and Waters, "The Reshaping and Dissolution."

69 Hayes, "Party Reputations, Journalistic Expectations."

70 Pakulski and Waters, "The Reshaping and Dissolution."

71 de Leon, Desai, and Tugal, eds., *Building Blocs*, 27.

72 de Leon, Desai, and Tugal, "Political Articulation," 198.

73 de Leon, Desai, and Tugal, eds., *Building Blocs*, 4–5.

74 Taggart, "New Populist Parties," 47.

75 Berezin, *Illiberal Politics in Neoliberal Times*; Betz, "The New Front National"; Kriesi, Grande, Lachat, Dolezal, Bornschier, and Frey, "Globalization and the Transformation."

76 Mudde, "The 2012 Stein Rokkan Lecture."

77 Betz, "The New Politics of Resentment"; Taggart, "New Populist Parties."

78 Rydgren, "Is Extreme Right-Wing Populism Contagious?"

79 Semyonov, Raijman, and Gorodzeisky, "The Rise of Anti-Foreigner Sentiment"; Yilmaz, "Right-Wing Hegemony"; Zuquete, "The European Extreme-Right."

80 Howard, "The Impact of the Far Right."

81 Schain, "The National Front in France," 232–3.
82 Veugelers, "A Challenge for Political Sociology."
83 Kriesi, Grande, Lachat, Dolezal, Bornschier, and Frey, "Globalization and the Transformation," 922; see also Müller, *What Is Populism?*; Mudde, "The Populist Radical Right," "The 2012 Stein Rokkan Lecture."
84 Berezin, *Illiberal Politics in Neoliberal Times*.
85 Veugelers, "A Challenge for Political Sociology," 79.
86 Taggart, "New Populist Parties."
87 Veugelers, "A Challenge for Political Sociology," 80.
88 Müller, *What Is Populism?*, 97.
89 Cas Mudde, "The Far Right in the 2014 European Elections: Of Earthquakes, Cartels, and Designer Fascists," *The Washington Post*, 30 May 2014.
90 de Leon, Desai, and Tugal, "Political Articulation."
91 Eidlin, "Why Is There No Labor Party in the United States?," 495.
92 Ibid., 505.
93 Rovny and Edwards, "Struggle over Dimensionality," 59.
94 Kitschelt, "European Party Systems."
95 Ladrech, "Social Movements and Party Systems."
96 Tiberj, "La politique des deux axes."
97 Andersen and Evans, "The Stability of French Political Space."
98 Anderson, "Economic Voting and Multilevel Governance."
99 Dufour, "From Protest to Partisan Politics"; Tanguay, "Sclerosis or a Clean Bill of Health?"
100 Benjamin Shingler, "Quebec Elects CAQ Majority Government, Liberals See Historic Losses," *CBC News*, 1 October 2018.
101 In the two previous provincial elections in which it presented candidates, the CAQ secured approximately one-quarter of the vote (27 per cent in 2012 and 23 per cent in 2014).
102 Brym, Gillespie, and Lenton, "Class Power, Class Mobilization."
103 Andersen, "The Class-Party Relationship"; Lipset, *Political Man*; Pinard, "Working Class Politics."
104 Bale, Green-Pedersen, Krouwel, Luther, and Sitter, "If You Can't Beat Them, Join Them?"; van Spanje, "Contagious Parties."
105 Bale, Green-Pedersen, Krouwel, Luther, and Sitter, "If You Can't Beat Them, Join Them?"
106 Hagelund, "A Matter of Decency?," 49.
107 Lamont and Molnar, "The Study of Boundaries."
108 Korteweg and Yurdakul, *The Headscarf Debates*, 3.

109 Pakulski and Waters, "The Reshaping and Dissolution."
110 Bohman, "Articulated Antipathies."
111 Schneider, "Branding in Politics."
112 In his study of the politics surrounding the Charter of Values, Iacovino contends that the lack of consensus around the religious signs issue in Quebec stems from the "heightened stakes" around issues of collective identity related to the province's status as minority nation. Iacovino, "Contextualizing the Quebec Charter."
113 Steinmetz, "Introduction: Culture and the State," 99.
114 Skrentny, *The Minority Rights Revolution*; see also Sewell, "A Theory of Structure."
115 Surel, "The Role of Cognitive and Normative Frames."

CHAPTER TWO

1 Bowen, *Why the French Don't Like Headscarves*; Brubaker, *Citizenship and Nationhood*; Laborde, *Critical Republicanism.*
2 Bowen, *Why the French Don't Like Headscarves*, 22.
3 Ibid., 22–3.
4 Weber, *Peasants into Frenchmen.*
5 Bowen, *Why the French Don't Like Headscarves*, 23.
6 Baubérot, "La laïcité française et ses mutations," 178–9; Rigoulot, "Protestants and the French Nation."
7 Muhlmann and Zalc, "La laïcité," 103.
8 Weber, *Peasants into Frenchmen.*
9 Celebrated every July 14th, "Bastille Day" commemorates the "Storming of the Bastille" on 14 July 1789, during which the people of Paris stormed a fortress-prison that housed political prisoners whose writings displeased the royal government. The event marks a key moment in the 1789 Revolution.
10 Noiriel, *A quoi sert "l'identité nationale,"* 26.
11 Weber, *Peasants into Frenchmen*, 332–5.
12 Bowen, *Why the French Don't Like Headscarves*, 25.
13 Noiriel, *Population, Immigration*, author's translation.
14 Baubérot, "La laïcité en France," 32.
15 Ibid., 34.
16 Scott, "Sexularism."
17 Noiriel, *Le creuset français*, 283.
18 Ibid., 281.
19 Weil, *Qu'est-ce qu'un français?*, author's translation.

20 Bowen, *Why the French Don't Like Headscarves*, 25.
21 Hollifield, "Immigration and Republicanism."
22 Noiriel, *A quoi sert "l'identité nationale,"* 37.
23 Ibid., 28, author's translation.
24 Ibid., 41.
25 In practice, however, there is a great deal of government activity on behalf of certain religions in France, including: government funds to finance the upkeep of religious buildings that existed in 1905, government management and financing of chaplains' offices for major religions, explicit provisions for religious representation in a number of domains, and government funds to pay teachers' salaries in private confessional schools that have entered into contact with the state (Bowen, *Why the French Don't Like Headscarves*, 28).
26 Baubérot, "La laïcité en France," 35.
27 Muhlmann and Zalc, "La laïcité," 105–6.
28 Weil, "Why the French Laïcité Is Liberal."
29 Fabre, "L'élaboration de la loi de 1905"; Terral, "Laïcité religieuse, antireligieuse, a-religieuse."
30 Hollifield, "Immigration and Republicanism," 149.
31 Weil, *Qu'est-ce qu'un français?*
32 Fredette, *Constructing Muslims in France*, 49.
33 Bertossi, "Country Report: France."
34 Noiriel, *A quoi sert "l'identité nationale."*
35 Ibid., 55.
36 Brubaker, *Citizenship and Nationhood.*
37 Bowen, *Why the French Don't Like Headscarves*, 67; Fredette, *Constructing Muslims in France*, 53.
38 Hollifield, "Immigration and Republicanism."
39 Bertossi, "Country Report: France."
40 Simon, "Nationality and National Sentiment," 116.
41 Bertossi, "Country Report: France," 18
42 Ibid., 19.
43 Noiriel, *A quoi sert "l'identité nationale,"* author's translation.
44 Blais and Loewen, "The French Electoral System."
45 Ladrech, "Social Movements and Party Systems."
46 Blais and Loewen, "The French Electoral System," 345.
47 Ibid., 349–52.
48 Ibid., 355.
49 Bornschier and Lachat, "The Evolution of the French Political Space," 360.

50 Ibid., 364
51 Ladrech, "Social Movements and Party Systems," 263; Schain, "The National Front in France," 231.
52 Ladrech, "Social Movements and Party Systems," 270.
53 Ibid., 267.
54 Ibid., 271.
55 Ibid., 272.
56 Ibid., 272–3.
57 Cole, "A Strange Affair"; Kuhn, "The French Presidential."
58 Cole, "A Strange Affair," 330.
59 Bornschier and Lachat, "The Evolution of the French Political Space," 364.
60 The UMP incorporated the former RPR, Démocratie Libérale (Liberal Democracy, DL), the Parti Radical (Radical Party, PR), and the Centre national des indépendants (National Center of Independents, CNI). The Rassemblement pour la France (Rally for France, RPF), which represents a "sovereigntist" movement on the French right, did not join the UMP, although most of its individual members supported the new party. The same is true of the Droite libérale et chrétienne (Liberal and Christiam Right, DLC) (Haegel, 2004: 188).
61 Haegel, "The Transformation of the French Right," 190–1.
62 Hargreaves, "The Political Mobilization," 353; Tiberj and Simon, "Civic Life and Political Participation."
63 Tiberj, "La politique des deux axes."
64 Kern, "Muslim Voters Change Europe."
65 Mestre, "Le FN n'est plus le même."
66 Berezin, *Illiberal Politics in Neoliberal Times*, 63.
67 Mitra, "The Front National in France"; Wieviorka, "The Front National."
68 The system introduced by Mitterrand used the "d'Hondt" method, a highest averages method for allocating seats in party-list proportional representation. This approach allocates seats "by dividing the votes by a series of divisors and at each stage of the process the party with the highest average vote is awarded a seat." That process "continues until all the seats have been filled" (Carter, "Proportional Representation," 145–6). When it was implemented in 1985, this system became the object of political controversy as the RPR/UDF opposition accused Mitterrand of adopting it as a way of splitting the right-wing vote by strengthening the Front National.
69 Schain, "Immigration and Changes in the French Party System," 612.
70 Ibid., 609.

71 Schain, "The Front National in France," 243–4.
72 Wieviorka, "The Front National," 448–9.
73 Le Monde, "Présidentielle 2017: Les résultats du second tour ville par ville," *Le Monde*, 8 May 2017.
74 Berezin, *Illiberal Politics in Neoliberal Times*, 89.
75 Ibid., 79.
76 Ibid., 149.
77 Ibid., 119.
78 Brechon and Mitra, "The Front National in France," 69–70.
79 Wieviorka, "The Front National."
80 Geva, "Marine Le Pen."
81 Ibid., 2.
82 Ibid., 4.
83 Berezin, *Illiberal Politics in Neoliberal Times*, 179.
84 Wieviorka, "The Front National," 467.
85 Ibid., 465.
86 This state of affairs – called "cohabitation" – in which the president and prime minister represent different parties, occurs when the president's party does not hold a majority of seats in parliament. In such cases, the president appoints a prime minister who will be acceptable to the majority party. This arrangement has been necessary three times since the 1980s: during the Mitterrand-Chirac period (1986–88), during the Mitterrand-Balladur period (1993–95), and during the Chirac-Jospin period (1997–2002).
87 Brubaker, *Citizenship and Nationhood*, 159–61.
88 Noiriel, *A quoi sert "l'identité nationale*," author's translation.
89 Wieviorka, "The Front National," 461.
90 Marthaler, "Nicolas Sarkozy."
91 Wieviorka, "The Front National," 461.
92 Ibid., 468.
93 Ibid., 478.
94 Swyngedouw and Ivaldi. "The Extreme Right Utopia."
95 Reynié, "Le tournant ethno-socialiste du Front National."
96 Wieviorka, "The Front National," 479.
97 Ibid., 490.
98 de Leon, Desai, and Tugal, eds., *Building Blocs*.
99 The term "Beurs" is used to designate the native-born children of Algerians in France from the 1980s onward. In 1983, members of this community took part in a series of large-scale anti-racist marches, ending in a demonstration in Paris on 3 December, attended by over 100,000 people.

100 Bowen, *Why the French Don't Like Headscarves*, 166.
101 de Leon, Desai, and Tugal, eds., *Building Blocs*.
102 Bowen, *Why the French Don't Like Headscarves*; Scott, "Symptomatic Politics."
103 Scott, "Symptomatic Politics."
104 Stasi, "Commission de réflexion."
105 Bowen, *Why the French Don't Like Headscarves*, 52.
106 Ibid., 50–60.
107 Ibid., 60.
108 Nicolas Sarkozy, "20eme rassemblement annuel de l'UOIF. Ministère de l'intérieur," 19 April 2003.
109 "Nicolas Sarkozy se prononce contre le voile à l'école," *Le Nouvel Observateur*, 12 September 2003, author's translation.
110 Mayer, "Comment Nicolas Sarkozy."
111 Bussi and Fourquet, "Élection présidentielle 2007," 413.
112 Strudel, "L'électorat de Nicolas Sarkozy," 463.
113 Noiriel, *A quoi sert "l'identité nationale,"* 106–10.
114 Mayer, "Comment Nicolas Sarkozy."
115 Bussi and Fourquet, "Élection présidentielle 2007."
116 Strudel, "L'électorat de Nicolas Sarkozy."
117 "Discours de Nicolas Sarkozy au Palais Du Latran le 20 décembre 2007," *Le Monde*, 21 December 2007, author's translation.
118 Front National, "La Laïcité," author's translation.
119 Noiriel, *A quoi sert "l'identité nationale,"* 103.
120 Kessel, *Ils ont volé la laïcité!*
121 Ibid., 177, author's translation.
122 Sugier, interview, author's translation.
123 Vianès, interview, author's translation.
124 Lépinard, "The Contentious Subject," 377.
125 Scott, *The Politics of the Veil*.
126 Lépinard, "The Contentious Subject," 380.
127 Ibid., 379.
128 As Lépinard points out, this is beginning to change as a new generation of scholars begins to make its mark in French feminist studies. "The Contentious Subject," 385.
129 Ibid., 381.
130 Rottmann and Ferree, "Citizenship and Intersectionality."
131 Dot-Pouillard, "Les recompositions politiques."
132 Bilge, "Beyond Subordination vs. Resistance"; Scott, "Symptomatic Politics."

133 Narayan, *Dislocating Cultures*; other scholars (see Farris 2016) have utilized the concept of "authentic insiders" to study the role of "femocrats" in Europe's Islamic signs debate.
134 Bilge, "Beyond Subordination vs. Resistance," 16.
135 "Harki" is a term used to designate Muslim Algerians who were loyal to France and fought for the French army in the Algerian war of 1954–62. Broad uses of the term include in its definition the repatriated French Muslims who have lived in France since 1962 and their descendants born in metropolitan France.
136 Field notes, April 2013, author's translation.
137 Dot-Pouillard, "Les recompositions politiques."
138 Habchi, *Toutes libres!*, 77.
139 Orloff and Shiff, "Feminists in Power."
140 Indigènes de la République, "L'appel des Indigènes," author's translation.
141 Robine, "Les 'Indigènes de la République.'"
142 See, for example: Delphy, "Antisexisme Ou Antiracisme?"
143 Chouder, interview, author's translation.
144 Ahmed, *Strange Encounters*; Bilge, "Beyond Subordination vs. Resistance"; Mohanty, "Under Western Eyes"; Yegenoglu, *Colonial Fantasies*.
145 Delphy, interview, author's translation.
146 Paye, interview, author's translation.
147 See also: Al-Saji, "The Racialization of Muslim Veils"; Beaman, "Battles over Symbols."
148 Tévanian, interview, author's translation.
149 Ibid.
150 Stéphanie Le Bars, "Des députés ouvrent le débat sur le port de la burqa," *Le Monde*, 18 June 2009.
151 Gerin, "Rapport d'information," author's translation.
152 "Le débat sur l'identité nationale est 'nécessaire' selon Sarkozy," *Le Monde*, 12 November 2009, author's translation.
153 Glavany, interview, author's translation.
154 Ibid.
155 Jean-François Copé, "Voile intégral: Une loi indispensable," *Le Figaro*, 15 December 2009, author's translation.
156 Conseil d'État, "Étude Relative aux Possibilités Juridique du Port du Voile Intégral," 30–5.

157 "La gauche confirme son succès, l'Alsace reste à droite," *Le Monde*, 21 March 2010.

158 Assemblée Nationale de France. *Proposition de loi interdisant le port de tenues ou d'accessoires ayant pour effet de dissimuler le visage dans les lieux ouverts au public et sur la voie publique*, Pub. L. No. 2283, 5 February 2010, http://www.assemblee-nationale.fr/13/propositions/pion2283.asp, author's translation.

159 Assemblée Nationale de France. *Scrutin public sur l'ensemble du projet de loi interdisant la dissimulation du visage dans l'espace public*, 13 July 2010, http://www.assemblee-nationale.fr/13/scrutins/jo0595.asp

160 *S.A.S. v France*, [2014] ECHR 43835/11.

161 European Court of Human Rights, *French Ban on the Wearing in Public of Clothing Designed to Conceal One's Face Does Not Breach the Convention*. European Court of Human Rights, 2014.

162 Adrian, *Religious Freedom at Risk*, 74.

163 Ibid., 56–67.

164 Ibid., 73.

165 Simon, "Contested Citizenship in France," 216.

CHAPTER THREE

1 Baubérot and Milot, *Laïcités sans frontières*.

2 Milot, *Laïcité dans le nouveau monde*.

3 Ibid.

4 McRoberts, *Québec*.

5 Juteau, "The Citizen Makes an Entrée."

6 McRoberts, *Québec*.

7 The sociologist and historian Gérard Bouchard has extensively analyzed the formation and articulation of these national narratives and their attendant "myths." See Bouchard, *La nation québécoise*; *La pensée impuissante*; "L'imaginaire de la Grande Noirceur."

8 Handler, *Nationalism and the Politics*.

9 Zubrzycki, "Aesthetic Revolt," 433.

10 Groulx, *L'appel de La Race*.

11 Zubrzycki, "Aesthetic Revolt," 437.

12 Dumont, *Genèse de la société québécoise*, 227, author's translation.

13 Zubrzycki, "Aesthetic Revolt."

14 Dumont, *Genèse de la société québécoise*.

15 Gérin-Lajoie, *Combats d'un révolutionnaire tranquille*.

16 Ibid., 94.
17 Behiels, *Prelude to Québec's Quiet Revolution*.
18 Hepburn, "Small Worlds in Canada and Europe," 535.
19 Lijphart, "Religious vs. Linguistic"; Lipset, *Political Man*; Medeiros, Gauvin, and Chhim, "Refining Vote Choice"; Pinard, "Working Class Politics."
20 Alford, "Class Voting"; Brym, Gillespie, and Lenton, "Class Power, Class Mobilization"; Lijphart, "Religious vs. Linguistic."
21 Henderson, "Regional Political Cultures."
22 Lijphart, "Religious vs. Linguistic."
23 Andersen, "The Class-Party Relationship."
24 Lipset, *Political Man*, 258.
25 Pinard, "Working Class Politics," 87.
26 Ibid., 88.
27 Ibid.
28 Medeiros, Gauvin, and Chhim, "Refining Vote Choice."
29 Tanguay, "Sclerosis or a Clean Bill of Health?," 223.
30 Lemieux, *Le Parti libéral du Québec*.
31 Hepburn, "Small Worlds in Canada and Europe."
32 Hamilton and Pinard, "The Bases of Parti Québécois Support," 3.
33 Medeiros, Gauvin, and Chhim, "Refining Vote Choice," 19.
34 Ibid., 18.
35 Hamilton and Pinard, "The Bases of Parti Québécois Support," 3.
36 Pinard and Hamilton, "The Parti Québécois Comes to Power," 739.
37 Tanguay, "Sclerosis or a Clean Bill of Health?," 225.
38 The original Bill 101 limited English-language instruction to children whose parent received elementary education in English anywhere in Quebec.
39 Hamilton and Pinard, "The Bases of Parti Québécois Support"; Pinard and Hamilton, "The Parti Québécois Comes to Power." This fact also led Susan Olzak ("Ethnic Mobilization in Canada") to conclude that it is the lessening, rather than the persistence, of a cultural division of labour in Quebec that fuels support for the sovereigntist project.
40 Pinard, "Political Ambivalence."
41 Tanguay, "Sclerosis or a Clean Bill of Health?," 235–6.
42 Québec solidaire, "Nos principes."
43 Behiels, *Prelude to Québec's Quiet Revolution*; Juteau, "'Pures Laines' Québécois"; McRoberts, *Québec*.
44 Co-founded by future prime minister Pierre Elliott Trudeau in 1950, *Cité Libre* was a political journal published in Quebec through the

1950s and 1960s. During these years, it served as a key voice of opposition to the Union Nationale government.

45 *Le Devoir* was founded by journalist and politician Henri Bourassa in 1910. The only independent large circulation newspaper in Quebec, its editorial line has historically favoured social democracy and Quebec independence.

46 For a description of this shift and its implications for the construction of Québécois nationhood, see Behiels, *Prelude to Quebec's Quiet Revolution*, and Thériault, "Entre la nation," "La nation francophone."

47 Fournier and Maheu, "Nationalismes et nationalisation du champ scientifique québécois."

48 Fournier, "Quebec Sociology and Quebec Society."

49 See for example Meunier and Warren, "L'horizon 'personnaliste.' "

50 See for example Létourneau (1997).

51 See for example Lemieux (1990, 2006); Meunier and Laniel, "Nation et catholicisme."

52 Coleman, *The Independence Movement.*

53 Balthazar, "The Québec Experience."

54 Coleman, *The Independence Movement*, 143.

55 This commission was nominated by then prime minister Lester Pearson to recommend steps for developing an equal partnership between Canada's English- and French-speaking nations. Among its key recommendations were: (1) that Ontario and New Brunswick be declared bilingual provinces, (2) that Ottawa be declared a bilingual city, and (3) that French and English be declared Canada's official languages.

56 Taylor, "The Politics of Recognition"; Taylor, *Sources of the Self.*

57 Gagnon and Iacovino, *Federalism, Citizenship, and Québec.*

58 Trudeau, *Federalism and the French Canadians.*

59 Lévesque, *An Option for Québec.*

60 Negotiated by Prime Minister Mulroney and the provincial premiers in 1987, the Meech Lake Accord proposed five modifications to the constitution: recognition of Quebec as a distinct society; a constitutional veto for all provinces; increased provincial jurisdiction over immigration; the extension of fiscal compensation to the provinces that seek to opt out of federal programs in areas of provincial jurisdiction; and provincial input in the appointment of Supreme Court judges. Because it proposed changes to the constitution's amending formula, ratification of the Meech Lake accord required the consent of all provincial legislatures within three years. By 1990, the accord had not been approved by the parliaments of Manitoba and Newfoundland and was therefore

abandoned. The Charlottetown accord represents a second attempt to resolve ongoing disagreement over the constitution. Key proposed amendments included: the recognition of Quebec as a distinct society in a "Canada clause"; the constitutional entrenchment of the requirement that three of Canada's nine Supreme Court judges be from Quebec; and the adoption of an elected Senate. Canadians struck down the Charlottetown accord in the nationwide referendum of 1992.

61 Juteau, "The Citizen Makes an Entrée."

62 This term is used throughout the document to designate immigrants and their offspring.

63 Gouvernement du Québec, Ministère des communautés culturelles et de l'immigration, "Autant de façons d'être québécois," 86.

64 Ibid., 18–20, author's translation.

65 Ibid., 29, author's translation.

66 Gouvernement du Québec, "Au Québec pour bâtir ensemble."

67 Ibid., 19, author's translation.

68 Ibid., 85.

69 Ibid., 15, author's translation.

70 Reitz, Simon, and Laxer, "Muslims' Social Inclusion."

71 This amendment did not prevent the Catholic Church from enjoying an "implicit" agreement, which secured its hold over the religious curriculum until 2005 (Meunier and Laniel, "Nation et catholicisme").

72 Two laws – one in 2000 and the other in 2005 – had already instituted de-confessionalization of the school boards (Assemblée Nationale du Québec. *Loi modifiant diverses dispositions législatives dans le secteur de l'éducation concernant la confessionalité*, Pub. L. No. 118, 2000; Assemblée Nationale du Québec. *Loi modifiant diverses dispositions législatives de nature confessionnelle dans le domaine de l'éducation*, Pub. L. No. 95, 2005). However, by using the notwithstanding clause on both occasions, the government of Quebec was able to maintain religious teaching in schools until 2008.

73 Zubrzycki, "Aesthetic Revolt"; Zubrzycki, *Beheading the Saint*, 23.

74 Zubrzycki, "Negotiating Pluralism."

75 Statistics Canada, "NHS Profile, Québec, 2011."

76 Institut national des études démographiques, "Trajectories and Origins."

77 *Syndicat Northcrest v. Amselem*, 2004 SCC 47, [2004] SCR 551.

78 *Multani v. Commission Scolaire Marguerite-Bourgeoys*, 2006 SCC 6, [2006] 1 SCR 256.

79 "'Un À-Plat-Ventrisme Qui Ne Mène Nulle Part,'" Radio-Canada, 17 November 2006.

80 The Bouchard-Taylor commission's final report contains a detailed description of the accommodation requests that served as the basis for the purported "crisis" in accommodations. For a journalistic account of these cases, see Dufour and Heinrich, *Circus Quebecus*. Social scientific analyses of the commission and its subject matter can be found in Bock-Coté, "Derrière la laïcité," Koussens, "Comment les partis politiques," and Laxer, Carson, and Korteweg, "Articulating Minority Nationhood."

81 The distinction between means and ends is central to the doctrine of secularism proposed in *Secularism and Freedom of Conscience*, by Maclure and Taylor (2011).

82 Bouchard and Taylor, "Building the Future," 115.

83 Ibid., 20.

84 Ibid., 134–5.

85 Ibid., 116.

86 Other scholars have considered the parameters of this struggle in the context of the Bouchard-Taylor commission. For instance, Bock-Coté, "Derrière la laïcité," has argued that, while the 2007–08 debate over reasonable accommodation in Quebec was ostensibly about secularism, it was in fact more about nationhood and its boundaries, and the extent to which the national majority could constitute itself as the keeper of collective norms in the context of migration.

87 Ibid., 19.

88 Bouchard, interview, author's translation.

89 Bouchard and Taylor, "Building the Future," 242.

90 Laxer, Carson, and Korteweg, "Articulating Minority Nationhood."

91 See, for example, Beauchemin, "Nationalisme québécois et crise du lien social," "La question nationale québécoise," and "Qu'est-ce qu'être Québécois?"

92 Robert Dutrisac, "Vers une nouvelle identité québécoise?," *Le Devoir*, 24 May 2008.

93 Beauchemin, interview, author's translation.

94 Ibid. For a further look at Beauchemin's reaction to the Bouchard-Taylor report, see his opinion piece, "Accueillir sans renoncer à soi-même," in *Le Devoir* on 22 January 2010.

95 The ADQ no longer exists in Quebec. Many of its members are now part of the Coalition avenir Québec (CAQ), currently the governing party in Quebec's National Assembly.

96 Zubrzycki, "Negotiating Pluralism."

97 Antoine Robitaille, "Le crucifix restera en place," *Le Devoir*, 23 May 2008.

98 Coalition avenir Québec, "A New Agenda."
99 Like the organizations from which it sprang, Québec solidaire has no "party leader"; the duties of leadership are instead entrusted to the president (a title afforded to one of the two spokespersons), the secretary general, and the male and female spokespeople.
100 Dufour, "From Protest to Partisan Politics," 57.
101 Ben Shingler, "Françoise David, Voice 'for the Disenfranchised,' Leaves Politics," *CBC News*, 19 January 2017.
102 Maillé, "Réception de La Théorie Postcoloniale."
103 Maillé, "The Québec Women's Movement," 288.
104 Ibid., 291.
105 Fédération des femmes du Québec, "Mémoire présenté."
106 Ibid.
107 Fédération des femmes du Québec, "Pour la laïcité sans domination," author's translation.
108 Conseil du statut de la femme, "Avis: Droit à l'égalité."
109 Conseil du statut de la femme, "Mémoire sur le projet de loi #60."
110 Latour, interview, author's translation.
111 "Céline," interview, author's translation. This interviewee chose to remain anonymous. Therefore, this is a pseudonym.
112 Manai, interview, author's translation; Riley, interview.
113 Claire Durand, "Ah! Les sondages," http://ahlessondages.blogspot.com/2014/06/generations-souverainete-parti-quebecois.html.
114 Mendelsohn, Parkin, and Pinard, "A New Chapter."
115 Beauchemin, interview, author's translation.
116 Léger Marketing, "Provincial Voting Intentions."
117 Turp, "Pour une charte québécoise de la laïcité."
118 Ibid., author's translation.
119 Parti Québécois, "Agir en toute liberté," author's translation.
120 This includes those working in the ministries, in government institutions, in public elementary and secondary schools, in *centres de petite enfance*, and private subsidized daycares, as well as judges, police officers, and employees of correctional institutions. Health care institutions, CEGEPs, universities, municipalities, and constituency offices would be exempt for five years on a renewable basis. Elected officials would also be exempt from the Charter's requirement regarding ostentatious religious signs.
121 This proposal echoes that put forward by Charest's Liberals in Bill 94, which never passed in the National Assembly.

122 "Charte des valeurs québécoises – Réactions mitigées sur la scène politique provinciale," *Le Devoir*, 11 September 2013.

123 Canadian Press, "Charte: Pauline Marois a trahi René Lévesque, selon Philippe Couillard," *Le Devoir*, 11 September 2013; Paul Journet, "Couillard veut scinder la 'charte de la chicane' pour l'adopter," *La Presse*, 11 September 2013.

124 Canadian Press, "Charte des valeurs québécoises – Réactions mitigées sur la scène politique provinciale," *Le Devoir*, 11 September 2013.

125 Ibid.

126 Tu Thanh Ha, "PQ Charter of Values Better Received by Francophones, Poll Shows," *Globe and Mail*, 16 September 2013.

127 Karim Benessaieh, "Mairie de Montréal: Unanimité contre la charte des valeurs," *La Presse*, 10 September 2013.

128 This was a somewhat ironic threat, given the Conservative Party's subsequent proposals to restrict the niqab in the federal election campaign of 2015.

129 Gérard Bouchard, "Charte des valeurs québécoises: Un mauvais projet pour le Québec," *Le Devoir*, 10 September 2013; Bouchard, "La démagogie au pouvoir," *La Presse*, 10 January 2014.

130 Guillaume Bourgault-Coté, "Point chaud – charte de la laïcité – Duceppe rejoint Parizeau et Bouchard: L'ex-chef du Bloc estime lue Le PQ interdit trop largement le port des signes religieux," *Le Devoir*, 2 December 2013.

131 Statistics Canada, "Linguistic characteristics of Canadians."

132 Durand, "Ah! Les sondages"; Mendelsohn, Parkin, and Pinard, "A New Chapter."

133 Marco Fortier, "L'effet PKP profite aux libéraux de Couillard," *Le Devoir*, 15 March 2014.

CHAPTER FOUR

1 Assemblée Nationale de France, *Proposition de résolution tendant à la création d'une commission d'enquête sur la pratique du port de la burqa ou du niqab sur le territoire national*, 9 June 2009, http://www.assemblee-nationale.fr/13/propositions/pion1725.asp, author's translation.

2 Parvez, "Debating the Burqa in France."

3 Gerin, *Les Ghettos de La République*.

4 Ibid., 116.

5 www.blogandregerin.fr/.

6 Gerin, interview, author's translation.

7 Ibid.

8 Ségolène Gros de Larquier, "Le 'combat républicain' d'André Gerin (PC)," *Le Point*, 19 June 2009, author's translation.

9 Ibid.

10 Gerin, interview, author's translation.

11 Assemblée Nationale de France. *Proposition de résolution tendant à la création d'une commission d'enquête sur la pratique du port de la burqa ou du niqab sur le territoire national*, 9 June 2009, http://www.assemblee-nationale.fr/13/propositions/pion1725.asp, author's translation.

12 Ibid.

13 In French politics, the term "group" refers to political parties and groupings of smaller political parties.

14 Thiers, interview, author's translation.

15 Gerin, interview.

16 In some cases, two or more representatives of the same association testified. Therefore, the total number of associations appearing before the commission is smaller than the total number of individuals.

17 A handful of other commission participants could arguably – by virtue of their ethnic or national origins – be included in this category. For the purpose of this analysis, though, I categorized participants according to the way the commission itself presented them. For example, although Sihem Habchi and Ismahane Chouder are of Muslim-Arab origin, they appeared before the commission in their capacity as representatives of recognized feminist associations, not as representatives, per se, of the Muslim community.

18 Gerin, "Rapport d'information," 39.

19 Ibid., 91.

20 Ibid., 113.

21 Ibid., 120.

22 Ibid., 187, author's translation.

23 Mothron, interview, author's translation.

24 Ameline, interview, author's translation.

25 Bataille, interview, author's translation.

26 Glavany, interview, author's translation.

27 "Marine Le Pen: Le voile intégral n'est que la partie émergée de l'iceberg," *Le Parisien*, 30 April 2010, author's translation.

28 Ameline, interview, author's translation.

29 This argument has been proffered, for instance, by Selby in "Islam in France Reconfigured."

30 Gerin, "Rapport d'information," 390–409, 447–56, 560–72.

31 Bowen, "A View from France," 1012.
32 Selby, "Islam in France Reconfigured," 383.
33 Gerin, "Rapport d'information," 392, author's translation.
34 Ibid., 563.
35 Ibid., 564.
36 Ibid., 36.
37 Ibid., 341.
38 Ibid.
39 Mothron, interview, author's translation.
40 The participation of veiled women was similarly limited in the Stasi commission, before which only two headscarf-wearing participants testified.
41 de Rugy, interview, author's translation.
42 Gerin, interview, author's translation.
43 Ibid.
44 Gerin, "Rapport d'information," 441, author's translation.
45 Ibid., 503.
46 Ibid., 435.
47 Ibid., 333; see also 271, 279, 293, 353, 380, 390, 410, 436, 483, 500, 538.
48 Ibid., 511.
49 Ibid., 337.
50 Ibid., 334.
51 Ibid., 300.
52 Ibid., 297.
53 Ibid., 295.
54 Ibid., 336.
55 Ibid., 608.
56 Ibid., 116.
57 Ibid., 306.
58 Ibid., 323.
59 Ibid., 457–66.
60 Ibid., 462.
61 Paye, interview, author's translation.
62 Killian, "From a Community of Believers," 317.
63 Mahmood, "Feminist Theory, Embodiment, and the Docile Agent."
64 Ibid.
65 Bilge, "Beyond Subordination vs. Resistance," 18.
66 Afshar, "Can I See Your Hair."
67 Korteweg, "The Sharia Debate in Ontario."
68 Annissa Fathi and Youssra H, interview, author's translation.

69 Youssra H, interview, author's translation.
70 Bowen, "A View from France," 1008.
71 Mazetier, interview, author's translation.
72 Hoffman-Rispal, interview, author's translation.
73 Gerin, interview, author's translation.
74 Ibid.
75 Ibid.
76 Gerin, "Rapport d'information," 350, author's translation.
77 Ibid., 413.
78 European Court of Human Rights, "French Ban on the Wearing in Public."
79 Vianès, interview, author's translation.
80 Gerin, "Rapport d'information," 416, author's translation.
81 Ibid., 547.
82 Ibid., 386–9.
83 Ibid., 422.
84 Ibid., 607.
85 Myard, interview, author's translation.
86 Gerin, "Rapport d'information," 555, author's translation.
87 Ibid., 557.
88 Ibid., 558.
89 Assemblée Nationale de France. *Proposition de loi interdisant le port de tenues ou d'accessoires ayant pour effet de dissimuler le visage dans les lieux ouverts au public et sur la voie publique*, Pub. L. No. 2283, 5 February 2010, http://www.assemblee-nationale.fr/13/propositions/pion2283.asp.
90 *S.A.S. v France*, [2014] ECHR 43835/11.
91 "Voile Intégral: La Mission Rend Son Rapport Dans La Division," *Libération*, 26 January 2010.
92 Hilout, interview, author's translation.
93 Myard, interview, author's translation.
94 Mothron, interview, author's translation.
95 Ibid.
96 Myard, interview, author's translation.
97 Ameline, interview, author's translation.
98 For a more thorough unpacking of the ways in which politicians in France and Quebec applied a particularistic reading to universal rights frames in their respective religious signs debates, see: Laxer and Korteweg, "Party Competition and the Production of Nationhood."
99 Mazetier, interview, author's translation.

100 de Rugy, interview, author's translation.
101 Hoffman-Rispal, interview, author's translation.
102 Mazetier, interview, author's translation.
103 Baubérot, *La laïcité falsifiée*; Glavany, *La laïcité*; Pena-Ruiz, *La laïcité pour L'égalité*.
104 Kessel, *Ils ont volé la laïcité!*, 11, author's translation.
105 Ibid., 15.
106 Bataille, interview, author's translation.
107 Operative from 1989 to 2012, the Haut Conseil à l'intégration (High Council of Integration, HCI) was a body attached to the French prime minister's office. Its major task was to submit an annual report as well as periodic advice to the government on the integration of foreign residents or residents of foreign origins. During its years in operation, the council was composed of a maximum of twenty members, appointed by the French president, mostly derived from the world of politics, research, management, culture, media, and sports (http://archives.hci.gouv.fr/Haut-Conseil-a-l-integration.html, accessed 13 July 2015).
108 Seksig, interview, author's translation. See also: Kessel, *Ils ont volé la laïcité!*, 17.
109 Gerin, interview, author's translation.
110 Jean-François Copé, "Voile intégral: Une loi indispensable," *Le Figaro*, 15 December 2009.
111 Glavany, interview, author's translation.
112 Ibid.
113 Bataille, interview, author's translation.
114 Hoffman-Rispal, interview, author's translation.
115 Gerin, interview, author's translation.
116 Alba, "Bright vs. Blurred Boundaries."
117 Gerin, interview, author's translation.
118 Glavany, *La laïcité*, 38, author's translation.
119 Glavany, interview, author's translation.
120 Glavany, *La laïcité;* Pena-Ruiz, *La laïcité pour l'égalité*.
121 Gerin, "Rapport d'information," 493, author's translation.
122 Ibid., 332.
123 Hoffman-Rispal, interview, author's translation.

CHAPTER FIVE

1 Regarding the presence of Catholic symbols in Quebec's public spaces and institutions, Québec solidaire proposed that religious recitations be prohibited in municipal and national assemblies, and that all religious symbols, including the infamous crucifix, be removed from the National Assembly. The Coalition avenir Québec took the opposite approach, opposing the removal of symbols representing Quebec's Catholic heritage from state buildings.

2 However, cleavages within the party opened it up to scrutiny by opponents. On 12 February 2014, without the support of her caucus, Liberal representative Fatima Houda-Pépin presented a bill, which (a) recommended that religiously based requests for accommodation in public service provision be prohibited, (b) proposed steps to outlaw polygamy and female genital mutilation, and (c) called for research to "identify and document manifestations of religious fundamentalism." As a result of this move, Houda-Pépin was thrown out of the PLQ.

3 Drainville, "Charte affirmant les valeurs."

4 "La Charte des valeurs, entre division et inclusion: 'Pas question de diluer la charte,' affirme le Ministre Drainville," *Radio-Canada*, 13 January 2014, author's translation.

5 Françoise David, *Point de presse de Mme Françoise David, députée de Gouin*, 15 January 2014, http://www.assnat.qc.ca/fr/actualites-salle-presse/conferences-points-presse/ConferencePointPresse-14733.html.

6 Guillaume Bourgault-Coté, "Charte: Au moins 200 heures d'audiences," *Le Devoir*, 28 December 2013, author's translation.

7 Ibid.

8 Marco Bélair-Cirino, "Marois propose de 'réfléchir de nouveau à notre avenir,'" *Le Devoir*, 8 March 2014.

9 Ibid.

10 Michel Corbeil, "Sondage Crop: Le PQ prend une confortable avance," *La Presse*, 18 February 2014.

11 "'La division est terminée, la réconciliation est arrivée' – Couillard," *Radio-Canada*, 7 April 2014, author's translation.

12 Research shows that there is broad consensus among the Québécois around the need for explicit guidelines to define the boundaries of state religious neutrality. There is also significant support for legislation to limit facial coverings among public services users and providers (Maclure, "Laïcité et fédéralisme").

13 Philippe Couillard, *Point de presse de M. Philippe Couillard, député de*

Roberval. 8 April 2014. http://www.assnat.qc.ca/fr/actualites-salle-presse/conferences-points-presse/ConferencePointPresse-16001.html.

14 Gauthier, "Mémoire: Charte affirmant des valeurs," author's translation.

15 Société nationale des Québécoises et des Québécois de Chaudière-Appalaches, "La ruralité a mis le Québec," author's translation.

16 Association québécoise des Nord-Africains pour la laïcité, "Mémoire sur le projet de loi 60," author's translation.

17 Mouvement des Janette, "Mémoire présenté par le mouvement des Janette," author's translation.

18 Gauthier, "Mémoire présenté à la commission," author's translation.

19 Laïcité citoyenne de la capitale nationale, "Les valeurs québécoises," author's translation.

20 Dionne, "Mémoire: Projet de loi no 60," author's translation.

21 Rassemblement pour la laïcité, "Mémoire sur le projet de loi 60," author's translation.

22 Dorion, interview, author's translation.

23 Laguitton, "Projet de loi #60," author's translation.

24 Ibid.

25 Seymour, "Le projet de loi 60," author's translation.

26 Centre d'études ethniques des universités montréalaises, "Mémoire du Centre d'études ethniques," author's translation.

27 Ligue des droits et libertés, "Un projet de loi dangereux," author's translation.

28 Collectif d'auteurs, "60 chercheurs universitaires pour la laïcité," author's translation.

29 Université de Sherbrooke, "Collectif de 66 professeur-e-s," author's translation.

30 Conseil du patronat du Québec, "Commentaires du Conseil du patronat," author's translation.

31 Bouchard, "L'imaginaire de la Grande Noirceur," 415–16.

32 Zubrzycki, *Beheading the Saint*.

33 Guilbault, interview, author's translation.

34 Lesbet, interview, author's translation.

35 Guilbault, interview, author's translation.

36 The critique of intersectional feminism was a central component of the PDFQ movement. For an account by the organization's president of the "divisive" effects of intersectionality, see: Michèle Sirois, "La pensée binaire du féminisme intersectionnel ne peut que mener à l'incohérence," *Sisyphe*, 26 October 2015.

37 Lesbet, interview, author's translation.
38 "Céline," interview, author's translation. This interviewee chose to remain anonymous. Therefore, this is a pseudonym.
39 Guilbault, interview, author's translation.
40 Lesbet, interview, author's translation.
41 Ibid.
42 Guilbault, interview, author's translation.
43 Maillé, "Réception de la théorie postcoloniale," author's translation.
44 For an in-depth analysis and historical account of Quebec feminists' reading of colonialism, and its relationship to nationhood, see Lamoureux, "Nationalisme et féminisme."
45 Hamelin, interview, author's translation.
46 Riley, interview.
47 Manai, interview, author's translation.
48 Ibid.
49 Ibid.
50 Ibid.
51 Ibid.
52 Chouder, interview, author's translation.
53 Manai, interview, author's translation.
54 Bergeron, "Mémoire 'pour' la charte."
55 Mouvement national des québécoises et Québécois, "Vers une politique de l'identité québécoise," author's translation.
56 See also: Joppke and Torpey, *Legal Integration of Islam*.
57 Barreau du Québec, "Mémoire du Barreau du Québec," author's translation.
58 *Syndicat Northcrest v. Amselem*, 2004 SCC 47, [2004] SCR 551.
59 Latour, interview, author's translation.
60 *Multani v. Commission Scolaire Marguerite-Bourgeoys*, 2006 SCC 6, [2006] 1 SCR 256.
61 *Bruker v. Marcovitz*, 2007 SCC 54, [2007] 3 SCR 607.
62 *Alberta v. Hutterian Brethren of Wilson Colony and Hutterian Brethren Church of Wilson*, 2009 SCC 37, [2009] 2 SCR 567.
63 Latour, "Assurer la protection législative."
64 Latour, interview, author's translation.
65 Gouvernement du Québec, *Charte Des Valeurs Québécoises*, author's translation.
66 Parti Québécois, *Nos Valeurs*, http://www.nosvaleurs.gouv.qc.ca/medias/pdf/Values.pdf, author's translation.

67 Marois, Quebec National Assembly, 23 October 2013, emphasis added, author's translation.

68 Drainville, Quebec National Assembly, 5 December 2013, author's translation.

69 Drainville, Quebec National Assembly, 23 October 2013, author's translation.

70 Marois, Quebec National Assembly, 7 November 2013, author's translation; see also Marois, Quebec National Assembly, 14 November 2013.

71 Ibid.

72 Drainville, Quebec National Assembly, 7 November 2013, author's translation.

73 Drainville, Quebec National Assembly, 13 November 2013, author's translation.

74 Drainville, Quebec National Assembly, 23 October 2013, author's translation.

75 Marco Bélair-Cirino, "Pour Bernard Drainville, les Libéraux ne savent pas défendre les valeurs québécoises," *Le Devoir*, 21 January 2014, author's translation.

76 Marco Bélair-Cirino, "Marois propose de 'réfléchir de nouveau à notre avenir,'" *Le Devoir*, 8 March 2014, author's translation.

77 Legault, Quebec National Assembly, 6 November 2013, author's translation.

78 Roy, interview, author's translation.

79 The capacity of "impossible" laws to create discourses around immigrant religious incorporation has been compellingly shown by Korteweg, "The 'Headrag Tax.'" Studying the "headrag tax" proposed by the Dutch anti-immigrant politician Geert Wilders in 2009, the author observed that, despite being "impossible" to implement, legislative proposals such as this one can nevertheless render "possible" certain articulations of the symbolic and material boundaries of nationhood.

80 Tanguay, Quebec National Assembly, 23 October 2013, author's translation.

81 "MNA" – for "member of the National Assembly" – is the term used on the English language website of Quebec's National Assembly: http://www.assnat.qc.ca/en/index.html.

82 Ibid.

83 Drainville, Quebec National Assembly, 23 October 2013, author's translation.

84 Tanguay, Quebec National Assembly, 23 October 2013, author's translation.

85 Coalition avenir Québec, "Religious Accommodations," 5.

86 Ibid., 3.

87 "Québec Election Campaign Kicks off for April 7 Vote," CBC, 5 March 2014.

88 Parti libéral du Québec, 2014, http://www.plq.org/fr/outils-en-ligne.

89 Roy, Quebec National Assembly, 23 October 2013, author's translation.

90 Deltell, Quebec National Assembly, 23 October 2013, author's translation.

91 Parti libéral du Québec, "Déclaration identité québécoise."

92 Robert Dutrisac, "Couillard met en garde le Québec contre la volonté de se distinguer," *Le Devoir*, 29 January 2014, author's translation.

93 Jean-Marc Salvet, "Laïcité et accommodements: Les fonctionnaires appuieront Drainville," *Le Soleil*, 10 September 2013, author's translation.

94 Dorion, interview, author's translation.

95 Bouchard, interview, author's translation.

96 Gérard Bouchard, "Charte des valeurs québécoises: Un mauvais projet pour le Québec," *Le Devoir*, 10 September 2013; Lynn Moore, "Video: Charter of Québec Values: Debate Will Be Heated and 'Useless,' Gérard Bouchard Says," *The Montreal Gazette*, 11 September 2013.

97 Jean Dorion, "Charte de la laïcité – Quand un séparatiste se sépare," *Le Devoir*, 22 September 2012, author's translation.

98 Indépendantistes pour une laïcité inclusive, "Rassembler plutôt qu'exclure," author's translation.

99 Dorion, interview, author's translation.

100 Maria Mourani, "Pour protéger nos foyers et nos droits," *La Presse*, 18 December 2013, author's translation.

101 Ibid.

CONCLUSION

1 Myrdal, *An American Dilemma*.

2 Zubrzycki, "'We, the Polish Nation.'"

3 Laxer, Carson, and Korteweg, "Articulating Minority Nationhood."

4 Brubaker and Cooper, "Beyond Identity."

5 Bowen, *Why the French Don't Like Headscarves*, 19.

6 Amiraux and Simon, "There Are No Minorities Here." Of course, there are numerous exceptions to this rule. For instance, there is a growing body of scholarship on Islamophobia in France, and the production – by politicians and public intellectuals alike – of a "Muslim problem."

See, for example: Hajjat and Mohammed, *Islamophobie*; Tévanian, *La république du mépris*. Numerous studies also consider the colonial roots of racial and ethnic relations in France. For instance: Amiraux, "De l'empire à la république"; Bancel, Blanchard, and Vergès, *La république coloniale*; Blanchard, Bancel, and Lemaire, eds., *La fracture coloniale*.

7 Korteweg and Yurdakul, *The Headscarf Debates*, 3.

8 Ibid.

9 Albright, "The Multidimensional Nature," 700–1.

10 Ibid., 701.

11 Ibid., 702.

12 Kriesi, Grande, Lachat, Dolezal, Bornschier, and Frey, "Globalization and the Transformation."

13 Andersen and Evans, "The Stability of French Political Space"; Marthaler, "'New' Politics for 'Old'?"

14 Medeiros, Gauvin, and Chhim, "Refining Vote Choice," 16.

15 Finkielkraut, *L'Ingratitude*.

EPILOGUE

1 Open Society Foundation, "After the Ban."

2 Ibid.

3 Ibid.

4 Suzanne Daley and Alissa J. Rubin, "French Muslims Say Veil Bans Give Cover to Bias," *New York Times*, 26 May 2015.

5 Open Society Foundation, "After the Ban."

6 Matthieu Ecoiffier and Tonino Serafini, "Sorties scolaries: Les mères voilées tolérées," *Libération*, 23 December 2013, author's translation.

7 Civil, commercial, social, or criminal cases that are first tried in courts of first instance (including *tribunaux d'instance* and *tribunaux de grande instance*, commercial courts, employment tribunals, etc.) and those that are appealed before a court of appeal may then be appealed to the Court of Cassation. It does not rule on the merits of a case. Rather, it decides whether the rules of law have been "correctly applied by the lower courts based on the facts." Thus, the Court of Cassation does not "strictly speaking deliver a ruling on the disputes which are at the origin of the decisions but on the decisions themselves." In other words, "it judges the decisions of the lower courts" (https://www.courdecassation.fr/about_the_court_9256.html, accessed 12 July 2015).

8 See for example: http://www.change.org/fr/pétitions/crèche-baby-loup-appel-à-toutes-les-consciences-républicaines.

9 Camille Hamet and Claire Rainfroy, "Baby Loup: La justice affirme la liberté religieuse," *Le Monde*, 20 March 2013.
10 Cour de Cassation, 19 March 2013.
11 Philippe Euzen, "Entreprises et religion, comment faire?," *Le Monde*, 1 April 2013.
12 Assemblée Nationale, *Compte rendu intégral, séance du jeudi 6 juin 2013*.
13 Angelique Chrisafis, "France's Headscarf War: 'It's an Attack on Freedom,'" *The Guardian*, 22 July 2013.
14 Observatoire de la laïcité, "Avis de l'Observatoire."
15 Cour de Cassation, 25 June 2014, author's translation.
16 Paul de Coustin, "L'UMP demande l'interdiction du voile à l'université," *Figaro*, 11 February 2015, author's translation.
17 Tristan Quinault Maupoil, "Porc dans les cantines, voile à l'université: La droite divisée," *Figaro*, 18 March 2015.
18 Ibid., author's translation.
19 Paul Laubacher, "Port du voile à l'université: La ministre des droits des femmes est 'contre,'" *Nouvel Observateur*, 3 March 2015, author's translation.
20 Ibid.
21 "Voile à l'université: Le FN dénonce un 'enfumage de fin de campagne,'" *Le Point*, 18 March 2015, author's translation.
22 Eric Conan, "Elisabeth Badinter: 'Je ne pardonne pas à la gauche d'avoir abandonné la laïcité,'" *Marianne*, 3 February 2015, author's translation.
23 "Ordonnance Du 26 Aout 2016," Conseil d'État, 26 August 2016.
24 "'Le burkini est une provocation' (Valls)," *Figaro*, 5 September 2016, author's translation.
25 "Sarkozy mène la charge contre le 'burkini,'" *Le Monde*, 24 August 2016, author's translation.
26 Front National, "Burkini: Le législateur doit prendre ses responsabilités," 26 August 2016, author's translation.
27 Yasmeen Serhan, "François Hollande's Legacy: Now That the French Head of State Won't Be Seeking Reelection, How Will His Presidency Be Remembered?," *The Atlantic*, 2 December 2016.
28 Guillaume Poingt, "Benoit Hamon 'gauchise' son programme économique," *Figaro*, 16 March 2017.
29 Manon Rescan and Lucie Soullier, "Hamon et Valls: Deux conceptions de la laïcité," *Le Monde*, 24 January 2017, author's translation.
30 Matthieu Goar, "Un discours de François Fillon à La Loupe, entre ombre de De Gaulle et fantome de Sarkozy," *Le Monde*, 15 December 2016.

31 Alexandre Lemarié, "A Strasbourg, Alain Juppé assume 'l'identité heureuse,'" *Le Monde*, 13 September 2016, author's translation.
32 Isabelle de Foucaud and Yohan Blavignat, "En direct – résultat primaire à droite: Fillon grand vainqueur," *Figaro*, 27 November 2016.
33 Angelique Chrisafis, "François Fillon under Formal Investigation for 'Fake Jobs Offences,'" *The Guardian*, 14 March 2017.
34 Gérard Courtois, "Mélenchon, les ressorts d'une percée spectaculaire," *Le Monde*, 19 April 2017.
35 "Présidentielle 2017: Les résultats du premier tour, commune par commune," *Le Monde*, 24 April 2017.
36 Following the 7 May 2017 election, the movement was renamed La République en marche ("Onward the Republic").
37 Angelique Chrisafis, "Emmanuel Macron: The French Outsider Who Would Be President," *The Guardian*, 17 February 2017.
38 Olivier Faye and Matthieu Goar, "François Fillon et Marine Le Pen, deux stratégies face à Emmanuel Macron," *Le Monde*, 14 March 2017.
39 Steven Poole, "'The Republic' or 'the People'? The Rhetoric of the French Presidential Election," *The Guardian*, 7 May 2017.
40 Angelique Chrisafis, "Emmanuel Macron Vows to Be 'President for All of France' and First Round Win," *The Guardian*, 23 April 2017.
41 Steven Poole, "'The Republic' or 'the People'? The Rhetoric of the French Presidential Election," *The Guardian*, 7 May 2017.
42 Angelique Chrisafis, "Marine Le Pen Springs Surprise Visit on Macron during Picket Line Campaign Trip," *The Guardian*, 27 April 2017.
43 "2017, Le Débat: Marine Le Pen - Emmanuel Macron," *France* 2, 3 May 2017, author's translation.
44 Ibid.
45 Sophie de Ravinel, "Macron défend sa vision de la laïcité," *Figaro*, 18 October 2016, author's translation.
46 Cécile Chambraud, "Laïcité et islam: Emmanuel Macron laisse des questions en suspens," *Le Monde*, 2 March 2017.
47 Front National, "144 Engagements Présidentiels."
48 Jonathan Bouchet-Petersen, "La laïcité de Marine Le Pen s'arrête aux portes de l'école," *Libération*, 10 February 2017.
49 Le Monde, "Présidentielle 2017: Les résultats du second tour ville par ville," *Le Monde*, 8 May 2017.
50 "Vidéo. 'La France l'a emporté': Le discours d'Emmanuel Macron devant ses partisans après son élection à la présidentielle," *France Info*, 7 May 2017.

51 "Vidéo. Présidentielle: Revivez en intégralité le discours de Marine Le Pen après sa défaite au second tour," *France Info*, 7 May 2017.

52 Katia Gagnon and Tommy Chouinard, "Femmes voilées: 'Augmentation dramatique' des agressions," *La Presse*, 2 October 2013; Olivier Parent, "Une femme voilée invectivée en plein centre commercial," *La Presse*, 15 September 2013.

53 "Montreal Bus Video Appears to Show Anti-Muslim Altercation," CBC *News Montreal*, 17 September 2013.

54 "Québec Muslim Badia Senouci Told: 'Change Your Religion,'" CBC, 16 September 2013.

55 "Montreal Bus Video Appears to Show Anti-Muslim Altercation," CBC *News Montreal*, 17 September 2013.

56 "Minister Calls for Calm Charter Debate, While Bigots Berate Hijab-Wearing Women," CTV *News Montreal*, 17 September 2013.

57 Marie-Ève Dumont, "Une attaque liée à la charte des valeurs: Une fenetre d'un centre islamique a été brisée avec une hache à Montréal," *Journal de Montréal*, 8 April 2014, author's translation.

58 Vallée, "Loi favorisant le respect de la neutralité."

59 Denis Lessard, "Laïcité de l'état: Couillard ne dérogera pas à son plan," *La Presse*, 15 June 2015.

60 Marco Bélair-Cirino, "La laïcité pourchasse Couillard: Le PQ attise le débat à l'aube de la nouvelle session parlementaire," *Le Devoir*, 23 January 2015; Presse Canadienne, "La loi sur la laïcité encore au programme de Couillard," *Le Devoir*, 14 January 2015.

61 Clément Sabourin, "Le gouvernement québécois va légiférer sur la laïcité d'ici l'été," *Le Devoir*, 11 March 2015, author's translation.

62 Caroline Plante, "Couillard Welcomes Charles Taylor's Change of Heart," *Montreal Gazette*, 14 February 2017.

63 Isabelle Porter and Marie-Michèle Sioui, "Un attentat terroriste dans une mosquée de Québec fait six morts," *Le Devoir*, 30 January 2017.

64 Charles Taylor, "Opinion: Neutralité de l'état: Le temps de la réconciliation," *La Presse*, 14 February 2017, author's translation.

65 Lisa-Marie Gervais, "La volte-face de Charles Taylor, une bénédiction pour Couillard," *Le Devoir*, 15 February 2017, author's translation.

66 Ibid.

67 Ibid.

68 Hall, "Liberalism and Statelessness."

69 "Péladeau, nouveau chef du PQ," *Radio-Canada*, 15 May 2015.

70 Antoine Robillard, "Laïcité: Péladeau fait marche arrière et met de

l'avant Bouchard-Taylor," *La Presse Canadienne*, 17 May 2015, author's translation.

71 "Débat au PQ: Vifs échanges sur la souveraineté," *Radio-Canada*, 16 April 2015, author's translation.

72 Philippe Teisceira-Lessard and Denis Lessard, "Pierre Karl Péladeau démissionne: 'J'ai choisi ma famille,'" *La Presse*, 2 May 2016, author's translation.

73 Marco Bélair-Cirino, "La laïcité au coeur d'un nouveau débat," *Le Devoir*, 16 September 2014.

74 Jean-Marc Salvet, "Lisée offre sa version de la laïcité," *La Presse*, 12 June 2016, author's translation.

75 "Jean-François Lisée élu nouveau chef du Parti Québécois," *Le Devoir*, 7 October 2016.

76 Martin Croteau, "Jean-François Lisée durcit sa position en matière d'identité," *La Presse*, 24 November 2016.

77 Maltais, Quebec National Assembly, 18 October 2017, author's translation.

78 Quebec National Assembly, 18 October 2017.

79 Chantale Hébert, "Québec's Bill 62 Declares War on Sunglasses," *Toronto Star*, 20 October 2017.

80 Presse Canadienne, "Bill 62: Lawyer Calls for Temporary Suspension of Face-Covering Law," *Montreal Gazette*, 17 November 2017.

81 Ingrid Peritz, "Quebec Judge Stays Controversial Face-Cover Law Bill 62," *Globe and Mail*, 1 December 2017.

82 Here, "reasonable" designates requests that do not "cause undue hardship on others or affect the quality of service or public health of others."

83 "Bill 62: Quebec Releases Criteria for Requesting, Granting Religious Accommodation," CBC, 9 May 2018.

84 Benjamin Shingler, "Judge Suspends Quebec Face-Covering Ban, Says It Appears to Violate Charter," *CBC News*, 28 June 2018.

85 Philip Authier, "Bill 62: Religious Accommodation Falls to Public Agencies, Quebec Says," *Montreal Gazette*, 10 May 2018.

86 Ibid.

87 Radio-Canada, "Québec présente les lignes directrices pour les accommodement religieux," *Radio-Canada*, 9 May 2018.

88 Jean-François Lisée, "Oser. Réussir. #AvecLisée," 2016. http://course.pq.org/jeanfrancoislisee.html.

89 Brian Myles, "Le PQ à l'ère Lisée: Le moment de lucidité," *Le Devoir*, 17 October 2016, author's translation.

90 Celine Cooper, "Jean-François Lisée Faces Big Challenges," *Montreal Gazette*, 15 January 2017.
91 Philip Authier, "Take Another Look at Us, Québec Solidaire Tells Left-Wing Anglos," *Montreal Gazette*, 27 May 2016; "Le PQ laisse toute la place à Québec Solidaire dans Gouin," *Radio-Canada*, 13 February 2017.
92 http://alliancepopulaire.quebec.
93 Marco Bélair-Cirino, "Nadeau-Dubois souhaite des alliances stratégiques avec le PQ," *Le Devoir*, 22 April 2017.
94 Philip Authier, "Lisée Downplays Bad Polls, Says He's Got the Right Election Plan," *The Montreal Gazette*, 27 January 2018.
95 Martin Croteau, "Lisée veut un 'État fort' pour promouvoir l'indépendance," *La Presse*, 27 January 2018.
96 Mahéo and Bélanger, "Is the Parti Québécois Bound to Disappear?"
97 Benjamin Shingler, "Quebec elects CAQ majority government, Liberals see historic losses," *CBC*, 1 October 2018.
98 Guillaume Bourgault-Côté, "La CAQ pourrait couper le tiers des immigrants économiques", *Le Devoir*, 7 September 2018.
99 Marie-Michèle Sioui, "La CAQ propose des testes de valeurs pour les immigrants," *Le Devoir*, 16 May 2018.
100 François Messier, "'On va respecter nos engagements,' assure François Legault," *Radio-Canada*, 2 October 2018.

Bibliography

PRIMARY SOURCES

Statistical Data and Reports

Institut national d'études démographiques. *Trajectories and Origins: Survey on Population Diversity in France*. Paris: INED, 2008.

Kern, S. *Muslim Voters Change Europe*. Gatestone Institute: International Policy Council, 2012. https://www.gatestoneinstitute.org/3064/muslim-voters-europe.

Léger Marketing. *Provincial Voting Intentions in Québec.* 2013. http://leger360.com/admin/voting_int/Provincial_Voting_Intentions_in_Québec2012.

Ministère de l'immigration et des communautés culturelles. *Donnés sur la population recensée en 2001 portant sur la religion*. Quebec: Gouvernement du Québec, 2003.

Statistics Canada. "Linguistic characteristics of Canadians." Ottawa: Minister of Industry, 2012. http://www12.statcan.gc.ca/census-recensement/2011/as-sa/98-314-x/98-314-x2011001-eng.cfm.

– "NHS Profile, Québec, 2011." Ottawa: Statistics Canada, 2011. http://www12.statcan.gc.ca/nhs-enm/2011/dp-pd/prof/details/page.cfm?Lang=EandGeo1=PRandCode1=24andData=CountandSearchText=QuébecandSearchType=BeginsandSearchPR=01andA1=AllandB1=AllandCustom=andTABID=1.

Government Reports, Party Documents, and Speeches

Bouchard, G., and Taylor, C. *Building the Future: A Time for Reconciliation*. Gouvernement du Québec, 2008.

Coalition avenir Québec. *A New Agenda for Québec Nationalists: Statement to the General Council of Coalition Avenir Québec*. 8 November 2015. https://coalitionavenirquebec.org/wp-content/uploads/2016/02/A-New-Nationalist-Project-2_1.pdf.

– *Religious Accommodations: For a Responsible Approach*. 2013.

Drainville, B. *Charter Affirming the Values of State Secularism and Religious Neutrality and of Equality between Women and Men, and Providing a Framework for Accommodation Requests*. Quebec: Quebec Official Publisher. Pub. L. No. 60. 2013.

Front National. *Burkini: Le législateur doit prendre ses responsabilités*. 26 August 2016. http://www.frontnational.com/2016/08/burkini-le-legislateur-doit-prendre-ses-responsabilites/.

– *La laïcité: Une valeur au coeur du projet républicain*. n.d. http://www.frontnational.com/le-projet-de-marine-le-pen/refondation-republicaine/laicite/.

– *144 engagements présidentiels*. 2017. https://www.marine2017.fr/wp-content/uploads/2017/02/projet-presidentiel-marine-le-pen.pdf.

Gerin, A. *Rapport d'information: Au nom de la misson d'information sur la pratique du port du voile intégral sur le territoire national* (No. 2262). Paris: Assemblée Nationale, 2010.

Gouvernement du Québec. *Au Québec pour bâtir ensemble: Énoncé de politique en matière d'immigration et d'intégration*. Quebec, 1991.

– *Charte des valeurs québécoises: Une affirmation de ce que nous sommes et de ce que nous voulons être*. Quebec, 7 November 2013.

Gouvernement du Québec: Ministère des communautés culturelles et de l'immigration. *Autant de façons d'être québécois*. Quebec, 1981.

Lisée, J.-F. *Oser. Réussir. #AvecLisée*. 2016. http://course.pq.org/jeanfrancois lisee.html.

Observatoire de la laïcité. *Avis de l'observatoire de la laïcité sur la définition et l'encadrement du fait religieux dans les structures qui assurent une mission d'accueil des enfants*. Paris, 2013.

Parti libéral du Québec. *Déclaration identité québécoise: Pour un Québec inclusif dans le respect de nos valeurs communes et de nos libertés individuelles*. Quebec, 5 September 2013.

Parti Québécois. *Agir en toute liberté – Programme 2011*. 2011

Québec solidaire. *Nos principes*. 2006. http://quebecsolidaire.net/propositions/nos-principes

Sarkozy, N. *20eme rassemblement annuel de l'UOIF*. Paris: Ministère de l'intérieur, 19 April 2003. http://www.interieur.gouv.fr/Archives/Archives-de-Nicolas-Sarkozy-2002-2004/Interventions/19.04.2003-20eme-rassemblement-annuel-de-l-UOIF.

Stasi, B. *Commission de réflexion sur l'application du principe de laïcité dans la République: Rapport au président de la République*. France: Présidence de la République, 2003. http://www.ladocumentationfrancaise.fr/var/storage/rapports-publics/034000725.pdf.

Vallée, S. *Loi favorisant le respect de la neutralité religieuse de l'État et visant notamment à encadrer les demandes d'accommodements religieux dans certains organismes*, Quebec: Quebec Official Publisher, *Pub. L. No.* 62. 2015.

Valls, M. *Déclaration de Manuel Valls, ministre de l'intérieur, en réponse à une question sur l'application de la loi du 11 octobre 2010 concernant le port du voile intégral, à l'Assemblée Nationale le 23 juillet 2013*. Paris: Ministère de l'intérieur, 2013. http://www.interieur.gouv.fr

Organizational Reports and Commission Briefs

Association québécoise des Nord-Africains pour la laïcité. *Mémoire sur le Projet de loi 60: Présenté à la Commission des institutions de l'assemblée nationale par M. Akli Ourdja et M. Ali Kaida*. 2013.

Barreau du Québec. *Mémoire du Barreau du Québec*. 2013.

Bergeron, S. *Mémoire "Pour" la charte: Pour une hiérarchisation des droits*. 2013.

Centre d'études ethniques des universités montréalaises. *Mémoire du Centre d'études ethniques des universités montréalaises relatif au projet de loi # 60 du gouvernement du Québec*. 2013.

Coalition laïcité Québec. *Mémoire présenté à la Commission des institutions de l'Assemblée nationale du Québec, dans le cadre de la consultation générale et des auditions publiques sur le projet de loi 60 présenté sous le titre: Charte affirmant les valeurs de laïcité et de neutralité de l'État ansi que l'égalité entre les femmes et les hommes et encadrant les demandes d'accommodement*. 2013.

Collectif d'auteurs. *60 chercheurs universitaires pour la laïcité, contre le Projet de Loi 60*. 2013.

Commission des droits de la personne et des droits de la jeunesse. *Mémoire à la commission des institutions de l'Assemblée nationale: Projet de loi #60, charte affirmant les valeurs de laïcité et de neutralité religieuse de l'état ainsi que l'égalité entre les femmes et les hommes et encadrant les demandes d'accommodement*. 2013.

Conseil du patronat du Québec. *Commentaires du Conseil du patronat du Québec sur le projet de loi # 60 Charte affirmant les valeurs de laïcité et de neutralité religieuse de l'État ainsi que d'égalité entre les femmes et les hommes et encadrant les demandes d'accommodement*. 2013.

Conseil du statut de la femme. *Avis: Droit à l'égalité entre les femmes et les hommes et liberté religieuse*. 2007.

– *Mémoire sur le projet de loi # 60: Charte affirmant les valeurs de laïcité et de neutralité religieuse de l'État ainsi que d'égalité entre les femmes et les hommes et encadrant les demandes d'accommodement*. 2013.

Dionne, C. *Mémoire: Projet de loi no 60, Charte affirmant des valeurs de laïcité et de neutralite de l'État ainsi que l'égalité entre les femmes et les hommes et enadrant les demandes d'accommodement*. 2013.

Fédération des femmes du Québec. *Mémoire présenté par la Fédération des femmes du Québec à la Commission de consultation sur les pratiques d'accommodements reliées aux différences culturelles*. 2007.

– *Pour la laïcité sans domination*. 2014.

Gauthier, M. *Mémoire présenté à la commission parlementaire chargée d'entendre les citoyens au sujet d'un projet de charte portant sur les signes religieux et les accommodements raisonnables*. 2013.

Gauthier, Y. *Mémoire: Charte affirmant des valeurs de laïcité et de neutralite de l'État ainsi que l'égalité entre les femmes et les hommes et enadrant les demandes d'accommodement*. 2013.

Indépendantistes pour une laïcité inclusive. *Rassembler plutot qu'exclure: Déclaration des Indépendantistes pour une laïcité inclusive sur la Charte des "valeurs québécoises."* 2013.

Indigènes de la République. (2005). L'Appel des Indigènes, 2014. http://indigenes-republique.fr/le-p-i-r/appel-des-indigenes-de-la-republique/.

Intellectuels pour la laïcité. "Pour un Québec laique et pluraliste: Déclaration des Intellectuels pour la laïcité." In *Pour une reconnaissance de la laïcité au Québec: Enjeux philosophiques, politiques et juridiques*, edited by D. Baril and Y. Lamonde. Laval: Presses de l'Université Laval, 2013.

Laguitton, D. *Projet de loi # 60: Une charte qui porte le voile*. 2013.

Laïcité citoyenne de la capitale nationale. *Les valeurs québécoises dans la capitale nationale*. 2013.

Ligue des droits et libertés. *Un projet de loi dangereux, incohérant et injustifié*. 2013.

Mouvement des Janette. *Mémoire présenté par le Mouvement des Janette dans le cadre de la consultation générale et des audiences publiques tenues par la Commission des institutions de l'Assemblée nationale du Québec sur le projet de loi # 60*. 2013.

Mouvement laique québécois. *Charte de la laïcité: Mémoire du Mouvement laique québécois*. 2013.

Mouvement national des québécoises et québécois. *Vers une politique de l'identité québécoise: Mémoire présenté dans le cadre de la commission parlementaire consacrée au projet de loi 60*. 2013.

Open Society Foundation. *After the Ban: The Experiences of 35 Women of the Full-Face Veil in France*. 2011.

Pour les droits des femmes du Québec. *Mémoire présenté à la Commission des Institutions de l'Assemblée nationale par Pour les droits des femmes du Québec*. 2014.

Rassemblement pour la laïcité. *Mémoire sur le Projet de loi 60 présenté à la Commission des institutions de l'Assemblée Nationale*. 2013.

Seymour, M. *Le Project de loi 60 et les signes ostentatoires*. 2014.

Société nationale des Québécoises et des Québécois de Chaudière-Appalaches. *La ruralité a mis le Québec au monde, on devrait peut-être l'écouter: Un point de vue du Québec rural sur la Charte des valeurs*. 2013.

Turp, D. "Pour une charte québécoise de la laïcité." In *Pour une reconnaissance de la laïcité au Québec: Enjeux philosophiques, politiques et juridiques*, edited by D. Baril and Y. Lamonde, 137–61. Laval: Presses de l'Université Laval, 2013.

Université de Sherbrooke. *Collectif de 66 professeur-e-s et chargé-e-s de cours de l'Université de Sherbrooke contre le Projet de loi # 60*. 2013.

SECONDARY SOURCES

Adrian, M. *Religious Freedom at Risk: The EU, French Schools, and Why the Veil Was Banned*. New York: Springer, 2016.

Ahmed, S. *Strange Encounters: Embodied Others in Post-Coloniality*. New York: Routledge, 2000.

Ahmed-Gosh, H. "Dilemmas of Islamic and Secular Feminists and Feminisms." *Journal of International Women's Studies* 9, no. 3 (2008): 99–116.

Alba, R., and N. Foner. "Comparing Immigrant Integration in North America and Western Europe: How Much do the Grand Narratives Tell Us?" *International Migration Review* 48, no. S1 (2014): S263–91.

Albright, J.J. "The Multidimensional Nature of Party Competition." *Party Politics* 16, no. 6 (2010): 669–719.

Alford, R. "Class Voting in the Anglo-American Political Systems." In *Party Systems and Voter Alignments: Cross-National Perspectives*, edited by S.M. Lipset and S. Rokkan, 65–127. New York: The Free Press, 1967.

Al-Saji, A. "The Racialization of Muslim Veils: A Philosophical Analysis." *Philosophy and Social Criticism* 36, no. 8 (2010): 875–902.

Amiraux, V. "De l'Empire à la République: À propos de l' 'Islam de France.'" *Cahiers de Recherche Sociologique* 46 (2008): 45–60.

Amiraux, V., and P. Simon. "There Are No Minorities Here: Cultures of Scholarship and Public Debate on Immigrants and Integration in France." *International Journal of Comparative Sociology* 47, no. 3–4 (2006): 191–215.

Andersen, R. "The Class-Party Relationship in Canada, 1965–2004." In *Political Choice Matters: Explaining the Strength of Class and Religious Cleavages in Cross-National Perspective*, edited by G. Evans and N.D. de Graaf, 165–84. Oxford: Oxford University Press, 2013.

Andersen, R., and J. Evans. "The Stability of French Political Space, 1988–2002. " *French Politics* 3 (2005): 282–301.

Anderson, B. *Imagined Communities: Reflections on the Origin and the Spread of Nationalism*. London and New York: Verso, 1991.

Anderson, C. D. "Economic Voting and Multilevel Governance: A Comparative Individual-Level Analysis." *American Journal of Political Science* 50, no. 2 (2006): 449–63.

Baehr, P., and D. Gordon. "From the Headscarf to the Burqa: The Role of Social Theorists in Shaping Laws against the Veil." *Economy and Society* 42, no. 2 (2013): 249–80.

Bale, T. "Cinderella and Her Ugly Sisters: The Mainstream and Extreme Right in Europe's Bipolarising Party Systems." *West European Politics* 26, no. 3 (2003): 67–90.

– "Politics Matters: A Conclusion." *Journal of European Public Policy* 15, no. 3 (2008): 453–64.

– "Turning Round the Telescope: Centre-Right Parties and Immigration and Integration Policy in Europe." *Journal of European Public Policy* 15, no. 3 (2008): 315–30.

Bale, T., C. Green-Pedersen, A. Krouwel, K.R. Luther, and N. Sitter. "If You Can't Beat Them, Join Them? Explaining Social Democratic Responses to the Challenge from the Populist Radical Right in Western Europe." *Political Studies* 58 (2010): 410–26.

Balthazar, L. "The Quebec Experience: Success or Failure?" *Regional and Federal Studies* 9, no.1 (1999): 153–69.

Bancel, N., P. Blanchard, and F. Vergès. *La République coloniale: Essai sur une utopie*. Paris: Albin-Michel, 2003.

Bannerji, H. "The Paradox of Diversity: The Construction of a Multicultural Canada and 'Women of Color.' *Women's Studies International Forum* 23, no. 5 (2000): 537–60.

Barth, F. "Introduction." In *Ethnic Groups and Boundaries: The Social Organization of Cultural Difference*, edited by F. Barth, 9–38. Long Grove, IL: Waveland Press, 1969.

Baubérot, J. "La laïcité en France: Histoire et défis actuels." In *La Laïcité en France*, edited by J. Baubérot and C. Dagens, 27–48. Paris: Parole et Silence, 2005.

– *La laïcité falsifiée*. Paris: Editions la Découverte, 2012.

– "La laïcité française et ses mutations." *Social Compass* 45, no. 1 (1998): 175–87.

– *Les sept laïcités françaises: Le modèle français de la laïcité n'existe pas*. Paris: Maison des sciences de l'homme, 2015.

Baubérot, J., and M. Milot. *Laïcités sans frontières*. Paris: Editions du Seuil, 2011.

Beaman, L.G. "Battles over Symbols: The 'Religion' of the Minority Versus the 'Culture' of the Majority." *Journal of Law and Religion* 28, no. 1 (2013): 67–104.

– "Conclusion: Alternatives to Reasonable Accommodation." In *Reasonable Accommodation: Managing Religious Diversity*, edited by L.G. Beaman, 208–23. Vancouver: UBC Press, 2012.

Beauchemin, J. "Chapitre 1: Qu'est-ce qu'être Québécois: entre la préservation de soi et l'ouverture à l'autre." In *État et société*, edited by Alain-G. Gagnon, 27–43. Montréal: Québec Amérique, 2003.

– "Nationalisme québécois et crise du lien social." *Les cahiers de recherche sociologique* 25 (1995): 101–23.

– "La question nationale québécoise: les nouveaux paramètres de l'analyse." *Recherches sociographiques* 39, no. 2–3 (1998): 249–69.

Behiels, M.D. *Prelude to Quebec's Quiet Revolution: Liberalism versus Neo-nationalism*. Montreal: McGill-Queen's University Press, 1985.

Benhabib, S. "The Return of Political Theology: The Scarf Affair in Comparative Constitutional Perspective in France, Germany and Turkey." *Philosophy and Social Criticism* 36, no. 4 (2010): 451–71.

Berezin, M. *Illiberal Politics in Neoliberal Times: Culture, Security and Populism in the New Europe*. Cambridge, MA: Cambridge University Press, 2009.

Bertossi, C. *Country Report: France* (No. Country Report, RSCAS/EUDO-CIT-CR 2010/14). Badia Fiesolana, San Domenico di Fiesole (FI), Italy: EUDO Citizenship Observatory, 2010.

Betz, H.G. "The New Front National: Still a Master Case?" Recode Working Paper Series, 2013.

– "The New Politics of Resentment: Radical Right-Wing Populist Parties in Western Europe." *Comparative Politics* 25, no. 4 (1993): 413–27.

Bilge, S. "Beyond Subordination vs. Resistance: An Intersectional Approach to the Agency of Veiled Muslim Women." *Journal of Intercultural Studies* 31, no. 1 (2010): 9–28.

Blad, C., and P. Couton. "The Rise of an Intercultural Nation: Immigration, Diversity and Nationhood in Québec." *Journal of Ethnic and Migration Studies* 35, no. 4 (2009): 645–67.

Blais, A., and P.J. Loewen. "The French Electoral System and Its Effects." *West European Politics* 32, no. 2 (2009): 345–59.

Blanchard, P., N. Bancel, and S. Lemaire, eds. *La fracture coloniale, la société française au prisme de l'héritage colonial*. Paris: La Découverte, 2005.

Bleich, E. "Integrating Ideas into Policy-Making Analysis: Frames and Race Policies in Britain and France." *Comparative Political Studies* 35, no. 9 (2002): 1054–76.

Bock-Coté, M. "Derrière la laïcité, la nation. Retour sur la controverse des accommodements raisonnables et sur la crise du multiculturalisme québécois." *Globe: Revue internationales d'études québécoises* 11, no. 1 (2008): 95–113.

Bohman, A. "Articulated Antipathies: Political Influence on Anti-Immigrant Attitudes." *International Journal of Comparative Sociology* 52, no. 6 (2011): 457–77.

Bornschier, S., and R. Lachat. "The Evolution of the French Political Space and Party System." *West European Politics* 32, no. 2 (2009): 360–83.

Bouchard, G. "L'imaginaire de la Grande Noirceur et de la Révolution tranquille: Fictions identitaires et jeux de mémoire au Québec." *Recherches sociographiques* 46, no. 3 (2005): 411–36.

– *L'interculturalisme. Un point de vue québécois*. Montreal: Les éditions du Boréal, 2012.

– *La nation québécoise au futur et au passé*. Montreal: VLB éditeur, 1999.

– *La pensée impuissante. Échecs et mythes nationaux canadiens-français, 1850–1960*. Montreal: Boréal, 2004.

– "What Is Interculturalism?" *McGill Law Journal* 56, no. 2 (2011): 435–68.

Bougrab, J. *Ma république se meurt*. Paris: Bernard Grasset, 2013.

Bowen, J. "A View from France on the Internal Complexity of National Models." *Journal of Ethnic and Migration Studies* 33, no. 6 (2007): 1003–16.

– *Why the French Don't Like Headscarves*. Princeton: Princeton University Press, 2007.

Brechon, P., and S.K. Mitra. "The Front National in France: The Emergence of an Extreme Right Protest Movement." *Comparative Politics* 25, no. 1 (1992): 63–82.

Brooks, C., and J. Manza. "Do Changing Values Explain the New Politics? A Critical Assessment of the Postmaterialist Thesis." *Sociological Quarterly* 35, no. 4 (1994): 541–70.

Brubaker, R. *Citizenship and Nationhood in France and Germany*. Cambridge, MA: Harvard University Press, 1992.

– "Immigration, Citizenship, and the Nation-State in France and Germany: A Comparative Historical Analysis." *International Sociology* 5, no. 4 (1990): 379–407.

– *Nationalism Reframed: Nationhood and the National Question in the New Europe*. New York: Cambridge University Press, 1996.

Brubaker, R., and F. Cooper. "Beyond Identity." *Theory and Society* 29 (2000): 1–47.

Brym, R.J., M.W. Gillespie, and R.L. Lenton. "Class Power, Class Mobilization, and Class Voting: The Canadian Case." *Canadian Journal of Sociology* 14, no. 1 (1989): 25–44.

Bussi, M., and J. Fourquet. "Election présidentielle 2007: Neuf cartes pour comprendre." *Presses de Sciences Po* 3, no. 57 (2007): 411–28.

Calhoun, C. *Nationalism*. Buckingham: Open University Press, 1997.

Campbell, J.L. "Ideas, Politics, and Public Policy." *Annual Review of Sociology* 28 (2002): 21–38.

Carter, E.L. "Proportional Representation and the Fortunes of Right-Wing Extremist Parties." *West European Politics* 25, no. 3 (2002): 125–46.

Clark, T.N., and S.M. Lipset. "Are Social Classes Dying?" *International Sociology* 6, no. 4 (1991): 397–410.

Clark, T.N., S.M. Lipset, and M. Rempel. "The Declining Political Significance of Social Class." In *The Breakdown of Class Politics: A Debate on Post-Industrial Stratification*, edited by T.N. Clark and S.M. Lipset, 77–104. Washington, DC: Woodrow Wilson Center Press, 2001.

Cole, A. "A Strange Affair: The 2002 Presidential and Parliamentary Elections in France." *Government and Opposition* 37, no. 3 (2002): 317–42.

Coleman, W.D. *The Independence Movement in Québec 1945–1980*. Toronto: University of Toronto Press, 1984.

de Cilia, R., M. Reisigl, and R. Wodak. "The Discursive Construction of National Identities." *Discourse and Society* 10, no. 2 (1999): 149–73.

de Leon, C., M. Desai, and C. Tugal. eds. *Building Blocs: How Parties Organize Society*. Stanford: Stanford University Press, 2015.

– "Political Articulation: Parties and the Constitution of Cleavages in the United States, India, and Turkey." *Sociological Theory* 27, no. 3 (2009): 193–219.

Delphy, C. "Antisexisme Ou Antiracisme? Un Faux Dilemme." *Nouvelles Questions Féministes* 25, no. 1 (2006): 59–83.

Dot-Pouillard, N. "Les recompositions politiques du mouvement féministe français au regard du hijab." *Sociologies*, 31 October 2007. http://journals.openedition.org/sociologies/246.

Dufour, P. "From Protest to Partisan Politics: When and How Collective Actors Cross the Line; Sociological Perspective on Québec Solidaire." *Canadian Journal of Sociology* 34, no. 1 (2009): 55–81.

Dufour, V., and J. Heinrich. *Circus Quebecus: Sous le chapiteau de la commission Bouchard-Taylor*. Montreal: Boréal, 2008.

Dumont, F. *Genèse de la société québécoise*. Montreal: Boréal, 1993.

Eidlin, B. "Why Is There No Labor Party in the United States? Political Articulation and the Canadian Comparison, 1932 to 1948." *American Sociological Review* 81, no. 3 (2016): 488–516.

Esping-Andersen, G. *Three Worlds of Welfare Capitalism*. Princeton: Princeton University Press, 1990.

Evans, P., D. Rueschemeyer, and T. Skocpol, eds. *Bringing the State Back In*. Cambridge: Cambridge University Press, 1985.

Fabre, R. "L'élaboration de la loi de 1905." In *Politiques de la laïcité au XXe siècle*, edited by P. Weil, 45–75. Paris: Presses universitaires de France, 2007.

Farris, S.R. *In the Name of Women's Rights: The Rise of Femonationalism*. Durham: Duke University Press, 2017.

Favell, A. *Philosophies of Integration: Immigration and the Idea of Citizenship in France and Britain*. New York: Palgrave, 1998.

Ferree, M.M. "Resonance and Radicalism: Feminist Framing in the Abortion Debates of the United States and Germany." *American Journal of Sociology* 109, no. 2 (2003): 304–44.

Finkielkraut, A. *L'Ingratitude: Conversation sur Notre Temps*. Folio, 1999.

Forester, J. "Bounded Rationality and the Politics of Muddling Through." *Public Administration Review*, January/February (1984): 23–31.

Fournier, M. "Quebec Sociology and Quebec Society: The Construction of a Collective Identity." *The Canadian Journal of Sociology / Cahiers Canadiens de Sociologie* 26, no. 3 (2001): 333–47.

Fournier, M., and L. Maheu. "Nationalismes et nationalisation du champ scientifique québécois." *Sociologie et sociétés* 7, no. 2 (1975): 89–114.

Fournier, P. "In the (Canadian) Shadow of Islamic Law: Translating Mahr as a Bargaining Endowment." *Osgoode Hall Law Journal* 44, no. 4 (2006): 649–78.

Fraser, N. "From Redistribution to Recognition: Dilemmas of Justice in a 'Post-Socialist' Age." *New Left Review* 212 (1995): 68–93.

Fraser, N., and A. Honneth. *Redistribution or Recognition? A Political-Philosophical Exchange*. London: Verso, 2003.

Fredette, J. *Constructing Muslims in France: Discourse, Public Identity, and the Politics of Citizenship*. Philadelphia: Temple Univerity Press, 2014.

Frosh, P., and G. Wolfsfeld. "ImagiNation: News Discourse, Nationhood, and Civil Society." *Media, Culture and Society* 29, no. 1 (2006): 105–29.

Gagnon, A.-G., and R. Iacovino. *Federalism, Citizenship, and Québec: Debating Multinationalism*. Toronto: University of Toronto Press, 2007.

Gellner, E. *Nations and Nationalism*. Ithaca: Cornell University Press, 1983.

Gerin, A. *Les ghettos de la république: Encore et toujours*. Paris: Le Publieur, 2012.

Gérin-Lajoie, P. *Combats d'un révolutionnaire tranquille*. Montreal: Centre éducatif et culturel, 1989.

Geva, D. "Marine Le Pen, Parité, and Right Wing Populism." Presented at the Annual Meeting of the Social Science History Association, Toronto, 2014.

Geys, B. "Success and Failure in Electoral Competition: Selective Issue Emphasis under Incomplete Issue Ownership." *Electoral Studies* 31, no. 2 (2012): 406–12.

Giry, S. "France and Its Muslims." *Foreign Affairs* 85, no. 5 (2006): 87–104.

Glavany, J. *La laïcité: Un combat pour la paix*. Paris: Heloise d'Ormesson, 2011.

Gokariksel, B., and K. Mitchell. "Veiling, Secularism, and the Neo-Liberal Subject: National Narratives and Supranational Desires in Turkey and France." *Global Networks* 5, no. 2 (2005): 147–65.

Groulx, L. *L'appel de la race*. Montreal: Action Française, 1923.

Habchi, S. *Toutes libres! Rebelles et insoumises, exigeons l'impossible*. Paris: Pygmalion, 2013.

Haegel, F. "The Transformation of the French Right: Institutional Imperatives and Organizational Changes." *French Politics* 2 (2004): 185–202.

Hagelund, A. "A Matter of Decency? The Progress Party in Norwegian Immigration Politics." *Journal of Ethnic and Migration Studies* 29, no. 1 (2003): 47–65.

Hajjat, A., and M. Mohammed. *Islamophobie: Comment les élites françaises fabriquent le "problème musulman."* Paris: La Découverte, 2013.

Hall, J.A. "Liberalism and Statelessness: Québec in Contexts." *Scottish Affairs* 37, no. 2 (2001): 42–53.

Hall, P. "Policy Paradigms, Social Learning and the State." *Comparative Politics* 25, no. 3 (1993): 275–96.

Hamilton, R., and M. Pinard. "The Bases of Parti Québécois Support in Recent Québec Elections." *Canadian Journal of Political Science* 9, no. 1 (1976): 3–26.

Handler, R. *Nationalism and the Politics of Culture in Québec*. Madison: University of Wisconsin Press, 1988.

Hargreaves, A.C. "The Political Mobilization of the North African Immigrant Community in France." *Ethnic and Racial Studies* 14, no. 3 (1991): 350–67.

Hayes, D. "Party Reputations, Journalistic Expectations: How Issue Ownership Influences Election News." *Political Communication* 25 (2008): 377–400.

Helbling, M., and A. Tresch. "Measuring Party Positions and Issue Salience from Media Coverage: Discussing and Cross-Validating New Indicators." *Electoral Studies* 30 (2011): 174–83.

Henderson, A. "Regional Political Cultures." *Canadian Journal of Political Science* 37, no. 3 (2004): 595–615.

Hepburn, E. "Small Worlds in Canada and Europe: A Comparison of Regional Party Systems in Québec, Bavaria and Scotland." *Regional and Federal Studies* 20, no. 4–5 (2010): 527–44.

Hollifield, J.F. "Immigration and Republicanism in France: The Hidden Consensus." In *Controlling Immigration: A Global Perspective*, edited by W.A. Cornelius, P.L. Martin, and J.F. Hollifield, 143–75. Stanford: Stanford University Press, 1994.

Howard, M.M. "The Impact of the Far Right on Citizenship Policy in Europe: Explaining Continuity and Change." *Journal of Ethnic and Migration Studies* 36, no. 5 (2010): 735–51.

Iacovino, R. "Contextualizing the Quebec Charter of Values: Belonging without Citizenship in Quebec." *Canadian Ethnic Studies* 47, no. 1 (2015): 41–60.

Inglehart, R. *Culture Shift in Advanced Industrial Societies*. Princeton: Princeton University Press, 1990.

Inglehart, R., and P.R. Abramson. "Economic Security and Value Change." *American Political Science Review* 88, no. 2 (1994): 336–54.

Inglehart, R., and J.-R. Rabier. "Political Realignment in Advanced Industrial Society: From Class-Based Politics to Quality-of-Life Politics." *Government and Opposition* 21 (1986): 456–79.

Jennings, J. "Citizenship, Republicanism and Multiculturalism in Contemporary France." *British Journal of Political Science* 30, no. 4 (2000): 575–97.

Joppke, C. "State Neutrality and Islamic Headscarf Laws in France and Germany." *Theory and Society* 36, no. 4 (2007): 313–42.

Joppke, C., and J. Torpey. *Legal Integration of Islam: A Transatlantic Comparison*. Cambridge, MA: Harvard University Press, 2013.

Juteau, D. "The Citizen Makes an Entrée: Redefining the National Community in Québec." *Citizenship Studies* 6, no. 4 (2002): 441–58.

– "'Pures laines' Québécois: The Concealed Ethnicity of Dominant Majorities." In *Rethinking Ethnicity: Majority Groups and Dominant Minorities*, edited by E.P. Kaufmann, 84–101. London: Routledge, 2004.

Kawar, L. "Juridical Framings of Immigrants in the United States and France: Courts, Social Movements, and Symbolic Politics." *International Migration Review* 46, no. 2 (2012): 414–55.

Kessel, P. *Ils ont volé la laïcité!* Paris: Jean-Claude Gawsewitch, 2012.

Killian, C. "From a Community of Believers of an Islam of the Heart: 'Conspicuous' Symbols, Muslim Practices, and the Privatization of Religion in France." *Sociology of Religion* 68, no. 3 (2007): 305–20.

– "The Other Side of the Veil: North African Women in France Respond to the Headscarf Affair." *Gender and Society* 17, no. 4 (2003): 567–90.

Kitschelt, H. "European Party Systems: Continuity and Change." In *Developments in West European Politics*, edited by M. Rhodes, P. Heywood, and V. Wright, 131–50. Houndmills, UK: Macmillan, 1997.

Korteweg, A.C. "The 'Headrag Tax': Impossible Laws and Their Symbolic and Material Consequences." *Social Identities* 19, no. 6 (2013): 759–74.

– "The Sharia Debate in Ontario: Gender, Islam, and Representations of Muslim Women's Agency." *Gender and Society* 22, no. 4 (2008): 434–54.

Korteweg, A.C., and G. Yurdakul. *The Headscarf Debates: Conflicts of National Belonging*. Stanford: Stanford University Press, 2014.

Koussens, D. "Comment les partis politiques québécois se représentent-ils la laïcité?" *Diversité Urbaine* 9, no. 1 (2009): 27–44.

– "Neutrality of the State and Regulation of Religious Symbols in Schools in Québec and France." *Social Compass* 56, no. 2 (2009): 202–13.

– "Religious Diversity and the Divergence of Secular Trajectories: Comparing Secularization Practices in Québec and France." *EUI Working Papers*: Florence, 2011.

Kriesi, H. "The Role of European Integration in National Election Campaigns." *European Union Politics* 8, no. 1 (2007): 83–108.

Kriesi, H., E. Grande, R. Lachat, M. Dolezal, S. Bornschier, and T. Frey. "Globalization and the Transformation of the National Political Space: Six European Countries Compared." *European Journal of Political Research* 45 (2006): 921–56.

Kuhn, R. "The French Presidential and Parliamentary Elections, 2002." *Representation* 39, no. 1 (2002): 44–56.

Kuru, A.T. "Passive and Assertive Secularism: Historical Conditions, Ideological Struggles, and State Policies toward Religion." *World Politics* 59, no. 4 (2007): 568–94.

Laborde, C. *Critical Republicanism: The Hijab Controversy and Political Philosophy*. Oxford: Oxford University Press, 2008.

– "On Republican Toleration." *Constellations* 9, no. 2 (2002): 167–83.

Ladrech, R. "Social Movements and Party Systems: The French Socialist Party and New Social Movements." *West European Politics* 12, no. 3 (1989): 262–79.

Lamont, M., and V. Molnar. "The Study of Boundaries in the Social Sciences." *Annual Review of Sociology* 28 (2002): 167–95.

Lamoureux, D. "Nationalisme et féminisme: Impasse et coïncidences." *Possibles* 8, no. 1 (1983): 43–59.

Langeron, P. "Diversité Québécoise et Tectonique des Cultures Juridiques." In *La diversité québécoise en débat: Bouchard, Taylor et les autres*, edited by B. Gagnon. Montreal: Editions Québec Amérique, 2010.

Latour, J. "Assurer la protection législative de la laïcité: Une démarche essentielle pour la cohésion sociale et la fraternité citoyenne." In *Pour Une Reconnaissance De La Laïcité Au Québec: Enjeux Philosophiques, Politiques Et Juridiques*, edited by D. Baril and Y. Lamonde, 111–36. Laval: Presses de l'Université Laval, 2013.

Laxer, E. "'We Are All Republicans': Political Articulation and the Production of Nationhood in France's Face Veil Debate." *Comparative Studies in Society and History* 60, no. 4 (2018): 938–67.

Laxer, E., R.D. Carson, and A.C. Korteweg. "Articulating Minority Nationhood: Cultural and Political Dimensions in Québec's Reasonable Accommodation Debate." *Nations and Nationalism* 20, no. 1 (2014): 133–53.

Laxer, E., and A.C. Korteweg. "Party Competition and the Production of Nationhood in the Immigration Context: Particularizing the Universal for Political Gain in France and Québec." *Ethnic and Racial Studies* 41, no. 11 (2018): 1915–33.

Leeper, T.J., and R. Slothuus. "Political Parties, Motivated Reasoning, and Public Opinion Formation." *Advances in Political Psychology* 35, no. 1 (2014): 129–56.

Lefebvre, E.L. "Republicanism and Universalism: Factors of Inclusion and Exclusion in the French Concept of Citizenship." *Citizenship Studies* 7, no. 1 (2003): 15–36.

Lemieux, V. *Le Parti libéral du Québec: Alliances, rivalités et neutralités*. Sainte-Foy: Les Presses de l'Université Laval, 1993.

Lépinard, E. "The Contentious Subject of Feminism: Defining Women in France from the Second Wave to Parity." *Signs* 32, no. 2 (2007): 375–403.

– "Doing Intersectionality: Repertoires of Feminist Practices in France and Canada." *Gender and Society* 18, no. 6 (2014): 1–27.

– "Impossible Intersectionality? French Feminists and the Struggle for Inclusion." *Politics and Gender* 10, no. 1 (2014): 124–30.

– "Migrating Concepts: Immigrant Integration and the Regulation of Religious Dress in France and Canada." *Ethnicities* 15, no. 5 (2015): 611–32.

Levesque, R. *An Option for Québec*. Toronto: McClelland and Stewart, 1968.

Lewis, J. "Gender and the Development of Welfare Regimes." *Journal of European Social Policy* 2, no. 3 (1992): 159–73.

Lijphart, A. "Religious vs. Linguistic vs. Class Voting: The 'Crucial Experiment' of Comparing Belgium, Canada, South Africa, and Switzerland." *American Political Science Review* 73, no. 2 (1979): 442–58.

Lindblom, C.E. "Still Muddling, Not Yet Through." *Public Administration Review* November/December (1979): 517–26.

Lipset, S.M. "The Decline of Class Ideologies: The End of Political Exceptionalism?" In *The Breakdown of Class Politics: A Debate on Post-Industrial Stratification*, edited by T.N. Clark and S.M. Lipset, 249–72. Washington, DC: Woodrow Wilson Center Press, 2001.

– *Political Man: The Social Bases of Politics*. New York: Doubleday, 1960.

Lipset, S.M., and S. Rokkan. "Cleavage Structure, Party Systems, and Voter Alignments: An Introduction." In *Party Systems and Voter Alignments: Cross-National Perspectives*, edited by S.M. Lipset and S. Rokkan, 1–64. New York: Free Press, 1967.

Maclure, J. "Laïcité et fédéralisme: Le débat sur la Charte de la laïcité dans le contexte federal canadien." *L'idée fédérale: Réseau québécois de réflexion sur le fédéralisme* (March 2014): 1–30.

Maclure, J., and C. Taylor. *Secularism and Freedom of Conscience*. Cambridge, MA: Harvard University Press, 2011.

Mahéo, V.-A., and E. Bélanger. "Is the Parti Québécois Bound to Disappear? A Study of the Current Generational Dynamics of Electoral Behaviour in Quebec." *Canadian Journal of Political Science* 51, no. 2 (2018): 335–56.

Maillé, C. "The Québec Women's Movement: Past and Present." In *Québec: State and Society*, vol 3, edited by A.-G. Gagnon, 287–306. Peterborough, Ontario: Broadview Press, 2004.

– "Réception de la théorie postcoloniale dans le féminisme québécois." *Recherches Féministes* 20, no. 2 (2007): 91–111.

Mair, P. "Political Parties, Popular Legitimacy and Public Privilege." *West European Politics* 18, no. 3 (1995): 40–57.

Marthaler, S. "'New' Politics for 'Old'? Value Change and the Voter-Party Relationship in France." *French Politics* 6 (2008): 187–213.

– "Nicolas Sarkozy and the Politics of French Immigration Policy." *Journal of European Public Policy* 15, no. 3 (2008): 382–97.

Mayer, N. "Comment Nicolas Sarkozy a rétréci l'électorat Le Pen." *Presses de Sciences Po* 3, no. 57 (2007): 429–45.

McRoberts, K. *Québec: Social Change and Political Crisis*. Toronto: McClelland and Stewart, 1988.

Medeiros, M., J.-P. Gauvin, and C. Chhim. "Refining Vote Choice in an Ethno-Regionalist Context: Three-Dimensional Ideological Voting in Catalonia and Québec." *Electoral Studies* 40 (2015): 14–22.

Mendelsohn, M., A. Parkin, and M. Pinard. "A New Chapter or the Same Old Story? Québec Public Opinion and the National Question from 1996–2003." In *Quebec and Canada in the New Century: New Dynamics, New Opportunities*, edited by M. Murphy, 25–52. Montreal: McGill-Queen's University Press, 2005.

Meunier, É.-M., and J.-F. Laniel. "Nation et catholicisme culturel au Québec: Signification d'une recomposition religio-politique." *Sciences religieuses / Studies in Religion* 41, no. 4 (2012): 595–617.

Meunier, É.-M., and J.-P. Warren. "L'horizon 'personnaliste' de la Révolution tranquille." *Société* 20–21 (1999): 347–448.

Milot, M. *Laïcité dans le nouveau monde: Le cas du Québec*. Paris: Brepols, 2002.

Minozzi, W. "Conditions for Dialogue and Dominance in Political Campaigns." *Political Communication* 31 (2014): 73–93.

Mitra, S.K. "The Front National in France – A Single-Issue Movement?" *West European Politics* 11, no. 2 (1988): 47–64.

Mohanty, C.T. "Under Western Eyes: Feminist Scholarship and Colonial Discourses." *Feminist Review* 30 (1988): 61–88.

Morel, A. "La coexistence des Chartes canadienne et québécoise: Problèmes d'intéraction." *Revue de droit de l'université Sherbrooke*, 17, no. 49 (1986): 82–3.

Mudde, C. *Populist Radical Right Parties in Europe*. Cambridge: Cambridge University Press, 2007.

– "The 2012 Stein Rokkan Lecture: Three Decades of Populist Radical

Right Parties in Western Europe: So What?" *European Journal of Political Research* 52 (2013): 1–19.

Muhlmann, G., and C. Zalc. "La laïcité, de la IIIe à la Ve République." *Le Seuil* 3, no. 126 (2008): 101–14.

Müller, J.-W. *What Is Populism?* Philadelphia: University of Pennsylvania Press, 2016.

Myrdal, G. *An American Dilemma: The Negro Problem and Modern Democracy.* New York: Harper and Brothers Publishers, 1944.

Noiriel, G. *Le Creuset français: Histoire de l'immigration XIXe-XXe siècles.* Paris: Editions du Seuil, 1988.

– *Population, immigration, et identité nationale en France: XIXe-XXe siècle.* Paris: Hachette, 1992.

– *A quoi sert "l'identité nationale."* Marseille: Agone, 2007.

Norris, P. *The Radical Right: Voters and Parties in the Electoral Market.* Cambridge: Cambridge University Press, 2005.

Oakes, L., and J. Warren. *Language, Citizenship, and Identity in Québec.* Basingstoke: Palgrave Macmillan, 2007.

Olzak, S. "Ethnic Mobilization in Québec." *Ethnic and Racial Studies* 5, no. 3 (1983): 253–75.

O'Neill, B., E. Gidengil, C. Côté, and L. Young. "Freedom of Religion, Women's Agency and Banning the Face Veil: The Role of Feminist Beliefs in Shaping Women's Opinion." *Ethnic and Racial Studies* 38, no. 11 (2014): 1886–901.

Orloff, A.S. "Gender and the Social Rights of Citizenship: The Comparative Analysis of Gender Relations and Welfare States." *American Sociological Review* 58 (1993): 303–28.

Orloff, A.S., and T. Shiff. "Feminism/s in Power: Rethinking Gender Equality after the Second Wave." *Perverse Politics? Feminism, Anti-Imperialism, Multiplicity* 30 (2016): 109–34.

Pakulski, J. "The Dying of Class or of Marxist Class Theory?" *International Sociology* 8, no. 3 (1993): 279–92.

Pakulski, J., and M. Waters. "The Reshaping and Dissolution of Social Class in Advanced Society." *Theory and Society* 25 (1996): 667–91.

Parvez, Z.F. "Debating the Burqa in France: The Antipolitics of Islamic Revival." *Qualitative Sociology* 34 (2011): 287–312.

Pena-Ruiz, H. *La laïcité pour l'égalité.* Paris: Mille et une nuits, 2011.

Pierson, P. "Increasing Returns, Path Dependence and the Study of Politics." *American Political Science Review* 94, no. 2 (2000): 251–76.

– *Politics in Time: History, Institutions, and Social Analysis.* Princeton: Princeton University Press, 2004.

Pinard, M. "Working Class Politics: An Interpretation of the Québec Case." *Canadian Review of Sociology and Anthropology* 7, no. 2 (1970): 87–109.

– "Political Ambivalence towards the Parti Québecois and Its Electoral Consequences, 1970–2003." *Canadian Journal of Sociology* 30, no. 3 (2005): 281–314.

Pinard, M., and R. Hamilton. "The Parti Québécois Comes to Power: An Analysis of the 1976 Québec Election." *Canadian Journal of Political Science* 11, no. 4 (1978): 739–75.

Putnam, R. "Bowling Alone: America's Declining Social Capital." *Journal of Democracy* 6, no. 1 (1995): 65–78.

Reitz, J., P. Simon, and E. Laxer. "Muslims' Social Inclusion in Canada, Québec and France: Does National Context Matter?" *Journal of Ethnic and Migration Studies* 43, no. 15 (2017): 2473–98.

Reynié, D. "Le tournant ethno-socialiste du Front National." *Etudes* 11, no. 415 (2011): 463–72.

Rigoulot, P. "Protestants and the French Nation under the Third Republic: Between Recognition and Assimilation." *National Identities* 11, no. 1 (2009): 45–57.

Robine, J. "Les 'Indigènes de la République': Nation et question postcoloniale." *Hérodote* 1, no. 120 (2006): 118–48.

Rooduijn, M., S.L. de Lange, and W. van der Brug. "A Populist Zeitgeist? Programmatic Contagion by Populist Parties in Western Europe." *Party Politics* 20, no. 4 (2014): 563–75.

Rovny, J., and E.E. Edwards. "Struggle over Dimensionality: Party Competition in Western and Eastern Europe." *East European Politics and Societies* 26, no. 1 (2012): 56–74.

Rydgren, J. "Is Extreme Right-Wing Populism Contagious? Explaining the Emergence of a New Party Family." *European Journal of Political Research* 44 (2005): 413–37.

Salzbrunn, M. "Performing Gender and Religion: The Veil's Impact on Boundary-Making Processes in France." *Women's Studies Journal* 41, no. 6 (2012): 682–705.

Schain, M.A. "Commentary: Why Political Parties Matter." *Journal of European Public Policy* 15, no. 3 (2008): 465–70.

– "Immigration and Changes in the French Party System." *European Journal of Political Research* 16 (1988): 597–621.

– "The National Front in France and the Construction of Political Legitimacy." *West European Politics* 10, no. 2 (1987): 229–52.

Schneider, H. "Branding in Politics – Manifestations, Relevance and Identity-

Oriented Management." *Journal of Political Marketing* 3, no. 3 (2004): 41–67.

Scott, J. *The Politics of the Veil*. Princeton: Princeton University Press, 2007.

– "Sexularism." Robert Schuman Centre for Advanced Studies, Ursula Hirschmann Annual Lecture on Gender and Europe, 2009.

– "Symptomatic Politics: The Banning of Islamic Headscarves in French Public Schools." *French Politics, Culture and Society* 23, no. 3 (2005): 106–27.

Selby, J.A. "Islam in France Reconfigured: Republican Islam in the 2010 Gerin Report." *Journal of Muslim Minority Affairs* 31, no. 3 (2011): 383–98.

Semyonov, M., R. Raijman, and A. Gorodzeisky. "The Rise of Anti-Foreigner Sentiment in European Societies, 1988–2000." *American Sociological Review* 71, no. 3 (2006): 426–49.

Sewell, W. "Historical Events as Transformations of Structures." *Theory and Society* 25 (1996): 841–81.

– "A Theory of Structure: Duality, Agency, and Transformation." *American Journal of Sociology* 98, no. 1 (1992): 1–29.

Sheehi, S. *Islamophobia: The Ideological Campaign against Muslims*. Atlanta, GA: Clarity Press, 2011.

Silverman, M. "The French Republic Unveiled." *Ethnic and Racial Studies* 30, no. 4 (2007): 628–42.

Simon, P. "Contested Citizenship in France: The Republican Politics of Identity and Integration." In *Developments in French Politics, Volume 5*, edited by A. Cole, S. Meunier, and V. Tiberj, 203–17. London: Palgrave Macmillan, 2013.

– "Nationality and National Sentiment." In *Trajectories and Origins: Survey on Population Diversity in France*, edited by C. Beauchemin, C. Hamelle, and P. Simon, 115–20. Paris: Institut d'études démographiques, 2010.

Skocpol, T. *States and Social Revolutions*. New York: Cambridge University Press, 1979.

Skrentny, J.D. *The Minority Rights Revolution*. Cambridge, MA: Harvard University Press, 2002.

Smith, A.D. *The Ethnic Origins of Nations*. New York: Blackwell, 1986.

Somers, M. "Narrativity, Narrative Identity, and Social Action: Rethinking English Working-Class Formation." *Social Science History* 16, no. 4 (1992): 591–630.

Somers, M., and G.D. Gibson. "Reclaiming the Epistemological 'Other': Narrative and the Social Constitution of Identity." In *Social Theory and the Politics of Identity*, edited by C. Calhoun, 37–99. London: Blackwell, 1994.

Soper, J.C., and J.S. Fetzer. "Explaining the Accommodation of Muslim Religious Practices in France, Britain, and Germany." *French Politics* 1, no. 1 (2003): 39–59.

– "Religious Institutions, Church-State History and Muslim Mobilisation in Britain, France and Germany." *Journal of Ethnic and Migration Studies* 33, no. 6 (2007): 933–44.

Statham, P., and A. Geddes. "Elites and the 'Organised Public': Who Drives British Immigration Politics and in Which Direction?" *West European Politics* 29, no. 2 (2006): 248–69.

Steinmetz, G. "Introduction: Culture and the State." In *State/Culture: State-Formation after the Cultural Turn*. Ithaca: Cornell Univerisity Press, 1999.

Surel, Y. "The Role of Cognitive and Normative Frames in Policy-Making." *Journal of European Public Policy* 7, no. 4 (2000): 495–512.

Swyngedouw, M., and G. Ivaldi. "The Extreme Right Utopia in Belgium and France: The Ideology of the Flemish Vlaams Blok and the French Front National." *West European Politics* 24, no. 3 (2001): 1–22.

Taggart, P. "New Populist Parties in Western Europe." *West European Politics* 18, no. 1 (1995): 34–51.

Tanguay, B. "Sclerosis or a Clean Bill of Health?" In *Quebec: State and Society (3rd ed.)*, edited by A.-G. Gagnon, 234–5. Peterborough: Broadview, 2004.

Terral, H. "Laïcité religieuse, antireligieuse, a-religieuse: L'évolution de l'école francaise entre 1880 et 1918." *Social Compass* 54, no. 2 (2007): 255–65.

Tévanian, P. *La République du mépris*. Paris: La Découverte, 2007.

Thériault, J.-Y. "Entre la nation et l'ethnie: Sociologie, société et communautés minoritaires francophones." *Sociologie et sociétés* 26, no. 1 (1994): 15–32.

– "La nation francophone d'Amérique: Canadiens, Canadiens français, Québécois." In *Dislocation et permanence: L'invention du Canada au quotiden*, edited by C. Andrew, 111–37. Ottawa: Ottawa University Press, 1999.

Thomas, E. "Keeping Identity at a Distance: Explaining France's New Legal Restrictions on the Islamic Headscarf." *Ethnic and Racial Studies* 29, no. 2 (2006): 237–59.

Tiberj, V. "La politique des deux axes." *Revue Française de Science Politique* 62 (2012): 71–106.

– "Values and the Votes from Mitterrand to Hollande: The Rise of the Two-axis Politics." *Parliamentary Affairs* 66 (2013): 69–86.

Tiberj, V., and P. Simon. "Civic Life and Political Participation." In *Trajectories and Origins: Survey on Population Diversity in France*, edited by C. Beauchemin, C. Hamelle, and P. Simon, 107–14. Paris: Institut d'études démographiques, 2010.

Tilly, C. *Stories, Identities, and Political Change*. Lanham, MD: Rowman and Littlefield, 2002.

– "To Explain Political Processes." *American Journal of Sociology* 100, no. 6 (1995): 1594–610.

Tilly, C., and S. Tarrow. *Contentious Politics*. London: Paradigm Publishers, 2007.

Triadafilopoulos, T., and A. Zaslove. "Influencing Migration Policy from Inside: Political Parties." In *Dialogues on Migration Policy*, edited by M. Giugni and F. Passy, 171–92. Lanham, MD: Lexington Books, 2006.

Trudeau, P.E. *Federalism and the French Canadians*. Toronto: Macmillan, 1968.

van Heerden, S., S.L. de Lange, W. ven der Brug, and M. Fennema. "The Immigration and Integration Debate in the Netherlands: Discursive and Programmatic Reactions to the Rise of Anti-Immigration Parties." *Journal of Ethnic and Migration Studies* 40, no. 1 (2014): 119–36.

van Kersbergen, K., and A. Krouwel. "A Double-Edged Sword! The Dutch Centre-Right and the 'Foreigners Issue.'" *Journal of European Public Policy* 15, no. 3 (2008): 398–414.

van Spanje, J. "Contagious Parties: Anti-Immigration Parties and Their Impact on Other Parties' Immigration Stances in Contemporary Western Europe." *Party Politics* 16 (2010): 563–86.

Veugelers, J. "A Challenge for Political Sociology: The Rise of Far-Right Parties in Contemporary Western Europe." *Current Sociology* 47, no. 4 (1999): 78–107.

Wagner, M. "When Do Parties Emphasise Extreme Positions? How Strategic Incentives for Policy Differentiation Influence Issue Importance." *European Journal of Political Research* 51 (2012): 64–88.

Walgrave, S., and K. De Swert. "Where Does Issue Ownership Come From? From the Party or from the Media? Issue-Party Identifications in Belgium, 1991–2005." *International Journal of Press/Politics* 12 (2007): 37–67.

Walgrave, S., J. Lefevere, and M. Nuytemans. "Issue Ownership Stability and Change: How Political Parties Claim and Maintain Issues through Media Appearances." *Political Communication* 26 (2009): 153–172.

Weber, E. *Peasants into Frenchmen: The Modernization of Rural France, 1870–1914*. Stanford: Stanford University Press, 1976.

Weil, P. *Qu'est-ce qu'un Français? Histoire de la nationalité française depuis la Révolution*. Paris: Grasset, 2002.

– "Why the French Laïcité Is Liberal." *Cardozo Law Review* 30, no. 6 (2008): 2699–714.

Weill, N. "What's in a Scarf? The Debate on Laïcité in France." *French Politics, Culture and Society* 24, no. 1 (2006): 59–73.

Wieviorka, M. "The Front National – Caught between Extremism, Populism and Democracy." In *Populist Fantasies: European Revolts in Context*, edited by C. Fieschi, M. Morris, and L. Caballero, 441–504. London: Counterpoint, 2013.

Wiles, E. "Headscarves, Human Rights, and Harmonious Multicultural Society: Implications of the French Ban for Interpretations of Equality." *Law and Society Review* 41, no. 3 (2007): 699–735.

Wimmer, A. "The Making and Unmaking of Ethnic Boundaries: A Multilevel Process Theory." *American Journal of Sociology* 113, no. 4 (2008): 970–1022.

Yegenoglu, M. *Colonial Fantasies: Towards a Feminist Reading of Orientalism*. Cambridge: Cambridge University Press, 1998.

Yilmaz, F. "Right-Wing Hegemony and Immigration: How the Populist Far-Right Achieved Hegemony through the Immigration Debate in Europe." *Current Sociology* 60, no. 3 (2012): 368–81.

Yuval-Davis, N. *The Politics of Belonging: Intersectional Contestations*. London: Sage, 2011.

Zimmer, O. "Boundary Mechanisms and Symbolic Resources: Towards a Process-Oriented Approach to National Identity." *Nations and Nationalism* 9, no. 2 (2003): 173–93.

Zubrzycki, G. "Aesthetic Revolt and the Remaking of National Identity in Québec, 1960–1969. " *Theory and Society* 42 (2013): 423–75.

– *Beheading the Saint: Nationalism, Religion, and Secularism in Québec*. Chicago: University of Chicago Press, 2016.

– "Negotiating Pluralism in Québec: Identity, Religion, and Secularism in the Debate over 'Reasonable Accommodation.'" In *Religion on the Edge: De-Centering and Re-Centering the Sociology of Religion*, edited by C. Bender, W. Cadge, P. Levitt, and D. Smilde, 215–37. Oxford: Oxford University Press, 2013.

– "'We, the Polish Nation': Ethnic and Civic Visions of Nationhood in Post-Communist Constitutional Debates." *Theory and Society* 30, no. 5 (2001): 629–68.

Zuquete, J.P. "The European Extreme-Right and Islam: New Directions?" *Journal of Political Ideologies* 13, no. 3 (2008): 321–44.

Index